TO READ ALOUD

Rediscovering the lost art of reading and listening

FRANCESCO DIMITRI

HEAD
of ZEUS

First published in 2017 by Head of Zeus Ltd
This paperback edition published in 2019 by Head of Zeus Ltd

Copyright in notes, introductions and selection
© Francesco Dimitri 2017

The moral right of Francesco Dimitri to be identified as the author
of this work has been asserted in accordance with the Copyright,
Designs and Patents Act of 1988.

The text credits on page 445 constitute an extension
of this copyright page.

1 3 5 7 9 10 8 6 4 2

A CIP catalogue record for this book is available
from the British Library.

ISBN (PB) 9781786693266
ISBN (E) 9781786693242

Printed in and bound in Great Britain by
CPI Group (UK) Ltd, Croydon CR0 4YY

Head of Zeus Ltd
First Floor East
5–8 Hardwick Street
London ECIR 4RG

www.headofzeus.com

For Paola,
who persisted

Contents

Introduction   1

LOVE   9

Francesco Dimitri, *Myth*: Baucis and Philemon   14

Alain de Botton, 'What Nice Men Never Tell   19
  Nice Women'

Kate Chopin, 'A Respectable Woman'   22

Cicero, *De Amicitia*   28

Jane Austen, *Pride and Prejudice*   31

Charles Dickens, *Great Expectations*   38

J. R. R. Tolkien, *The Return of the King*   44
  (third volume of *The Lord of the Rings*)

Julie de L'Espinasse, letter to Hippolyte de Guibert   47

LOSS   49

Francesco Dimitri, *Myth*: Alcestis   55

Neil Gaiman, 'The Sweeper of Dreams'   60

Simone de Beauvoir, *A Very Easy Death*   63

Oscar Wilde, *De Profundis*   67

Edith Nesbit, 'Uncle Abraham's Romance'   71

Joe Hill, 'Scheherazade's Typewriter'   77

Daphne du Maurier, *Rebecca*   82

Graham Joyce, *The Limits of Enchantment*   85

CHANGE   89
Francesco Dimitri, *Myth*: Persephone and Demeter   94
Ray Bradbury, *Dandelion Wine*   98
Joyce Carol Oates, 'The Scarf'   105
Lewis Carroll, *The Life and Letters of Lewis Carroll*   112
Francesco Dimitri, 'The Oak in my Garden'   114
Olive Schreiner, 'The Woman's Rose'   119
Zora Neale Hurston, *Dust Tracks on a Road*   125
Rebecca Solnit, *A Field Guide to Getting Lost*   128

PLEASURE   131
Francesco Dimitri, *Myth*: Psyche and Eros   137
Jim Dodge, *Stone Junction*   143
Joanne Harris, *Chocolat*   146
Anaïs Nin, 'Manuel'   150
Jorge Amado, *Gabriela, Clove and Cinnamon*   155
Lillian Beckwith, *The Hills is Lonely*   161
Epicurus, *Letter to Menoeceus*   164
D. H. Lawrence, *Lady Chatterley's Lover*   167
John Cleland, *Fanny Hill: or, Memoirs of a Woman   172
    of Pleasure*
Giacomo Leopardi, 'Dialogue of Torquato Tasso   179
    and his Familiar Genius', from *Operette morali*

WORK   181
Francesco Dimitri, *Myth*: Pygmalion   186
Joe R. Lansdale, *Captains Outrageous*   190
George Orwell, *Down and Out in Paris and London*   194
Virginia Woolf, 'Professions for Women'   197
Anthony Trollope, *Autobiography*   203

H. G. Wells, *Kipps*   206

Elizabeth Gaskell, *Cranford*   211

John Fante, *The Brotherhood of the Grape*   214

NATURE   219

Francesco Dimitri, *Myth*: Adonis   224

Rob Cowen, *Common Ground*   228

John Muir, *My First Summer in the Sierra*   234

Ralph Waldo Emerson, 'Nature'   238

Dorothy Wordsworth, *Recollections of a Tour Made*   241
  in Scotland A.D. 1803

Robert Macfarlane, *The Old Ways*   245

Isabella Bird, *The Hawaiian Archipelago*   249

Chris Yates, *Nightwalk*   256

Amy Leach, 'Radical Bears in the Forest Delicious'   260

CHAOS   267

Francesco Dimitri, *Myth*: The Daughters of Minyas   273

Rosalind Kerven, 'The Dead Moon'   277

Gregory Bateson, 'Why Do Things Get in a Muddle?',   282
  from *Steps to an Ecology of Mind*

Alice Hoffman, *Practical Magic*   290

E. M. Forster, *A Room with a View*   296

David Mitchell, *Black Swan Green*   298

Vernon Lee, 'A Pontifical Mass at the Sixtine Chapel'   302

Maurice Baring, 'Half a Minute's Silence'   306

LIGHTNESS   311

Francesco Dimitri, *Myth*: The Birth of Hermes   316

Katherine Mansfield, 'Bank Holiday'   321

Mark Twain, Speech made on his seventieth birthday   326

Aleister Crowley, *The Confessions of Aleister Crowley:*   330
  an Autohagiography

P. G. Wodehouse, 'The Secret Pleasures of Reginald'   333

G. K. Chesterton, 'On Running After One's Hat'   337

WONDER   343

Francesco Dimitri, *Myth*: The Death of Pan   348

Olaf Stapledon, *Star Maker*   352

Dion Fortune, *Glastonbury: Avalon of the Heart*   357

W. B. Yeats, 'Enchanted Woods', from *The Celtic Twilight*   363

Algernon Blackwood, 'The Messenger'   369

Jo Walton, *Among Others*   374

Kenneth Grahame, *The Wind in the Willows*   379

Tana French, *The Secret Place*   384

Kelly Link, 'Going to hell. Instructions and advice'   388

CODA: DELICACIES FOR DISCUSSION   391

H. D. Thoreau, *Civil Disobedience*   395

Arthur Conan Doyle, *The Coming of the Fairies*   401

Catherine Millet, *The Sexual Life of Catherine M.*   405

THE 'READ ALOUD' TOOLKIT   409

1. Reading prescriptions   411

2. List of reading times   423

3. Index of tags   429

4. Notes on the authors   431

5. How to organise a 'Read Aloud party' in your home   441

Text acknowledgements   445

Toasts   451

Introduction

Around a campfire and over mammoth steaks, our pre-historic ancestors were already telling tall tales.

> That was the biggest mammoth that ever was!
> It wasn't even a mammoth – I'm telling you, it was
> a monster!
> It cried with a human voice!

By sharing stories, they gathered; by gathering, they became stronger. Sharing stories is what makes humans human: more than the fire, it was the campfire that allowed *Homo sapiens* to come together and create tribes, cities and states.

When we use the word 'story' today, we think of writing on a page, or images on a screen. A story is an object, a thing. And yet for most of human history the only way you could experience a story was to hear it from the lips of a storyteller. A story was not a *thing* but an *event* that people would be drawn to. They would meet, listen, laugh – and perhaps fight and then make up. The story was the campfire, the campfire was the story.

Many kinds of fires have been lit throughout the millennia. We say that a person called Homer wrote the *Iliad* and the *Odyssey*, but we don't actually know if he was the one who wrote them down – or if he even existed at all. What we do know is that in the ancient Greek city-states there were epic poets who told extraordinary tales to people as they feasted: tales of kings and princes and the duels they fought, of wooden horses used as subterfuges in war, of beautiful creatures – part-woman, part-bird – who lured unsuspecting mariners to their deaths. Their words weren't meant to be written down and read, but spoken and heard.

In Gaelic halls, bards would turn petty politics into engrossing narratives, singing their words in ways not dissimilar to the Greek poets. You would listen to a bard; you had to be there with him, breathing the same air, making eye contact, to decide whether he was any good.

It was not only stories that were told aloud, but also items of news, pieces of wisdom – everything that now belongs to ink and paper and screen. In Greece and Rome, skilled orators would attract crowds. Socrates would make philosophy by talking to people in the streets. Folk tales were repeated at harvest bonfires; strange news travelled from mouth to mouth and market to market; ghost stories were whispered on long winter nights. There is something powerful in *being there*, in person, while words happen. It creates a bond, a sense of community; it generates conversations about matters more interesting than the weather. Listening to words read aloud is, quite simply, a lovely experience. So why don't we do it any more?

It is not that we don't share art. We do, every day. Part of the pleasure of going to the cinema comes from your being there with other people (crossing your fingers they won't be of the keeping-their-phone-on persuasion). Television can be shared also: you might not have watched *How I Met Your Mother* if your partner had not asked you to, just as your partner only watched *Breaking Bad* because you were doing so. Together you crack jokes, gorge on popcorn. Sure, many of us also watch films and TV series on our own, but it is just as common – indeed, probably more so – to watch them in company. The same goes for most forms of art: few people go to a concert to be alone; the ceiling of the Sistine Chapel wasn't painted for the private enjoyment of Pope Julius II; even video games, touted for decades as the loneliest form of entertainment, created online communities as soon as the internet made it feasible (those of us who remember playing games in arcades, know that even then this was anything but lonely).

We don't share words anymore, though. Words belong to books, and you are supposed to relish a book all on your own. Let me be clear: that sense of taking a solitary walk in the woods, as Umberto Eco put it, is a wonderful, special thing books do, an authentic form of magic. But books can work a different magic as well.

Books can be for sharing.

Fast forward from bardic halls to a living room in present-day London, and you will see me taking coffee with my wife, a friend of ours and her two-year-old daughter. Our friend was visiting for an early winter weekend, armed with the tools of a young mother's trade – toys and puppets and miniature drums. And a book about a witch.

My friend knows that I have some odd interests, the history of magic being one, so, during a second round of coffee, she picked up the book and started reading it to me. It was meant to be a joke – but I found myself engrossed. Groggy and sleep-deprived as I was (we had had a late night), I was drawn into the world of a witch on a broomstick, who flew over the country having adventures that weren't exactly thought-provoking, but were strangely fascinating to me. I glanced at my wife and the little girl: the spell was working on them as well. So we all sat, two adults and one child, listening to the story. My friend, somewhat bemused, was kind enough to read it out to the very end.

The story obliterated the last traces of doziness in a way that caffeine hadn't managed to do – and the witch remained stuck in my head. Why had my wife and I enjoyed that reading so much? Neither of us would have read the story on our own, and yet both of us had been delighted by it. There was something mysterious at work there – but what was it?

A few days later, I was clearing the last autumn leaves from the garden when my eyes fell on the small, rusty firepit we have in a corner. The penny dropped, and I understood.

We had built a campfire.

The idea of reading aloud to grown-ups is not new. In the past, people would read aloud for a variety of reasons: to woo their beloved, to inspire a friend, to persuade someone in their care to take a particular course of action. The novelist Flaubert read aloud everything he wrote, to check the quality of his writing. It was not only stories that were read aloud, but also reflections, meditations, pieces of practical philosophy. Reading aloud – and listening – used to be a widely enjoyed leisure activity and a way of giving and receiving advice. The time has come to rediscover it.

The US psychiatrist Edward Hallowell coined the expression 'human moment': he pointed out that, useful as digital communication is, it makes us forget how important it is to talk face-to-face to other people. We have a 'human moment' when we share a physical space with another person, actively listening to that person, while that person listens to us in turn. We are both present, concentrating on the here and now, with no hurry to move on. Such moments foster friendship, creativity and wellbeing: they are vital to our mental health, and yet we have fewer and fewer of them, even with our closest friends and family. We are so busy, and digital communication technologies have become so ubiquitous, that we don't always remember how a 'human moment' is supposed to happen. Surely, replying to John's tweet is almost as good as buying him a drink, right?

I am not saying we should ditch our technology, of course not. But we do need to find a new balance. When my friend started reading aloud, she made a 'human moment' *happen*: she, my wife and I were all mindfully present, just happy to be there, and we didn't need anything more than that.

Mindfulness (in its modern, Western form) can be broadly defined as the capacity for living in the moment, enjoying all the qualities for the present; a state of mind that fosters creativity, relieves stress and helps with problem solving. It is not an easy state to achieve: mindfulness requires some training, which can be frustrating and brings results only after a while, and our pace of life certainly doesn't make it any easier. Reading aloud is a gentle, effortless way to reach that state. The physical presence of the person you read to, or who reads to you, in a small, intimate setting, as well as the time-limit naturally imposed by the length of the piece of writing, conspire to anchor you to the here and now, making you mindful without you even noticing it. This is what makes the experience so refreshing; this is what captivated my wife and me when my friend read us the story of the witch.

Many pieces of literature are less good when voiced than they are on the page: some fall flat, some have an uneasy flow. Not the ones in this book. They will give of their best when read aloud. Go on, give it a try, in the bookshop, right now. You will see what I mean. If you attract strange looks, nod to the person, smile and read to them. (Yes, I *am* being serious.)

As a non-native speaker, I have an odd relationship with English: I love it profoundly, but I am also very aware of its formal qualities. It is not *nature* but *nurture* to me. When researching this book, I was looking for pieces that have an oral quality to them, and yet I couldn't exactly define what an 'oral quality' was supposed to be. I still can't. Some writings work when read aloud because of the aural texture they create; others because of their conceptual rhythm. There is not one road to orality, but a myriad of small paths. I have tried to explore a few of them. I hope you'll enjoy what I found, and make use of it.

This book is a toolbox for well-being: literary self-help, if you like. I unashamedly aim to improve your life, through literature and human connection rather than the umpteenth step-by-step programme. Take ten minutes off, sit down with somebody you care about and share a passage of writing: you will both feel more relaxed and connected, as if you had spent two hours together in a spa.

If this sounds too good to be true, you only need, well, ten minutes to put it to the test.

All the pieces in this book are short: the longer ones take fifteen minutes to be read aloud, many of them a lot less. You don't need to make time for a lengthy session: you can just flip the pages and give it a go. Also, you don't need any training. This is not a book for actors, bards and public speakers: using it does not require any skill at all. What matters is being there, experiencing the moment for what it is – whether you are the one who reads or the one who listens, the one who gives the gift or the one who receives it, the reader or the readee.

The pieces are organised into nine sections, tackling nine different aspects of life. Each piece also has a number of tags (*companionship, comfort, magic, happiness, married life, calm, resilience, anxiety, regret, self-knowledge* and so on) attached to it. They identify themes, moods, qualities, states of life, and states of mind, on which the piece in question sheds light. By consulting the Index of tags at the back of the book, you can search for and identify pieces to suit the specific needs of a specific moment.

Each section opens with a short introduction and with a personal rewriting of a classic myth. The roots of our culture are in the classics, after all, and they remain a precious reservoir of wisdom.

So dip into *To Read Aloud*, my friend. Turn its pages, seek out a piece to read to a friend, partner, or lover – and make a gift of words.

Your next 'human moment' begins now.

LOVE

YOU FALL IN LOVE. You don't decide to go there, you don't walk in, no, you just stumble into it. Love is a wonderland you can reach only by chance, mistake or luck, though it is not a rabbit (well, we *hope* not) but a person who is leading you there. He might become your partner, if you play your cards right.

Love is not your breath inside the hut, but the hurricane outside, an external force of its own. It belongs not to you, but to the same elemental realm as fire and moonlight. It might be quiet or all-consuming, it might grow slowly, or it might suddenly hit you with a sucker punch, but love will always bring out the best and worst in you. When you are in love you make your most idiotic mistakes and you come up with your best ideas. You are anxious, even terrified (*is Mum going to like her?*), and you are bold (*he's right, let's quit this soul-crushing job*). You are at your most selfish and most generous. You are not very coherent. That's the point of it.

I am not sure anybody can define love. We can say what it does to us: it makes our hands tremble and our stomachs churn. Love is like the Invisible Man, we can't see him, but we can see the ripples he leaves behind. Even art does not try to define love, but, more humbly, points at it and says, *Look, that is something you know.* Love has inspired some of the greatest music ever composed, paintings ever made – and stories ever told. Ask any artist, and if she is sincere she will tell you that one of the reasons why we make art in the first place is, well, to make love. And that's not such a bad reason, after all.

Love comes in many shapes. The ancient Greeks had at least six words for it, from *eros*, the passion of sensual lovers, to *philia*, the joy of friendship, passing from the empathic bonds of *storge* and the transport of *agape*, from the playfulness of *ludus* and the *pragma* of seasoned lovers. There are no hard boundaries between these different kinds. *Eros* can spark a relationship, but you need *philia* to make it last.

*

The writings in this chapter deal with some of the shapes of love. You can read them to a lover, or to a person who has made you fall in love with them and whom you now hope might fall for you; you could read them to entertain your long-time partner on a rainy Sunday, or to charm the cute stranger you met on Tinder. Reading aloud creates a bond, as love does. Use these writings to put *eros* on fire, fuel *agape*, or nourish *philia*.

As with every chapter in *To Read Aloud*, we start with a myth. In this case, the story of Baucis and Philemon, a couple who go through all the forms of love, from *eros* to *pragma*, and, with some help from the gods, eventually win the most precious prize for lifelong lovers.

Then it is the turn of Alain de Botton, one of the subtlest

of modern explorers of love, to make us wonder whether there is a secret to the niceness of nice men. Are there things that 'nice men' never tell us, in order to stay nice?

After nice men, we turn to respectable women: in her short story, Kate Chopin shows us the limits of respectability, the unexpected ways of seduction and the alluring power of the human voice. Are romantic and sexual love necessarily one and the same? The ending of this story is slightly mysterious. What happens next? What do the respectable woman's words mean? No one really knows, but you might have your own ideas.

In a celebrated treatise, the great Roman orator and statesman Cicero talks about a different kind of love – friendship.

Jane Austen and Charles Dickens focus their attention on two different stages of love: Austen tells of the 'falling in' stage, while Dickens recounts a possibly happy ending to a love story that has followed a tangled course.

Julie de L'Espinasse, with French ardour, writes a beautiful declaration of love. Borrow her words: they have survived since the eighteenth century, so there must be something to them.

And, finally, we come to J. R. R. Tolkien, an intense writer on friendship. *Philia* can be as powerful as *eros*: you would do anything for a real friend, even travel to the end of the world, and beyond.

Baucis and Philemon

FRANCESCO DIMITRI

───◆───

⏳ 10 minutes

This is a classical myth, told by the Roman
poet Ovid in his *Metamorphoses*. It is about
a love as long and as beautiful as life itself.
It goes like this...

───◆───

I don't know when Baucis and Philemon got together. I
don't know who fell in love with whom first, whether it
was Baucis with Philemon or Philemon with Baucis, or if
perhaps their love grew in time, organically, like a tapestry
they wove between them. I can't tell for sure. What I *can*
tell is that they married very young, and lived in a small,
clean cottage whose roof was made of twigs and reeds
they harvested from the swamp nearby. In that cottage
they laughed, and cried, and fought, and made peace,
and watched the seasons pass. In that cottage they had a
long, good life together, and when old age finally caught
up with them, it found them in love more than ever. They
didn't have riches and they didn't have children and their

neighbours never visited them, but Baucis and Philemon were perfectly happy. They had the kind of love that only comes with time, they had food enough not to starve, and wisdom enough to appreciate their luck: the company of some chicken and a grumpy goose was all they needed. If you asked them who was the boss of the house, they would laugh.

One evening, just after dusk, two strangers appeared.

One was a young, handsome man; tired and covered in dust, he made a bad job of hiding the grin on his lips. The other was taller, older, with broad shoulders and a curly beard, and even though he walked wearily, he still walked as if he owned the road. Baucis saw them from the window and told her husband that two travellers were coming. The old man stood up carefully, his bones cracking with age from toes to neck, and slowly headed to the door to welcome the travellers inside.

The younger traveller did the talking. He said (without exactly lying) that he and his friend came from afar, and they needed a place to spend the night, and food – if Baucis and Philemon had any to spare. Before he had finished talking Philemon was already clearing an old bench and Baucis was throwing a rough blanket on it. Baucis and Philemon had already had their meagre supper and they had been ready to go to bed, but they knew that not everybody was as lucky as they were, and they wanted to help.

Baucis asked the younger man about his travels, and Philemon asked the bearded man if he liked the country. Baucis and Philemon didn't want their guests to feel awkward, or in their debt.

Baucis lit the fire. There wasn't enough wood to keep it going, so she picked twigs from the roof and used those. Once the fire was crackling away, she put a pot of water on to boil and chopped into it what few vegetables they had inside the house. Philemon took their only chine of meat down from the ceiling, where it was hanging. It was small and leathery, and it had to last the year, but he cut a good slice to throw into the bubbling water.

With the slow movements of age, Baucis and Philemon put their mattress on a willow frame to make a couch of it. They covered the couch with their more prized possessions – some worn, threadbare clothes they took out only when the time came for a sacred feast. Their three-legged table was rickety; Baucis stuck a piece of broken pottery under the uneven leg, and then swept its top with mint leaves, so it was sweet-smelling and clean.

The meal began: there were the black and green olives sacred to Athena, good cheese, nuts and dried figs and dates, and plums and honeycomb and radishes and wine – Baucis and Philemon gave to their guests as much as they could. They gave all with a smile on their lips and sincere happiness in their hearts. Soon the bowl of wine was empty, and then it was full again.

But Baucis hadn't filled it, nor had Philemon.

The wine had appeared from nowhere.

Baucis and Philemon exchanged a look: this was surely a message from the gods. They whispered a prayer. Yes, they hadn't given enough; yes, they could do more. Philemon stood up and reached for the grumpy goose, who was sleeping in a corner. The goose jumped to its feet and ran away. It ran towards the guests, the bearded man and the younger one.

The bearded man laughed heartily and raised a hand, stopping Philemon from coming near. He said, 'You don't need to kill your goose.'

The younger man said, 'I am Hermes, and this one here, he is Zeus. We are the gods you were praying to: don't waste your goose on us.'

Zeus stood on his feet. 'Come,' he said.

Speechless, Baucis and Philemon followed the gods out of the cottage, through the moonlit countryside, up a high hill. They climbed slowly, leaning on their frail sticks. The gods slowed their step to the pace of the old couple. 'None of your neighbours gave us shelter,' Zeus said, as they climbed.

'They didn't even bother to open the door,' Hermes chimed in.

'And for that, they will pay,' Zeus said. 'But not you.'

Hermes said, 'Not you.'

They made it to the top of the hill, and with a grand sweeping gesture, Zeus showed the countryside around. All their neighbours' houses were gone, swallowed by the swamp. Only one cottage was still standing, the one they had just left; and now it started to change before their eyes.

Tall columns took the place of the shabby doorway, the dirt on the pavement became marble, and the reeds that made up the roof turned into solid gold. The ramshackle cottage was gone; a beautiful temple stood in its place.

'Ask what you wish,' Zeus said, calmly. 'And I will grant it.'

Baucis and Philemon talked very briefly. They were of

one mind. 'We want to be your priests,' Baucis said, 'for what is left of our lives.'

Philemon added, 'But when our lives are over, we want to go together. I wish never to see my wife's grave.'

Baucis said, 'And I wish never to bury my husband.'

'Of course,' Zeus smiled.

Baucis and Philemon spent many bountiful years as a priestess and priest of the gods. Then one morning came when they were on the steps of the temple, enjoying the warm kiss of the springtime sun, talking, as they did, feeling blessed by their being together. On that morning Philemon felt something in his chest, his heart skipping a beat, a gentle pain spreading. Baucis opened her eyes wide: she saw Philemon's wizened skin turn into bark, and she saw strong, green shoots sprout from his head. Baucis looked at her hands: they too were turning into wood and leaves.

She knew what was happening, and so did Philemon. They reached out to each other while they still could.

Baucis said, 'Farewell, my love.'

'Farewell, my love,' Philemon answered.

Then bark covered their mouths, and they spoke no more.

And those trees still stand on the steps of the temple in Phrygia, entwined in a close embrace; I saw them myself. I saw offerings and garlands hanging from their branches.

If you visit there, you might want to leave one too.

companionship · comfort · magic · happiness · married life

'What Nice Men Never Tell Nice Women'

ALAIN DE BOTTON

———◆———

⏳ 7 minutes

We all have hidden sides; sides hidden not just
from others, but from ourselves, too. Let's see
what really goes on in a nice man's mind.

———◆———

The nice man has learnt not to say everything; that's why he seems so nice. There's a lot going on in his mind that he's not quite allowing himself to express. He loves you too much: he'd rather be kind than entirely honest – and feels, perhaps quite rightly, that he cannot really be both. Such is the condition of the nice man. The nice man is intent on not being the lad or the bad boy. He had enough of that macho rowdy behaviour at school and never wants to be exposed to it again. He is tender towards his mother and his little sister. He likes women a lot, as friends and not just as lovers.

This makes it hard for him to live with the sides of himself that seem very focused on some awkward priorities. He's very easy to shame. For example, when you're in a restaurant and you're explaining about your aunt's recent operation (the doctors had to sew the whole tendon back together), half of his attention at least will be on the waitress, bending over to collect some bottles from a box by the door, or perhaps one of the other diners. He's haunted by the idea of a rapid meaningless encounter – possibly with one of your very best friends.

When you say that all those porn sites are revolting and humiliating for women and what no-hopers those who go there might be, he agrees wholeheartedly – then, with some guilt, spends many absurdly exciting hours on them when you're out. The nice man is democratic, egalitarian and deeply sympathetic to the feminist agenda – and yet in sexual fantasy, he loves the idea of being tyrannical, bullying and really very rough. He himself can't understand the disjuncture between competing parts of his nature; he is spooked by the drastic switch in his value-system that occurs the very second after orgasm. The nice man is your brother, your father, your friend.

The nice man doesn't feel that he can be loved and reveal the true sources of his sexual excitement. Without noticing or meaning to in any way, you are silencing him. It takes very little to keep the nice man quiet – he picks up on the slightest hint of your displeasure and censors himself accordingly. Maybe you're by now thinking the nice man isn't really nice at all. He's just a fake and a phoney. Far from it: he truly is nice. It's just that niceness isn't what we might think it is. Niceness isn't about having no harmful desires inside oneself, it's about knowing how to keep these very quiet. Niceness is, to a crucial extent, about secrecy. It's an achievement of repression. Nice guys don't not have bad thoughts: they're just unusually committed to keeping them at the level of muffled feelings rather than statements or actions. The nice man wants to do everything to avoid paining those he loves with the more troubled sides of his imagination. Of course, there is a price to be paid for all this niceness. There's invariably a degree of buried resentment – and distance – whenever we aren't able to be fully ourselves. This could get rather dispiriting, across decades.

It's clearly very hard for the partners of the nice to take on board the darker sides of their lovers. But if they are robust enough to dare to give them some attention, the result can be an extraordinary flowering of the relationship beyond anything yet experienced. However close we may be to someone because they have been nice to us, it's as nothing next to the closeness we'll achieve if we allow them to show us, without shaming or humiliating them, what really isn't quite so nice about them. Out there, in the politer corners of society, nice guys are – without saying a thing, that's not their style – waiting for nice women to start to gently take the weighty burden of their 'badness' off them. And, of course, vice versa too, for no gender has any monopoly on the sense of being bad.

anxiety · honesty · irony · self-knowledge · shift of perspective

'A Respectable Woman'
KATE CHOPIN

◆

⧗ 14 minutes

This is a short story – written in the 1890s by an author
who lived in America's Deep South – about doing the
right thing, whatever the right thing might be.

◆

Mrs Baroda was a little provoked to learn that her husband
expected his friend, Gouvernail, up to spend a week or
two on the plantation.

They had entertained a good deal during the winter;
much of the time had also been passed in New Orleans
in various forms of mild dissipation. She was looking
forward to a period of unbroken rest, now, and undis-
turbed tête-a-tête with her husband, when he informed
her that Gouvernail was coming up to stay a week or two.

This was a man she had heard much of but never seen.
He had been her husband's college friend; was now a journalist, and in no sense a society man or 'a man about town,'
which were, perhaps, some of the reasons she had never
met him. But she had unconsciously formed an image of
him in her mind. She pictured him tall, slim, cynical; with

eye-glasses, and his hands in his pockets; and she did not like him. Gouvernail was slim enough, but he wasn't very tall nor very cynical; neither did he wear eye-glasses nor carry his hands in his pockets. And she rather liked him when he first presented himself.

But why she liked him she could not explain satisfactorily to herself when she partly attempted to do so. She could discover in him none of those brilliant and promising traits which Gaston, her husband, had often assured her that he possessed. On the contrary, he sat rather mute and receptive before her chatty eagerness to make him feel at home and in face of Gaston's frank and wordy hospitality. His manner was as courteous toward her as the most exacting woman could require; but he made no direct appeal to her approval or even esteem.

Once settled at the plantation he seemed to like to sit upon the wide portico in the shade of one of the big Corinthian pillars, smoking his cigar lazily and listening attentively to Gaston's experience as a sugar planter.

'This is what I call living,' he would utter with deep satisfaction, as the air that swept across the sugar field caressed him with its warm and scented velvety touch. It pleased him also to get on familiar terms with the big dogs that came about him, rubbing themselves sociably against his legs. He did not care to fish, and displayed no eagerness to go out and kill grosbecs when Gaston proposed doing so.

Gouvernail's personality puzzled Mrs Baroda, but she liked him. Indeed, he was a lovable, inoffensive fellow. After a few days, when she could understand him no better than at first, she gave over being puzzled and remained piqued. In this mood she left her husband and her guest, for the most part, alone together. Then finding that Gouvernail took no manner of exception to her action, she imposed her society upon him, accompanying him in his idle strolls to the mill and walks along the batture. She persistently sought to penetrate the reserve in which he had unconsciously enveloped himself.

'When is he going – your friend?' she one day asked her husband. 'For my part, he tires me frightfully.'

'Not for a week yet, dear. I can't understand; he gives you no trouble.'

'No. I should like him better if he did; if he were more like others, and I had to plan somewhat for his comfort and enjoyment.'

Gaston took his wife's pretty face between his hands and looked tenderly and laughingly into her troubled eyes. They were making a bit of toilet sociably together in Mrs Baroda's dressing-room.

'You are full of surprises, ma belle,' he said to her. 'Even I can never count upon how you are going to act under given conditions.' He kissed her and turned to fasten his cravat before the mirror.

'Here you are,' he went on, 'taking poor Gouvernail seriously and making a commotion over him, the last thing he would desire or expect.'

'Commotion!' she hotly resented. 'Nonsense! How can you say such a thing? Commotion, indeed! But, you know, you said he was clever.'

'So he is. But the poor fellow is run down by overwork

now. That's why I asked him here to take a rest.'

'You used to say he was a man of ideas,' she retorted, unconciliated. 'I expected him to be interesting, at least. I'm going to the city in the morning to have my spring gowns fitted. Let me know when Mr Gouvernail is gone; I shall be at my Aunt Octavie's.'

That night she went and sat alone upon a bench that stood beneath a live oak tree at the edge of the gravel walk.

She had never known her thoughts or her intentions to be so confused. She could gather nothing from them but the feeling of a distinct necessity to quit her home in the morning.

Mrs Baroda heard footsteps crunching the gravel; but could discern in the darkness only the approaching red point of a lighted cigar. She knew it was Gouvernail, for her husband did not smoke. She hoped to remain unnoticed, but her white gown revealed her to him. He threw away his cigar and seated himself upon the bench beside her; without a suspicion that she might object to his presence.

'Your husband told me to bring this to you, Mrs Baroda,' he said, handing her a filmy, white scarf with which she sometimes enveloped her head and shoulders. She accepted the scarf from him with a murmur of thanks, and let it lie in her lap.

He made some commonplace observation upon the baneful effect of the night air at that season. Then as his gaze reached out into the darkness, he murmured, half to himself:

'Night of south winds – night of the large few stars!

Still nodding night—'

She made no reply to this apostrophe to the night, which indeed, was not addressed to her.

Gouvernail was in no sense a diffident man, for he was not a self-conscious one. His periods of reserve were not constitutional, but the result of moods. Sitting there beside Mrs Baroda, his silence melted for the time.

He talked freely and intimately in a low, hesitating drawl that was not unpleasant to hear. He talked of the old college days when he and Gaston had been a good deal to each other; of the days of keen and blind ambitions and large intentions. Now there was left with him, at least, a philosophic acquiescence to the existing order – only a desire to be permitted to exist, with now and then a little whiff of genuine life, such as he was breathing now.

Her mind only vaguely grasped what he was saying. Her physical being was for the moment predominant. She was not thinking of his words, only drinking in the tones of his voice. She wanted to reach out her hand in the darkness and touch him with the sensitive tips of her fingers upon the face or the lips. She wanted to draw close to him and whisper against his cheek – she did not care what – as she might have done if she had not been a respectable woman.

The stronger the impulse grew to bring herself near him, the further, in fact, did she draw away from him. As soon as she could do so without an appearance of too great rudeness, she rose and left him there alone.

Before she reached the house, Gouvernail had lighted a fresh cigar and ended his apostrophe to the night.

Mrs Baroda was greatly tempted that night to tell her

husband – who was also her friend – of this folly that had seized her. But she did not yield to the temptation. Beside being a respectable woman she was a very sensible one; and she knew there are some battles in life which a human being must fight alone.

When Gaston arose in the morning, his wife had already departed. She had taken an early morning train to the city. She did not return till Gouvernail was gone from under her roof.

There was some talk of having him back during the summer that followed. That is, Gaston greatly desired it; but this desire yielded to his wife's strenuous opposition.

However, before the year ended, she proposed, wholly from herself, to have Gouvernail visit them again. Her husband was surprised and delighted with the suggestion coming from her.

'I am glad, chère amie, to know that you have finally overcome your dislike for him; truly he did not deserve it.'

'Oh,' she told him, laughingly, after pressing a long, tender kiss upon his lips, 'I have overcome everything! you will see. This time I shall be very nice to him.'

▶

adventure · instinct · irony · married life · rules · self-knowledge · temptation

De Amicitia

CICERO

⧗ 6 minutes

In this short extract from his treatise *De Amicitia*,
the Roman statesman and orator Marcus Tullius
Cicero tells us why friends matter, and why
being a good friend matters even more.

The benefits of friendship are almost more than I can say.
To begin with, how can life be worth living [...] without
the peace of mind coming from the mutual good will of a
friend? What can be better than to have someone to whom
you can say everything with the same absolute confidence
as to yourself? Is not prosperity robbed of half its value if
you have no one to share your joy? And, on the other hand,
misfortunes would be hard to bear if there were not someone to feel them even more acutely than yourself. Other
objects of desire serve for specific ends – riches for use,
power for securing homage, office for reputation, pleasure for enjoyment, health for freedom from pain and for
using the full functions of the body. But friendship has
innumerable advantages. Turn which way you please, you

will find it at work. It is everywhere, and yet never out of place, never unwelcome. Fire and water themselves, to use a common expression, are not more useful than friendship. [...] [It] enhances prosperity, and relieves adversity of its burden by halving and sharing it.

*

[...] Friendship gives us bright hopes for the future and forbids weakness and despair. A man sees the face of a true friend as if it were a second self. So that where his friend is, he is; if his friend be rich, he is not poor; though he be weak, his friend's strength is his; and in his friend's life he enjoys a second life after his own is finished. This last thing is perhaps the most difficult to conceive, but such is the effect of the respect, the loving remembrance, and the regret of friends which follow us to the grave. While they take the sting out of death, they add a glory to the life of the survivors. Nay, if you eliminate from nature the tie of affection, no house or city will survive, and we would even stop to cultivate the soil.

If you don't see the virtue of friendship and harmony, you may learn it by looking at the effects of quarrels. Was any family ever so well established, any State so firmly settled, as to be beyond the reach of utter destruction from animosities and factions? This may teach you the immense advantage of friendship.

*

They say that a certain philosopher of Agrigentum, in a Greek poem, said, with the authority of an oracle, that whatever in nature and the universe was unchangeable, was so in virtue of the binding force of friendship; and whatever was changeable, was so by the solvent power of discord. This is a truth that everybody understands and practically attests by experience. For if any marked instance of loyal friendship in confronting or sharing danger comes to light, everyone applauds it. What cheers there were, for example, all over the theatre at a passage in the new play of my friend and guest Pacuvius; where, the king not knowing which of two men was Orestes, [a man the king wanted to kill], the real Orestes asserted it was he, while his friend Pylades declared himself also to be Orestes, so that he might die instead of his friend. The audience rose en masse and clapped their hands. And this was at an incident in fiction: what would they have done, must we suppose, if it had been in real life? [...]

*

I don't think I have any more to say about friendship. If there is any more, and I have no doubt there is much, you must, if you care to do so, consult those who profess to discuss such matters.

◗

companionship · honesty · hope

Pride and Prejudice

JANE AUSTEN

◆

⏳ 15 minutes

Is there *anyone* who has not read *Pride and Prejudice*
or seen one of the many film and TV adaptations of
Jane Austen's much-loved novel? At its heart is the
love story between Mr Darcy and Elizabeth Bennet.
This extract shows us the moment when – against
his best intentions – Darcy starts falling for Elizabeth.
If you think it is chock-full of memorable quotes,
that's probably because it is.

◆

Occupied in observing Mr Bingley's attentions to her
sister, Elizabeth was far from suspecting that she was
herself becoming an object of some interest in the eyes
of his friend. Mr Darcy had at first scarcely allowed her
to be pretty; he had looked at her without admiration at
the ball; and when they next met, he looked at her only
to criticise. But no sooner had he made it clear to himself
and his friends that she hardly had a good feature in her
face, than he began to find it was rendered uncommonly
intelligent by the beautiful expression of her dark eyes. To

this discovery succeeded some others equally mortifying. Though he had detected with a critical eye more than one failure of perfect symmetry in her form, he was forced to acknowledge her figure to be light and pleasing; and in spite of his asserting that her manners were not those of the fashionable world, he was caught by their easy playfulness. Of this she was perfectly unaware; to her he was only the man who made himself agreeable nowhere, and who had not thought her handsome enough to dance with.

He began to wish to know more of her, and as a step towards conversing with her himself, attended to her conversation with others. His doing so drew her notice. It was at Sir William Lucas's, where a large party were assembled.

'What does Mr Darcy mean,' said she to Charlotte, 'by listening to my conversation with Colonel Forster?'

'That is a question which Mr Darcy only can answer.'

'But if he does it any more I shall certainly let him know that I see what he is about. He has a very satirical eye, and if I do not begin by being impertinent myself, I shall soon grow afraid of him.'

On his approaching them soon afterwards, though without seeming to have any intention of speaking, Miss Lucas defied her friend to mention such a subject to him; which immediately provoking Elizabeth to do it, she turned to him and said:

'Did you not think, Mr Darcy, that I expressed myself uncommonly well just now, when I was teasing Colonel Forster to give us a ball at Meryton?'

'With great energy; but it is always a subject which makes a lady energetic.'

'You are severe on us.'

'It will be *her* turn soon to be teased,' said Miss Lucas. 'I am going to open the instrument, Eliza, and you know what follows.'

'You are a very strange creature by way of a friend! – always wanting me to play and sing before anybody and everybody! If my vanity had taken a musical turn, you would have been invaluable; but as it is, I would really rather not sit down before those who must be in the habit of hearing the very best performers.' On Miss Lucas's persevering, however, she added, 'Very well, if it must be so, it must.' And gravely glancing at Mr Darcy, 'There is a fine old saying, which everybody here is of course familiar with: "Keep your breath to cool your porridge"; and I shall keep mine to swell my song.'

Her performance was pleasing, though by no means capital. After a song or two, and before she could reply to the entreaties of several that she would sing again, she was eagerly succeeded at the instrument by her sister Mary, who having, in consequence of being the only plain one in the family, worked hard for knowledge and accomplishments, was always impatient for display.

Mary had neither genius nor taste; and though vanity had given her application, it had given her likewise a pedantic air and conceited manner, which would have injured a higher degree of excellence than she had reached. Elizabeth, easy and unaffected, had been listened to with much more pleasure, though not playing half so well; and Mary, at the end of a long concerto, was glad to purchase praise and gratitude by Scotch and Irish airs, at the request of her younger sisters, who, with some of the Lucases, and two or three officers, joined eagerly in dancing at one end of the room.

Mr Darcy stood near them in silent indignation at such a mode of passing the evening, to the exclusion of all conversation, and was too much engrossed by his thoughts to perceive that Sir William Lucas was his neighbour, till Sir William thus began:

'What a charming amusement for young people this is, Mr Darcy! There is nothing like dancing after all. I consider it as one of the first refinements of polished society.'

'Certainly, sir; and it has the advantage also of being in vogue amongst the less polished societies of the world. Every savage can dance.'

Sir William only smiled. 'Your friend performs delightfully,' he continued after a pause, on seeing Bingley join the group; 'and I doubt not that you are an adept in the science yourself, Mr Darcy.'

'You saw me dance at Meryton, I believe, sir.'

'Yes, indeed, and received no inconsiderable pleasure from the sight. Do you often dance at St James's?'

'Never, sir.'

'Do you not think it would be a proper compliment to the place?'

'It is a compliment which I never pay to any place if I can avoid it.'

'You have a house in town, I conclude?'

Mr Darcy bowed.

'I had once had some thought of fixing in town myself – for I am fond of superior society; but I did not feel quite certain that the air of London would agree with Lady Lucas.'

He paused in hopes of an answer; but his companion was not disposed to make any; and Elizabeth at that instant moving towards them, he was struck with the action of doing a very gallant thing, and called out to her:

'My dear Miss Eliza, why are you not dancing? Mr Darcy, you must allow me to present this young lady to you as a very desirable partner. You cannot refuse to dance, I am sure when so much beauty is before you.' And, taking her hand, he would have given it to Mr Darcy who, though extremely surprised, was not unwilling to receive it, when she instantly drew back, and said with some discomposure to Sir William:

'Indeed, sir, I have not the least intention of dancing. I entreat you not to suppose that I moved this way in order to beg for a partner.'

Mr Darcy, with grave propriety, requested to be allowed the honour of her hand, but in vain. Elizabeth was determined; nor did Sir William at all shake her purpose by his attempt at persuasion.

'You excel so much in the dance, Miss Eliza, that it is cruel to deny me the happiness of seeing you; and though this gentleman dislikes the amusement in general, he can have no objection, I am sure, to oblige us for one half-hour.'

'Mr Darcy is all politeness,' said Elizabeth, smiling.

'He is, indeed; but, considering the inducement, my dear Miss Eliza, we cannot wonder at his complaisance – for who would object to such a partner?'

Elizabeth looked archly, and turned away. Her resistance had not injured her with the gentleman, and he was thinking of her with some complacency, when thus accosted by Miss Bingley:

'I can guess the subject of your reverie.'

'I should imagine not.'

'You are considering how insupportable it would be to pass many evenings in this manner – in such society; and indeed I am quite of your opinion. I was never more annoyed! The insipidity, and yet the noise – the nothingness, and yet the self-importance of all those people! What would I give to hear your strictures on them!'

'Your conjecture is totally wrong, I assure you. My mind was more agreeably engaged. I have been meditating on the very great pleasure which a pair of fine eyes in the face of a pretty woman can bestow.'

Miss Bingley immediately fixed her eyes on his face, and desired he would tell her what lady had the credit of inspiring such reflections. Mr Darcy replied with great intrepidity:

'Miss Elizabeth Bennet.'

'Miss Elizabeth Bennet!' repeated Miss Bingley. 'I am all astonishment. How long has she been such a favourite? – and pray, when am I to wish you joy?'

'That is exactly the question which I expected you to ask. A lady's imagination is very rapid; it jumps from admiration to love, from love to matrimony, in a moment. I knew you would be wishing me joy.'

'Nay, if you are serious about it, I shall consider the matter is absolutely settled. You will be having a charming mother-in-law, indeed; and, of course, she will always be at Pemberley with you.'

He listened to her with perfect indifference while she chose to entertain herself in this manner; and as his composure convinced her that all was safe, her wit flowed long.

irony · music · rules

Great Expectations

CHARLES DICKENS

◆

⏳ **15 minutes**

Stories can deliver the happy endings that life
all too often fails to provide. Here is one which
manages to be sweet without being sugary:
Pip and Estella have been in love for a long time,
and separated for a long time. But now, the
alignment of the stars is changing.

◆

For eleven years, I had not seen Joe nor Biddy with my
bodily eyes – though they had both been often before my
fancy in the East – when, upon an evening in December,
an hour or two after dark, I laid my hand softly on the
latch of the old kitchen door. I touched it so softly that I
was not heard, and looked in unseen. There, smoking his
pipe in the old place by the kitchen firelight, as hale and
as strong as ever, though a little grey, sat Joe; and there,
fenced into the corner with Joe's leg, and sitting on my
own little stool looking at the fire, was – I again!

'We giv' him the name of Pip for your sake, dear old
chap,' said Joe, delighted, when I took another stool by the

child's side (but I did not rumple his hair), 'and we hoped he might grow a little bit like you, and we think he do.'

I thought so too, and I took him out for a walk next morning, and we talked immensely, understanding one another to perfection. And I took him down to the churchyard, and set him on a certain tombstone there, and he showed me from that elevation which stone was sacred to the memory of Philip Pirrip, late of this Parish, and Also Georgiana, Wife of the Above.

'Biddy,' said I, when I talked with her after dinner, as her little girl lay sleeping in her lap, 'you must give Pip to me one of these days; or lend him, at all events.'

'No, no,' said Biddy, gently. 'You must marry.'

'So Herbert and Clara say, but I don't think I shall, Biddy. I have so settled down in their home, that it's not at all likely. I am already quite an old bachelor.'

Biddy looked down at her child, and put its little hand to her lips, and then put the good matronly hand with which she had touched it into mine. There was something in the action, and in the light pressure of Biddy's wedding-ring, that had a very pretty eloquence in it.

'Dear Pip,' said Biddy, 'you are sure you don't fret for her?'

'O no – I think not, Biddy.'

'Tell me as an old, old friend. Have you quite forgotten her?'

'My dear Biddy, I have forgotten nothing in my life that ever had a foremost place there, and little that ever had any place there. But that poor dream, as I once used to call it, has all gone by, Biddy – all gone by!'

Nevertheless, I knew, while I said those words, that I secretly intended to revisit the site of the old house that evening, alone, for her sake. Yes, even so. For Estella's sake.

I had heard of her as leading a most unhappy life, and as being separated from her husband, who had used her with great cruelty, and who had become quite renowned as a compound of pride, avarice, brutality, and meanness. And I had heard of the death of her husband, from an accident consequent on his ill-treatment of a horse. This release had befallen her some two years before; for anything I knew, she was married again.

The early dinner hour at Joe's, left me abundance of time, without hurrying my talk with Biddy, to walk over to the old spot before dark. But, what with loitering on the way to look at old objects and to think of old times, the day had quite declined when I came to the place.

There was no house now, no brewery, no building whatever left, but the wall of the old garden. The cleared space had been enclosed with a rough fence, and looking over it, I saw that some of the old ivy had struck root anew, and was growing green on low quiet mounds of ruin. A gate in the fence standing ajar, I pushed it open, and went in.

A cold silvery mist had veiled the afternoon, and the moon was not yet up to scatter it. But, the stars were shining beyond the mist, and the moon was coming, and the evening was not dark. I could trace out where every part of the old house had been, and where the brewery had been, and where the gates, and where the casks. I had done so, and was looking along the desolate garden walk, when I beheld a solitary figure in it.

The figure showed itself aware of me, as I advanced. It had been moving towards me, but it stood still. As I drew nearer, I saw it to be the figure of a woman. As I drew nearer yet, it was about to turn away, when it stopped, and let me come up with it. Then, it faltered, as if much surprised, and uttered my name, and I cried out—

'Estella!'

'I am greatly changed. I wonder you know me.'

The freshness of her beauty was indeed gone, but its indescribable majesty and its indescribable charm remained. Those attractions in it, I had seen before; what I had never seen before, was the saddened, softened light of the once proud eyes; what I had never felt before was the friendly touch of the once insensible hand.

We sat down on a bench that was near, and I said, 'After so many years, it is strange that we should thus meet again, Estella, here where our first meeting was! Do you often come back?'

'I have never been here since.'

'Nor I.'

The moon began to rise, and I thought of the placid look at the white ceiling, which had passed away. The moon began to rise, and I thought of the pressure on my hand when I had spoken the last words he had heard on earth.

Estella was the next to break the silence that ensued between us.

'I have very often hoped and intended to come back, but have been prevented by many circumstances. Poor, poor old place!'

The silvery mist was touched with the first rays of the moonlight, and the same rays touched the tears that dropped from her eyes. Not knowing that I saw them, and setting herself to get the better of them, she said quietly—

'Were you wondering, as you walked along, how it came to be left in this condition?'

'Yes, Estella.'

'The ground belongs to me. It is the only possession I have not relinquished. Everything else has gone from me, little by little, but I have kept this. It was the subject of the only determined resistance I made in all the wretched years.'

'Is it to be built on?'

'At last, it is. I came here to take leave of it before its change. And you,' she said, in a voice of touching interest to a wanderer, 'you live abroad still?'

'Still.'

'And do well, I am sure?'

'I work pretty hard for a sufficient living, and there-fore – yes, I do well.'

'I have often thought of you,' said Estella.

'Have you?'

'Of late, very often. There was a long hard time when I kept far from me the remembrance of what I had thrown away when I was quite ignorant of its worth. But since my duty has not been incompatible with the admis-sion of that remembrance, I have given it a place in my heart.'

'You have always held your place in my heart,' I answered. And we were silent again until she spoke.

'I little thought,' said Estella, 'that I should take leave of you in taking leave of this spot. I am very glad to do so.'

'Glad to part again, Estella? To me, parting is a painful thing. To me, the remembrance of our last parting has been ever mournful and painful.'

'But you said to me,' returned Estella, very earnestly, '"God bless you, God forgive you!" And if you could say that to me then, you will not hesitate to say that to me now – now, when suffering has been stronger than all other teaching, and has taught me to understand what your heart used to be. I have been bent and broken, but – I hope – into a better shape. Be as considerate and good to me as you were, and tell me we are friends.'

'We are friends,' said I, rising and bending over her, as she rose from the bench.

'And will continue friends apart,' said Estella.

I took her hand in mine, and we went out of the ruined place; and, as the morning mists had risen long ago when I first left the forge, so the evening mists were rising now, and in all the broad expanse of tranquil light they showed to me, I saw no shadow of another parting from her.

◗▬◖

desire · happiness · hope · resilience

The Return of the King

(third volume of *The Lord of the Rings*)

J. R. R. TOLKIEN

❖

⌛ 5 minutes

A true friend will stay with you in the face of
everything: even death, even the end of the
world. Frodo and Sam have completed their task
of destroying the ring of power, but now they
are trapped on a fiery mountain and Frodo is
wounded. All seems lost. And yet...

❖

'I am glad that you are here with me,' said Frodo. 'Here at
the end of all things, Sam.'

'Yes, I am with you, Master,' said Sam, laying Frodo's
wounded hand gently to his breast. 'And you're with me.
And the journey's finished. But after coming all that way I
don't want to give up yet. It's not like me, somehow, if you
understand.'

'Maybe not, Sam,' said Frodo; 'but it's like things are in
the world. Hopes fail. An end comes. We have only a little
time to wait now. We are lost in ruin and downfall, and
there is no escape.'

'Well, Master, we could at least go further from this dangerous place here, from this Crack of Doom, if that's its name. Now couldn't we? Come, Mr Frodo, let's go down the path at any rate!'

'Very well, Sam. If you wish to go, I'll come,' said Frodo; and they rose and went slowly down the winding road; and even as they passed towards the Mountain's quaking feet, a great smoke and steam belched from Sammath Naur, and the side of the cone was riven open, and a huge fiery vomit rolled in slow thunderous cascade down the eastern mountain-side.

Frodo and Sam could go no further. Their last strength of mind and body was swiftly ebbing. They had reached a low ashen hill piled at the Mountain's foot; but from it there was no more escape. It was an island now, not long to endure, amid the torment of Orodruin. All about it the earth gaped, and from deep rifts and pits smoke and fumes leaped up. Behind them the Mountain was convulsed. Great rents opened in its side. Slow rivers of fire came down the long slopes towards them. Soon they would be engulfed. A rain of hot ash was falling.

They stood now; and Sam still holding his master's hand caressed it. He sighed. 'What a tale we have been in, Mr Frodo, haven't we?' he said. 'I wish I could hear it told! Do you think they'll say: *Now comes the story of Nine-fingered Frodo and the Ring of Doom?* And then everyone will hush, like we did, when in Rivendell they told us the tale of Beren One-hand and the Great Jewel. I wish I could hear it! And I wonder how it will go on after our part.'

But even while he spoke so, to keep fear away until the

very last, his eyes still strayed north, north into the eye of the wind, to where the sky far off was clear, as the cold blast, rising to a gale, drove back the darkness and the ruin of the clouds.

*

And so it was that Gwaihir saw them with his keen far-seeing eyes, as down the wild wind he came, and daring the great peril of the skies he circled in the air: two small dark figures, forlorn, hand in hand upon a little hill, while the world shook under them, and gasped, and rivers of fire drew near. And even as he espied them and came swooping down, he saw them fall, worn out, or choked with fumes and heat, or stricken down by despair at last, hiding their eyes from death.

Side by side they lay; and down swept Gwaihir, and down came Landroval and Meneldor the swift, and in a dream, not knowing what fate had befallen them, the wanderers were lifted up and borne far away out of the darkness and the fire.

companionship · hope · resilience

Letter to Hippolyte de Guibert

JULIE DE L'ESPINASSE

⏳ 3 minutes

Julie de l'Espinasse hosted a salon in eighteenth-century Paris. A well-educated, witty, intelligent woman, she wrote a large number of letters.
In this one she leads us – with passion and eloquence – to three words that are very simple, and yet very difficult to say.

Ah, my dear friend, you hurt me, and a great curse for you and for me is the feeling which animates me. You were right in saying that you did not need to be loved as I know how to love; no, that is not your measure; you are so perfectly lovable, that you must be or become the first object of desire of all these charming ladies, who stick upon their heads all they had in it, and who are so lovable that they love themselves by preference above everything. You will give pleasure, you will satisfy the vanity of nearly all women. By what fatality have you held me to life, and you make me die of anxiety and of pain? My friend, I do not complain; but it distresses me that you pay no heed to my repose; this thought chills and tears my heart alternately. How can one have an instant's tranquillity with a man whose head is as defective as his coach, who counts for nothing the dangers, who never foresees anything, who is incapable of taking care, of exactitude, to whom it never happens to do what he has projected; in a word, a man who everything attracts, and whom nothing can stay nor give stability... Good night. My door has not been opened once today, but my heart palpitated. There were moments when I feared to hear your voice, and then I was disconsolate that it was not your voice. So many contradictions, so many contrary movements are true, and can be explained in three words: *I love you*.

anxiety · desire

LOSS

ALMOST EVERY PUBLISHER IN the UK rejected J. K. Rowling's first *Harry Potter* novel: they did not consider it to be 'commercial' enough. But she and her agent persisted, until they finally convinced one publisher to take it on. You know how the story ends: millions of readers the world over – adults as well as children – entranced by the magical world of Potter; multiple awards; film adaptations; riches beyond measure for Harry's creator; a charitable trust founded to fight poverty and disease. It's an uplifting success story if ever there was one.

There are times when we are J. K. Rowling: we lose until we win.

But consider the case of Herman Melville. He wrote *Moby Dick*, arguably one of the greatest and most influential novels in literary history – and a pretty good yarn too, if you are into seafaring adventures. Melville managed to sell it to a publisher, but never to readers: the book tanked, and so did his career after that. Melville died forgotten and certainly not wealthy. His work was rediscovered only after he died. Melville's is not a success story, other than in the sense that he was vindicated by history and won, posthumously, the reputation that he never had in life (which I find, to be honest, a lousy deal).

The thing is, there are also times when we are Herman Melville: we lose and that's it.

Just as music is also made of silence, so life is also made of loss. We miss our chance with the person we fall in love with. Our parents die. Our friends betray us. We realise our band will never make it. We screw up. Some losses are not a stepping-stone to future gain, some losses just suck. Life does not have a story arc, in which setback is followed by advance and failure by success: all too often, when something goes wrong, it is not the prelude to a bigger and better happiness.

I don't mean to sound bleak, but life *can* be – and the sooner we realise that, the better we can equip ourselves to deal with it. Sometimes good, healthy people die young. Sometimes we have to leave a place we love. When we lose something – a person, a chance, a part of ourselves – we should give ourselves time to come to terms with the loss, rather than fretting that we need to 'move on' (as contemporary cliché has it). We should *celebrate* loss, not for what it might lead to, but in and of itself: there might be a happy ending waiting for us round the next corner or there might not, we don't know, but what we *do* know is that here and now we are hurt. That is nothing to be ashamed of, not something to be brushed under the carpet.

*

The writings in this section will help us to deal with loss, to understand it and embrace it. You can read them to help your friends to acknowledge the pain, and to shoulder its burden with them. You can read them to articulate the feelings that loss brings, making them less frightening. Or you can read them to *train* your friends and yourself to come to terms with loss, for the moment when that training will come in handy. Not all of these pieces are sad ones; quite the contrary. Sadness is one of the dimensions of loss, but not the only one.

The myth of Alcestis is a famous celebration of loss, with a happy ending. Alcestis decides to die in order to save her husband, but her husband would rather be the one who dies than go on living without his wife.

Neil Gaiman reminds us that we should never lose our way when we walk the boundaries between dreams and reality.

Simone de Beauvoir's is a devastating piece on the loss of her mother. She lucidly articulates the doubts and fears we face when tragedy strikes.

Devastating also is Oscar Wilde's *De Profundis*. If you ever find yourself thinking that the better part of your life is behind you, and that you haven't done as much with it as you should have done, you may find solace in realising that others share your feelings.

Edith Nesbit's short story is a poignant tale of wasted opportunity.

Joe Hill offers a different take on grief. A woman loses her father, an unpublished writer, who now communicates with her by writing short stories – and they're better than ever.

Daphne du Maurier describes the feelings of loss we experience when we leave a hotel room behind, or any place where we have spent a part of our life, large or small.

Never again will we be the person occupying that time or that space.

From Graham Joyce comes another perspective on grief: what would happen if we could have one last conversation with someone who has died?

Alcestis

FRANCESCO DIMITRI

———◆———

⏳ 9 minutes

This is the story of Queen Alcestis. It raises
questions about selfishness and generosity, and
about what we are willing to renounce,
and what we are not, for a greater good.

———◆———

Alcestis was very much in love with King Admetus, her husband. Getting her father to agree to the marriage had not been easy. Before granting his blessing, her father gave Admetus an impossible task: Admetus had to tame a lion and a boar, and harness them to a carriage. But Alcestis' father didn't know that Admetus was friends with Apollo. With the god's help the young man met the challenge without breaking a sweat, and he could marry the woman he loved.

Admetus turned out to be a good king and a better husband, and he and Alcestis had many good years. They would walk the woods together, and when night came, read stories to each other. Alcestis loved the special pitch of Admetus' voice when he laughed – the only moment when he would let his regal mask slip. She loved how tender he could be in the secrecy of their bedroom: and when their pet cat died, Admetus allowed himself to cry. But he was strong, too, the best hunter ever seen and a skilled wrestler. They had many good years. Until Admetus fell ill.

It started one morning, when Admetus woke with a headache and an upset stomach. The night before they had drunk too much at a feast. He shrugged it off and said it was just the effects of the wine. Only it wasn't. The next day Admetus stayed in bed with a high fever, and on the day after that, he was barely conscious. Alcestis called in doctors and priests, but no one could help: Admetus' hour had come. Alcestis spent the night at her husband's bedside, and dawn found her taking a break, sitting on the steps of the palace staircase. She wept, not minding who might see her.

A pair of legs appeared by her side, and someone sat down next to her. 'Hello Alcestis,' the man said.

She knew him: he was no man. He was her husband's old friend Apollo.

'Are you here...' she said, her voice breaking. 'Are you here to bid him farewell?'

'Not exactly, no. I might... have done something.'

Alcestis looked at him. 'I'm listening.'

'I got the Fates drunk, years ago, and they gave me a little gift for Admetus. They agreed that when his hour came, they would let him live. Only...'

'Only?'

'Only, the world needs symmetry, you know. Someone else has to die in his place. Willingly,' Apollo added, in a regretful voice.

Alcestis stood up, all her tears suddenly gone: she didn't have time for misery. 'I'll find someone,' she said.

'I'm sure you will.'

Alcestis ran to Admetus' best human friend. Admetus had saved his life once, during a hunt, putting himself between his friend and a wild boar. When Alcestis explained the situation, he shook his head. 'But he's the King,' Alcestis said. 'It's not only about him! There's going to be trouble when he dies.'

'I guess so,' Admetus' best friend said. 'Such a shame.'

Alcestis ran out of the house and went to talk to Admetus' head servant, a man who had been a slave and Admetus had liberated. He refused too. Alcestis said, 'The king's life is much more important than yours!'

'Not to me it's not.'

Alcestis realised she was wasting her time. There were only two people who would give their life for the King. She went to his parents. They were elderly and frail, and they didn't have much longer to live.

They laughed in Alcestis' face.

'But you're going to die soon anyway!' she cried.

The father replied, 'I'd rather die *soon* than *now*.'

And the mother said, 'Besides, you never know. We might be made immortal. Such things happen.'

Alcestis left their room feeling desperate. How could they not understand? She thought they would be happier to die than live to see their son die. How could they bear the thought of going on without him, the sweetest man in the world? She certainly couldn't.

She certainly couldn't.

Of course, she thought. *She* would rather die than suffer the loss of her beloved, rather die than go through the night without hearing his voice reading stories to her. She loved him so much that taking his place was the least painful option for her. This time, she would be selfish.

'I'll go,' she said to the air, to the nymphs, to the invisible gods who were listening. 'I'll go, but let my Admetus live.'

She knew that Admetus would never forgive her, but she also knew he would love her nonetheless.

And so Alcestis died, and her beloved lived. And when he found out what had happened, he cried, and shouted to the stars that he didn't want to live this way, without his Alcestis. He thought of killing himself, but that would be disrespectful to her memory. Admetus, wishing that *he* was the one who had died, sat in his palace, in the darkness, with his sorrow and his pain.

But he wouldn't suffer for long.

When Alcestis reached the Underworld, Persephone was waiting for her, and Persephone knew one or two things about loss. 'Tell me your story,' the goddess said, and Alcestis did, as best she could.

When she was done, there was a long silence.

'Go back,' Persephone said after a while. 'Go to your husband.'

'But the balance...'

'I am the Queen of the Underworld,' Persephone said. '*I* decide what the balance is.'

That night Admetus was in the room that had been his and Alcestis', exhausted after a day spent weeping. He was in bed, trying to catch some sleep. The shadows in the room were wobbling like smoke, and his grieving mind thought he could catch in them a glimpse of the face he loved and missed.

'Are you a dream, or a spirit?' he asked.

Alcestis sat on the bed.

'Neither,' she said.

companionship · generosity · hope

'The Sweeper of Dreams'

NEIL GAIMAN

———◆———

⏳ **3 minutes**

There is a balance we must keep, between
our nocturnal dream world and the sun-
drenched reality. Neil Gaiman warns us
against the danger of losing it.

———◆———

After all the dreaming is over, after you wake, and leave
the world of madness and glory for the mundane day-lit
daily grind, through the wreckage of your abandoned
fancies walks the sweeper of dreams.

Who knows what he was when he was alive? Or if, for
that matter, he ever was alive. He certainly will not answer
your questions. The sweeper talks little, in his gruff grey
voice, and when he does speak it is mostly about the
weather and the prospects, victories and defeats of certain
sports teams. He despises everyone who is not him.

Just as you wake he comes to you, and he sweeps up
kingdoms and castles, and angels and owls, mountains
and oceans. He sweeps up the lust and the love and the

lovers, the sages who are not butterflies, the flowers of meat, the running of the deer and the sinking of the *Lusitania*. He sweeps up everything you left behind in your dreams, the life you wore, the eyes through which you gazed, the examination paper you were never able to find. One by one he sweeps them away: the sharp-toothed woman who sank her teeth into your face; the nuns in the woods; the dead arm that broke through the tepid water of the bath: the scarlet worms that crawled in your chest when you opened your shirt.

He will sweep it up – everything you left behind when you woke. And then he will burn it, to leave the stage fresh for your dreams tomorrow.

Treat him well, if you see him. Be polite with him. Ask him no questions. Applaud his teams' victories, commiserate with him over their losses, agree with him about the weather. Give him the respect he feels he is due.

For there are people he no longer visits, the sweeper of dreams, with his hand-rolled cigarette and his dragon tattoo.

You've seen them. They have mouths that twitch, and eyes that stare, and they babble and they mewl and they whimper. Some of them walk the cities in ragged clothes, their belongings under their arms. Others in their number are locked in the dark, in places where they can no longer harm themselves or others. They are not mad, or rather, the loss of their sanity is the lesser of their problems. It is worse than madness. They will tell you, if you let them: they are the ones who live, each day, in the wreckage of their dreams.

And if the sweeper of dreams leaves you, he will never come back.

magic · resilience

A Very Easy Death

SIMONE DE BEAUVOIR

◆

⏳ 8 minutes

This is a sad, lucid piece, by a celebrated twentieth-century French existentialist philosopher, about the loss of her mother. It is soothing, but very dark also, confronting us as it does with some of our deepest anxieties.

◆

What would have happened if Maman's doctor had detected the cancer as early as the first symptoms? No doubt it would have been treated with rays and Maman would have lived two or three years longer. But she would have known or at least suspected the nature of her disease, and she would have passed the end of her life in a state of dread. What we bitterly regretted was that the doctor's mistake had deceived us; otherwise Maman's happiness would have become our chief concern. The difficulties that prevented Jeanne and Poupette from having her in the summer would not have counted. I should have seen more of her; I should have invented things to please her.

And is one to be sorry that the doctors brought her

back to life and operated, or not? She, who did not want to lose a single day, 'won' thirty: they brought her joys; but they also brought her anxiety and suffering. Since she did escape from the martyrdom that I sometimes thought was hanging over her, I cannot decide for her. [...] And as for me? Those four weeks have left me pictures, nightmares, sadnesses that I should never have known if Maman had died that Wednesday morning. But I cannot measure the disturbance that I should have felt since my sorrow broke out in a way that I had not foreseen. We did derive an undoubted good from this respite: it saved us, or almost saved us, from remorse. When someone you love dies you pay for the sin of outliving her with a thousand piercing regrets. Her death brings to light her unique quality; she grows as vast as the world that her absence annihilates for her and whose whole existence was caused by her being there; you feel that she should have had more room in your life – all the room, if need be. You snatch yourself away from this wildness: she was only one among many. But since you never do all you might for anyone – not even within the arguable limits that you have set yourself – you have plenty of room left for self-reproach. With regard to Maman we were above all guilty, these last years, of care-lessness, omission and abstention. We felt that we atoned for this by the days that we gave her, and by the victories gained over fear and pain. Without our obstinate watch-fulness she would have suffered far more.

For indeed, comparatively speaking, her death was an easy one. 'Don't leave me in the power of the brutes.' I thought of all those who have no one to make that appeal to: what agony it must be to feel oneself a defenceless thing, utterly at the mercy of indifferent doctors and overworked nurses. No hand on the forehead when terror seizes them; no sedative as soon as pain begins to tear them; no lying prattle to fill the silence of the void. 'She aged forty years in twenty-four hours.' That phrase too had obsessed my mind. Even today – why? – there are horrible agonising deaths. And then in the public wards, when the last hour is coming near, they put a screen round the dying man's bed: he has seen this screen round other beds that were empty the next day: he knows. I pictured Maman, blinded for hours by the black sun that no one can look at directly: the horror of her staring eyes with their dilated pupils. She had a very easy death; an upper-class death.

[...]

Time vanishes behind those who leave this world, and the older I get the more my past years draw together. The 'Maman darling' of the days when I was ten can no longer be told from the inimical woman who oppressed my adolescence; I wept for them both when I wept for my old mother. I thought I had made up my mind about our failure and accepted it; but its sadness comes back to my heart. There are photographs of both of us, taken at about the same time: I am eighteen, she is nearly forty. Today I could almost be her mother and the grandmother of that sad-eyed girl. I am so sorry for them – for me because I am so young and I understand nothing; for her because her future is closed and she has never understood anything. But I would not know how to advise them. It was not in my power to wipe out the unhappiness in her childhood that condemned Maman to make me unhappy and to suffer in her turn from having done so. For if she embittered several years of my life, I certainly paid her back though I did not set out to do so. [...]

*

You do not die from being born, nor from having lived, nor from old age. You die from *something*. The knowledge that because of her age my mother's life must soon come to an end did not lessen the horrible surprise: she had sarcoma. Cancer, thrombosis, pneumonia: it is as violent and unforeseen as an engine stopping in the middle of the sky. My mother encouraged one to be optimistic when, crippled with arthritis and dying, she asserted the infinite value of each instant; but her vain tenaciousness also ripped and tore the reassuring curtain of everyday triviality. There is no such thing as a natural death: nothing that happens to a man is ever natural, since his presence calls the world into question. All men must die: but for every man his death is an accident and, even if he knows it and consents to it, an unjustifiable violation.

▶

anxiety · regret · self-knowledge

De Profundis

OSCAR WILDE

———◆———

⏳ 9 minutes

Do you ever feel like you have squandered
your talents, wasted your chances?
Oscar Wilde did.

———◆———

The gods had given me almost everything. But I let myself
be lured into long spells of senseless and sensual ease. I
amused myself with being a *flâneur*, a dandy, a man of
fashion. I surrounded myself with the smaller natures and
the meaner minds. I became the spendthrift of my own
genius, and to waste an eternal youth gave me a curious
joy. Tired of being on the heights, I deliberately went to the
depths in the search for new sensation. What the paradox
was to me in the sphere of thought, perversity became
to me in the sphere of passion. Desire, at the end, was
a malady, or a madness, or both. I grew careless of the
lives of others. I took pleasure where it pleased me, and
passed on. I forgot that every little action of the common
day makes or unmakes character, and that therefore what

one has done in the secret chamber one has some day to cry aloud on the housetop. I ceased to be lord over myself. I was no longer the captain of my soul, and did not know it. I allowed pleasure to dominate me. I ended in horrible disgrace. There is only one thing for me now, absolute humility.

I have lain in prison for nearly two years. Out of my nature has come wild despair; an abandonment to grief that was piteous even to look at; terrible and impotent rage; bitterness and scorn; anguish that wept aloud; misery that could find no voice; sorrow that was dumb. I have passed through every possible mood of suffering. Better than Wordsworth himself I know what Wordsworth meant when he said –

> 'Suffering is permanent, obscure, and dark
> And has the nature of infinity.'

But while there were times when I rejoiced in the idea that my sufferings were to be endless, I could not bear them to be without meaning. Now I find hidden somewhere away in my nature something that tells me that nothing in the whole world is meaningless, and suffering least of all. That something hidden away in my nature, like a treasure in a field, is Humility.

It is the last thing left in me, and the best: the ultimate discovery at which I have arrived, the starting-point for a fresh development. It has come to me right out of myself, so I know that it has come at the proper time. It could not have come before, nor later. Had any one told me of it, I would have rejected it. Had it been brought to me,

I would have refused it. As I found it, I want to keep it. I must do so. It is the one thing that has in it the elements of life, of a new life, *Vita Nuova* for me. Of all things it is the strangest. One cannot acquire it, except by surrendering everything that one has. It is only when one has lost all things, that one knows that one possesses it.

Now I have realised that it is in me, I see quite clearly what I ought to do; in fact, must do. And when I use such a phrase as that, I need not say that I am not alluding to any external sanction or command. I admit none. I am far more of an individualist than I ever was. Nothing seems to me of the smallest value except what one gets out of oneself. My nature is seeking a fresh mode of self-realisation. That is all I am concerned with. And the first thing that I have got to do is to free myself from any possible bitterness of feeling against the world.

I am completely penniless, and absolutely homeless. Yet there are worse things in the world than that. I am quite candid when I say that rather than go out from this prison with bitterness in my heart against the world, I would gladly and readily beg my bread from door to door. If I got nothing from the house of the rich I would get something at the house of the poor. Those who have much are often greedy; those who have little always share. I would not a bit mind sleeping in the cool grass in summer, and when winter came on sheltering myself by the warm close-thatched rick, or under the penthouse of a great barn, provided I had love in my heart. The external things of life seem to me now of no importance at all. You can see to what intensity of individualism I have arrived – or am arriving rather, for the journey is long, and 'where I walk there are thorns.'

Of course I know that to ask alms on the highway is not to be my lot, and that if ever I lie in the cool grass at night-time it will be to write sonnets to the moon. When I go out of prison, R. will be waiting for me on the other side of the big iron-studded gate, and he is the symbol, not merely of his own affection, but of the affection of many others besides. I believe I am to have enough to live on for about eighteen months at any rate, so that if I may not write beautiful books, I may at least read beautiful books; and what joy can be greater? After that, I hope to be able to recreate my creative faculty.

But were things different: had I not a friend left in the world; were there not a single house open to me in pity; had I to accept the wallet and ragged cloak of sheer penury: as long as I am free from all resentment, hardness and scorn, I would be able to face the life with much more calm and confidence than I would were my body in purple and fine linen, and the soul within me sick with hate.

anxiety · hope · meaning · regret

'Uncle Abraham's Romance'

EDITH NESBIT

◆———◆

⏳ 10 minutes

Edith Nesbit's gothic short story evokes
that most poignant of losses – of a love that
might have been, of a once-in-a-lifetime
opportunity for happiness.

◆———◆

'No, my dear,' my Uncle Abraham answered me, 'no –
nothing romantic ever happened to me... unless... but no;
that wasn't romantic either...'

I was. To me, I being eighteen, romance was the world.
My Uncle Abraham was old and lame. I followed the
gaze of his faded eyes, and my own rested on a miniature
that hung at his elbow-chair's right hand, a portrait of a
woman, whose loveliness even the miniature-painter's
art had been powerless to disguise – a woman with large
lustrous eyes and perfect oval face.

I rose to look at it. I had looked at it a hundred times.
Often enough in my baby days I had asked, 'Who's that,

uncle?' and always the answer was the same: 'A lady who died long ago, my dear.'

As I looked again at the picture, I asked, 'Was she like this?'

'Who?'

'Your – your romance!'

Uncle Abraham looked hard at me. 'Yes,' he said at last. 'Very – very like.'

I sat down on the floor by him. 'Won't you tell me about her?'

'There's nothing to tell,' he said. 'I think it was fancy mostly, and folly; but it's the realest thing in my life, my dear.'

A long pause. I kept silent. You should always give people time, especially old people.

'I remember,' he said in the dreamy tone always promising so well to the ear that loves a story – 'I remember, when I was a young man, I was very lonely indeed. I never had a sweetheart. I was always lame, my dear, from quite a boy; and the girls used to laugh at me.'

He sighed. Presently he went on:

'And so I got into the way of mooning off by myself in lonely places, and one of my favourite walks was up through our churchyard, which was set on a hill in the middle of the marsh country. I liked that because I never met anyone there. It's all over, years ago. I was a silly lad; but I couldn't bear of a summer evening to hear a rustle and a whisper from the other side of the hedge, or maybe a kiss, as I went by.

'Well, I used to go and sit all by myself in the churchyard, which was always sweet with the thyme and quite light (on account of it's being so high) long after the marshes were dark. I used to watch the bats flitting about in the red light, and wonder why God didn't make everyone's legs straight and strong, and wicked follies like that. But by the time the light was gone I had always worked it off, so to speak, and could go home quietly, and say my prayers without bitterness.

'Well, one hot night in August, when I had watched the sunset face and the crescent moon grow golden, I was just stepping over the low stone wall of the churchyard when I heard a rustle behind me. I turned around, expecting it to be a rabbit or a bird. It was a woman.'

He looked at the portrait. So did I.

'Yes,' he said, 'that was her very face. I was a bit scared and said something – I don't know what – she laughed and said, did I think she was a ghost? and I answered back; and I stayed talking to her over the churchyard wall till 'twas quite dark, and the glow-worms were out in the wet grass all along the way home.

'Next night, I saw her again; and the next, and the next. Always at twilight time; and if I passed any lovers leaning on the stiles in the marshes it was nothing to me now.'

Again my uncle paused. 'It was very long ago,' he said shyly, 'and I'm an old man; but I know what youth means, and happiness, though I was always lame, and the girls used to laugh at me. I don't know how long it went on – you don't measure time in dreams – but at last your grandfather said I looked as if I had one foot in the grave, and he would be sending me to stay with our kin in Bath, and take the waters. I had to go. I could not tell my father why I would rather die than go.'

'What was her name, Uncle?' I asked.

'She never would tell me her name, and why should she? I had names enough in my heart to call her by. Marriage? My dear, even then I knew marriage was not for me. But I met her night after night, always in our churchyard where the yew-trees were, and the old crooked gravestones so thick in the grass. It was there we always met and always parted. The last time was the night before I went away. She was very sad, and dearer than life itself. And she said—

"If you come back before the new moon, I shall meet you here just as usual. But if the new moon shines on this grave and you are not here – you will never see me again any more."

'She laid her hand on the tomb against which we had been leaning. It was an old, lichened, weather-worn stone, and its inscription –

SUSANNAH KINGSNORTH
Ob. 1723

"I shall be here," I said.

"I mean it," she said, very seriously and slowly, "it is no fancy. You will be here when the new moon shines?"

'I promised, and after a while we parted.

'I had been with my kinsfolk in Bath for nearly a month. I was to go home on the next day when, turning over a case in the parlour, I came upon that miniature. I could not speak for a minute. At last I said, with dry tongue, and heart beating to the tune of heaven and hell—

"Who is this?"

"That?" said my aunt. "Oh! She was betrothed to one of our family years ago, but she died before the wedding. They say she was a bit of a witch. A handsome one, wasn't she?"

'I looked again at the face, the lips, the eyes of my dear lovely love, whom I was to meet tomorrow night when the new moon shone on that tomb in our churchyard.

"Did you say she was dead?" I asked, and hardly knew my own voice.

"Years and years ago! Her name's on the back, and the date—"

'I took the portrait from its faded, red-velvet bed, and read on the back – SUSANNAH KINGSNORTH, *Ob.* 1723.

'That was in 1823.' My uncle stopped short.

'What happened?' I asked breathlessly.

'I believe I had a fit,' my uncle answered slowly, 'at any rate, I was very ill.'

'And you missed the new moon on the grave?'

'I missed the new moon on the grave.'

'And you never saw her again?'

'I never saw her again...'

'But, Uncle, do you really believe? Can the dead... was she... did you...'

My uncle took his pipe and filled it. 'It's a long time ago,' he said, 'a many, many years. Old man's tales, my dear! Old man's tales. Don't you take any notice of them.'

He lighted the pipe, puffed silently a moment or two

before he said: 'But I know what youth means, and love and happiness, though I was always lame, and the girls used to laugh at me.'

magic · regret · time

'Scheherazade's Typewriter'

JOE HILL

⏳ 10 minutes

When we lose someone we love, how long does
it take to make sense of the loss?

Elena's father had gone into the basement every night, after work, for as far back as she could remember, and did not come up until he had written three pages on the humming IBM electric typewriter he had bought in college, when he still believed he would someday be a famous novelist. He had been dead for three days before his daughter heard the typewriter in the basement, at the usual time: a burst of rapid bang-bang-banging, followed by a waiting silence, filled out only by the idiot hum of the machine.

Elena descended the steps, into darkness, her legs weak. The drone of his IBM filled the musty-smelling dark, so the gloom itself seemed to vibrate with electrical current, as before a thunderstorm. She reached the lamp beside her father's typewriter, and flipped it on just as the

Selectrix burst into another bang-bang flurry of noise. She screamed, and then screamed again when she saw the keys moving on their own, the chrome typeball lunging against the bare black platen.

That first time Elena saw the typewriter working on its own, she thought she might faint from the shock of it. Her mother almost did faint, when Elena showed her, the very next night. When the typewriter jumped to life and began to write, Elena's mother threw her hands up and shrieked and her legs wobbled under her, and Elena had to grab her by the arm to keep her from going down.

But in a few days they got used to it, and then it was exciting. Her mother had the idea to roll a sheet of paper in, just before the typewriter switched itself on at 8 p.m. Elena's mother wanted to see what it was writing, if it was a message for them from beyond. *My grave is cold. I love you and I miss you.*

But it was only another of his short stories. It didn't even start at the beginning. The page began midway, right in the middle of a sentence.

It was Elena's mother who thought to call the local news. A producer from channel five came to see the typewriter. The producer stayed until the machine turned itself on and wrote a few sentences, then she got up and briskly climbed the stairs. Elena's mother hurried after her, full of anxious questions.

'Remote control,' the producer said, her tone curt. She looked back over her shoulder with an expression of distaste. 'When did you bury your husband, ma'am? A week ago? What's wrong with you?'

None of the other television stations were interested. The man at the newspaper said it didn't sound like their kind of thing. Even some of their relatives suspected it was a prank in bad taste. Elena's mother went to bed and stayed there for several weeks, flattened by a terrible migraine, despondent and confused. And in the basement, every night, the typewriter worked on, flinging onto paper in noisy chattering bursts.

The dead man's daughter attended to the Selectrix. She learned just when to roll a fresh sheet of paper in, so that each night the machine produced three new pages of story, just as it had when her father was alive. In fact, the machine seemed to wait for her, humming in a jovial sort of way, until it had a fresh sheet to stain with ink.

Long after no one else wanted to think about the typewriter any more, Elena continued to go into the basement at night, to listen to the radio, and fold laundry, and roll a new sheet of paper into the IBM when it was necessary. It was a simple enough way to pass the time, mindless and sweet, rather like visiting her father's grave each day to leave fresh flowers.

Also, she had come to like reading the stories when they were finished. Stories about masks and baseball and fathers and their children... and ghosts. Some of them were ghost stories. She liked those the best. Wasn't that the first thing you learned in every fiction course everywhere? Write what you know? The ghost in the machine wrote about the dead with great authority.

After a while, the ribbons for the typewriter were only available by special order. Then even IBM stopped making them. The typeball wore down. She replaced it, but then the carriage started sticking. One night, it looked up, wouldn't move forward, and oily smoke began to trickle from under the iron hood of the machine. The typewriter hammered letter after letter, one right on top of the other, with a kind of mad fury, until Elena managed to scramble over and shut it off.

She brought it to a man who repaired old typewriters and other appliances. He returned it in perfect operating condition, but it never wrote on its own again. In the three weeks it was at the shop, it lost the habit.

As a little girl, Elena had asked her father why he went into the basement each night to make things up, and he had said it was because he couldn't sleep until he had written. Writing things warmed his imagination up for the work of creating an evening full of sweet dreams. Now she was unsettled by the idea that his death might be a restless, sleepless thing. But there was no help for it.

She was by then in her twenties and when her mother died – an unhappy old woman, estranged not just from her family but the entire world – she decided to move out, which meant selling the house and all that was in it. She had hardly started to sort the clutter in the basement, when she found herself sitting on the steps, rereading the stories her father had written after he died. In his life, he had given up the practice of submitting his work to publishers, had wearied of rejection. But his postmortem work seemed to the girl to be much – *livelier* – than his earlier work, and his stories of hauntings and the unnatural seemed especially arresting. Over the next few weeks, she collected his best into a single book, and began to send it to publishers. Most said there was no market in collections by writers of no reputation, but in time she heard from an editor at a small press who said he liked it, that her father had a fine feel for the supernatural.

'Didn't he?' she said.

Now this is the story as I first heard it myself from a friend in the publishing business. He was maddeningly ignorant of the all-important details, so I can't tell you where the book was finally published or when or, really, anything more regarding this curious collection. I wish I knew more. As a man who is fascinated with the occult, I would like to obtain a copy.

Unfortunately, the title and author of the unlikely book are not common knowledge.

comfort · creativity · magic · time

Rebecca

DAPHNE DU MAURIER

---◆---

⏳ 4 minutes

The Italians have a saying, *'partire è un po' morire'*,
'leaving is a bit like dying'. When you leave a
house in which you have lived, or even just a
hotel room where you have spent the weekend,
you are leaving behind a part of yourself.

---◆---

Packing up. The nagging worry of departure. Lost key,
unwritten labels, tissue paper lying on the floor. I hate
it all. Even now, when I have done so much of it, when
I live, as the saying goes, in my boxes. Even today, when
shutting drawers and flinging wide an hotel wardrobe, or
the impersonal shelves of a furnished villa, is a method-
ical matter of routine, I am aware of sadness, of a sense of
loss. Here, I say, we have lived, we have been happy. This
has been ours, however brief the time. Though two nights
only have been spent under a roof, yet we leave something
of ourselves behind. Nothing material, not a hair-pin on a
dressing table, not an empty bottle of Aspirin tablets, not

82

a handkerchief beneath a pillow, but something indefinable, a moment of our lives, a thought, a mood.

This house sheltered us, we spoke, we loved within those walls. That was yesterday. Today we pass on, we see it no more, and we are different, changed in some infinitesimal way. We can never be quite the same again. Even stopping for luncheon at a wayside inn, and going to a dark, unfamiliar room to wash my hands, the handle of the door unknown to me, the wallpaper peeling in strips, a funny little cracked mirror above the basin; for this moment, it is mine, it belongs to me. We know one another. This is the present. There is no past and no future. Here I am washing my hands, and the cracked mirror shows me to myself, suspended as it were, in time; this is me, this moment will not pass.

And then I open the door and go to the dining-room, where he is sitting waiting for me at a table, and I think how in that moment I have aged, passed on, how I have advanced one step towards an unknown destiny.

We smile, we choose our lunch, we speak of this and that, but – I say to myself – I am not she who left him five minutes ago. I am another woman, older, more mature...

I saw in a paper the other day that the Hôtel Côte d'Azur at Monte Carlo had gone to new management, and had a different name. The rooms have been redecorated, and the whole interior changed. Perhaps Mrs Van Hopper's suite on the first floor exists no more. Perhaps there is no trace of the small bedroom that was mine. I knew I should never go back, that day I knelt on the floor and fumbled with the awkward catch of her trunk.

The episode was finished, with the snapping of the lock. I glanced out of the window, and it was like turning the page of a photograph album. Those roof-tops and that sea were mine no more. They belonged to yesterday, to the past. The rooms already wore an empty air, stripped of our possessions, and there was something hungry about the suite, as though it wished us gone, and the new arrivals, who would come tomorrow, in our place. The heavy luggage stood ready strapped and locked in the corridor outside. The smaller stuff would be finished later. Waste-paper baskets groaned under litter. All her half empty medicine bottles and discarded face-cream jars, with torn-up bills and letters. Drawers in tables gaped, the bureau was stripped bare.

time · memory

The Limits of Enchantment

GRAHAM JOYCE

◆

⧖ 4 minutes

How we all wish we could have had one more
conversation with someone we loved deeply and
who has now passed on! By magic, or by using
our imaginations, or a bit of both, that wish
can be made a reality.

◆

I went to Mammy's grave in the night – not the fake grave, the real one in the woods. I sat with my back against the broad oak and I talked with Mammy. The moon was strong and clear and if I half closed my eyes I could easily see her, sitting with her back to a neighbouring oak, talking to me in the silvery light, talking to the moon.

Now perhaps I was going a little bit mad at that time, and I'm not sure if I saw it or I simply remembered it. Or perhaps in remembering it I somehow saw it all over again. What's the difference between memory and imagination if there is no one who can tell you whether a thing happened? Mammy was talking to me about my singing, how

I was a chanter and I shouldn't hide my gift. 'See them little babies?' she says. 'What's the first thing they do when they're out?'

'They wail,' I says.

'That's right,' she says, 'they wail, because they're hurting at the world, blinking and smarting at the sudden violence of the light. But after a while they stop, because the hurt falls away and they only see the beauty, but they don't know what it is. And when you're a-chanting, that's what you're doing.'

'What, hurting?'

'Yes. You're wailing. But you're on the way to mending it. To making the hurt fall away. All singing is about a hurting, ain't it? Oh, there's funny songs here and there, but there's a hurt even in them if you listen. And though the song can't put it right, it makes the hurt fall away for a moment, and lets you see what's behind it. And a fine chanter like you, well, that's what you give people.'

I said I understood. I thought perhaps I did.

But Mammy would never stay serious too long. She got to her feet and she kicked off her shoes. 'Come on Fern, count me in. Our little last dance afore we go in. One little last dance.'

I got to my feet, too, and with the moonlight drenching the woods and pouring between the trees I clapped my hands to count time and I gave her a lively Marrowbones, that being her favourite tune for ever. And she hitched up her skirts around her knees and she danced, with such a look of happiness and wicked joy etched on her features that I could barely hold the tune for laughing.

'Look at these old bones!' Mammy called as she kicked up her legs among the bluebells. 'Look at this old bag of bones a-dancing under the moon! And we don't care what they'll think of us!'

And I clapped my hands for her and I just couldn't keep the song going for laughter. The moon was on her. She seemed to call it to her and it soaked her as she capered and danced. It drizzled from her. It was her mantle. I could never love her more than at that moment.

And then in the next moment I was alone, under the tree where she was buried, and Mammy was gone, and I didn't know if I'd just recalled her shade to the world or only remembered something that happened, and I knew that dwelling on such an idea could tip you over the edge.

beauty · companionship · consolation · magic · memory

CHANGE

THE ANCIENT GREEK PHILOSOPHER Heraclitus main-
tained that there is one basic truth to the universe,
namely that everything changes all the time. The fact that
change happens is the only thing that never changes. You
can enter a river many times, Heraclitus said, but the river
will never be quite the same as the time before. The water
in which you bathed will have moved on, replaced by new
water. Different herbs will be growing on the banks, different fish will be swimming with you. Plato – a slightly
later Greek philosopher – described Heraclitus' theory
thus: 'No man ever steps in the same river twice.' When
we say that some things never change, we are not looking
at them carefully enough.

Modern science agrees with Heraclitus. The very solid-
ity of matter is an illusion: at a subatomic level, we are a
kaleidoscope whose component parts are in a state of constant flux. Inside our bodies, cells are continually dying
and new ones continually being born. Across a broader
time-frame, the same goes for planets and galaxies and,
possibly, parallel universes. And the same goes also for
ideas in our mind, the strangest space of all.

If that's not enough change for you, think of all the cogs
that are already in motion that will turn your life upside

down. The person you will fall in love with is slowly but surely getting closer to you; the process that will bring you your next job is already under way.

This makes life beautiful; but it makes it hard too.

Change is natural, but that doesn't make it automatically *good*. Change can be frightening, disorienting and yes, damaging. The process that was set in motion might be one that makes you redundant. But when we learn to negotiate change, to be gracious with it rather than afraid of it, we can enjoy it when it is good, and make it hurt a little less when it is not.

I selected the pieces in this section with this goal in mind: to help you accept change for what it is, a mysterious force. As long as you survive it, any experience in life is just that, experience, and can be enriching in its own way.

*

The myth I have chosen here is the story of Persephone and Demeter. It is the story of a young goddess, Persephone, who is kidnapped by the Lord of the Underworld, and then fought over by him and her mother Demeter. It helps us to see change as a fundamental part of life.

Ray Bradbury tells us about one of the saddest moments of change in any child's life, the end of summer. But it can be an uplifting experience as well as a sad one, a prelude to something new.

Joyce Carol Oates writes about the passing of the torch from one generation to the next: a woman who now finds herself having to take care of her ageing mother remembers the time when she was her mother's young daughter.

Writing to a young girl, Lewis Carroll gives her some practical advice on how to deal with change and enjoy the process: his letter is a hymn to change itself, and a guide to how to make the most of it.

In a piece that I wrote myself, I describe an oak tree in my garden. It is a very small oak, so small that a squirrel could destroy it. Will it ever get to be a tall, majestic tree?

Olive Schreiner's short story is about a change in a relationship, and about the importance of holding onto one's faith in other people.

Zora Neale Hurston writes charmingly about herself as a young girl, imagining the joys and sorrows she will go through in life.

Persephone and Demeter

FRANCESCO DIMITRI

———◆———

⏳ 7 minutes

This is the story of beautiful Persephone, the
Lord of the Underworld who stole her, and her
mother Demeter, who wanted her back.

———◆———

A long time ago, in a long-lost land, Persephone was
picking flowers with her girlfriends. She was the daughter
of Demeter, goddess of the harvest, and her brother Zeus,
king of the Gods. Such a heritage – she believed – kept
her safe. The day was blessed by a warm sun and a cool
breeze, and Persephone was gathering violets, crocuses
and roses. She would always keep herself to herself: even
Hermes, with all his wiles, hadn't managed to get past her
mother, Demeter, and marry her. But Hermes, unfortunately, wasn't the only one who had fallen for her.

A sweet scent wafted through the air of that glorious
day, making its way to Persephone. It filled her head like a
song. Charmed, she followed the scent to its source, leaving
her friends behind. The scent came from a gorgeous

daffodil, standing in a sunny glade. Persephone closed her eyes to inhale every last drop; then she crouched, and touched the flower.

The earth opened beneath her feet.

The earth opened, in that long-lost land, and Hades, Lord of the Underworld, came out of it, riding in a golden chariot. With a swift movement he seized Persephone. And she screamed, and she cried, but the Lord of the Underworld was much stronger than she was, and she couldn't wriggle free. He took her down, down, down, into the darkness and cold that lies beneath us, unseen, unheard, but always present, and the earth closed above their heads. It was as if Persephone had never existed.

Her mother, Demeter, heard her cry, and ran to help, but it was too late. Persephone was nowhere to be seen. The daffodil was still in its place, untouched, unscathed, sweet-smelling and innocent. Persephone was lost.

Demeter resolved to find her.

She took two torches, one in each hand, and by their light she travelled the world for nine days, without eating, without sleeping, without bathing, calling for her daughter. On the tenth day Hecate, goddess of the Moon, joined her: Hecate too had heard Persephone's cry, and she had seen her being kidnapped, but the face of the man who stole her had been covered by night's dark veil.

Hecate, though, knew who could help. She and Demeter went to talk with the sun-god, Helios, who sees everything that happens. He respected Demeter too much to hide anything from her: he told her that Hades, Lord of the Underworld, had stolen her daughter, and that Zeus himself had allowed it to happen. Helios tried to appease Demeter, saying that Hades was a great Lord, and would be a good husband, which was true, but the fact remained that Persephone had been taken against her will and that of her mother, and this could not be tolerated.

Zeus had betrayed Demeter, his own sister. For her part, Demeter was disgusted with her fellow-gods: she wanted nothing more to do with them. She started wandering the land, and neglecting her divine duties.

Without her, plants withered and the land began to die. Without her, everything was lost for gods and mortals alike. So Zeus told Hades to give Persephone back.

Hades had made Persephone Queen of the Underworld, and she was not unhappy there: indeed, Hades was a good husband. But she wanted to go back to her mother, and Zeus had spoken. Hades gave her one last gift, some pomegranate seeds, and she left. She walked up, up, up, through the dark caves of the Underworld, up, up, up, across the River Styx, and so she returned to the light, and to the fair world of sun and moon.

Demeter was overjoyed to see her daughter again, and to hold her, and to speak to her: here she was, alive, and beautiful, and young.

Something had changed, though; something was different.

Demeter asked, 'Did you eat something in the Underworld?'

'I ate some pomegranate seeds,' Persephone replied.

Demeter knew that those who eat the food of the Underworld are bound to stay there for ever. This rule is older and stranger even than the gods, and they have to abide by it. Her daughter should have known better. She asked, 'Why did you do that?'

'Hades used magic to trick me.'

Life was returning to the land; flowers were springing up again, and fruit was growing on the trees. 'We'll find a way,' Demeter said.

She asked Zeus to figure something out, and Zeus, who had learnt his lesson, did just that. It was decided that Persephone would spend one-third of the year in the Underworld, ruling as its queen, equal in all respects to Hades; and two-thirds of the year above, with the other gods, and nymphs, and beautiful humans.

Since that time, long past but not forgotten, there is a moment, every year, when sadness falls; when Persephone leaves us, and we feel everything is lost. But then the season changes, and Persephone comes back. Time is not an arrow, time is a circle, and everything has to change so that everything can survive.

Persephone is happy now, a queen in the world below, a daughter in the world above, a goddess in both. The Lord of the Underworld didn't get his way, not completely, and nor did Demeter. While Hades and Demeter remain prisoners of their roles, always the same, unchanging, fixed in time, Persephone can travel between worlds. She can change.

Yes, Persephone is very happy now.

▶

adventure · desire · happiness

Dandelion Wine

RAY BRADBURY

◆

⏳ 13 minutes

Do you remember the end of summer, when
you were a child? That sense of one thing ending
and something else beginning? This is about all
that, about the bittersweet flavour of change.

◆

And then, quite suddenly, summer was over.

He knew it first when walking downtown. Tom grabbed
his arm and pointed gasping at the dime store window.
They stood there unable to move because of the things
from another world displayed so neatly, so innocently, so
frighteningly, there.

'Pencils, Doug, ten thousand pencils!'

'Oh, my gosh!'

'Nickel tablets, dime tablets, notebooks, erasers, water
colors, rulers, compasses, a hundred thousand of them!'

'Don't look. Maybe it's just a mirage.'

'No,' moaned Tom in despair. 'School. School straight
on ahead! Why, why do dime stores show things like that

in windows before summer's even over! Ruin half the vacation!'

They walked on home and found Grandfather alone on the sere, bald-spotted lawn, plucking the last few dandelions. They worked with him silently for a time and then Douglas, bent in his own shadow, said:

'Tom, if this year's gone like this, what will next year be, better or worse?'

'Don't ask me.' Tom blew a tune on a dandelion stem. 'I didn't make the world.' He thought about it. 'Though some days I feel like I did.' He spat happily.

'I got a hunch,' said Douglas.

'What?'

'Next year's going to be even bigger, days will be brighter, nights longer and darker, more people dying, more babies born, and me in the middle of it all.'

'You and two zillion other people, Doug, remember.'

'Day like today,' murmured Douglas, 'I feel it'll be... just me!'

'Need any help,' said Tom, 'just yell.'

'What could a ten-year-old brother do?'

'A ten-year-old brother'll be eleven next summer. I'll unwind the world like the rubber band on a golf ball's insides every morning, put it back together every night. Show you how, if you ask.'

'Crazy.'

'Always was.' Tom crossed his eyes, stuck out his tongue. 'Always will be.'

Douglas laughed. They went down in the cellar with Grandpa and while he decapitated the flowers they looked at all the summer shelves and glimmering there in the motionless streams, the bottles of dandelion wine. Numbered from one to ninety-odd, there the ketchup bottles, most of them full now, stood burning in the cellar twilight, one for every living summer day.

'Boy,' said Tom, 'what a swell way to save June, July, and August. Real practical.'

Grandfather looked up, considered this, and smiled.

'Better than putting things in the attic you never use again. This way, you get to live the summer over for a minute or two here or there along the way through the winter, and when the bottles are empty the summer's gone for good and no regrets and no sentimental trash lying about for you to stumble over forty years from now. Clean, smokeless, efficient, that's dandelion wine.'

The two boys pointed along the rows of bottles.

'There's the first day of summer.'

'There's the new tennis shoes day.'

'Sure! And there's the Green Machine!'

'Buffalo dust and Ching Ling Soo!'

'The Tarot Witch! The Lonely One!'

'It's not really over,' said Tom. 'It'll never be over. I'll remember what happened on every day of this year, forever.'

'It was over before it began,' said Grandpa, unwinding the wine press. 'I don't remember a thing that happened except some new type of grass that wouldn't need cutting.'

'You're joking!'

'No, sir, Doug, Tom, you'll find as you get older the days kind of blur... can't tell one from the other...'

'But, heck,' said Tom. 'On Monday this week I roller-skated at Electric Park, Tuesday I ate chocolate cake, Wednesday I fell in the crick, Thursday fell off a swinging vine, the week's been full of things! And today, I'll remember today because the leaves outside are beginning to get all red and yellow. Won't be long they'll be all over the lawn and we'll jump in piles of them and burn them. I'll never forget today! I'll always remember, I know!'

Grandfather looked up through the cellar window at the late-summer trees stirring in a colder wind. 'Of course you will, Tom,' he said. 'Of course you will.'

And they left the mellow light of the dandelion wine and went upstairs to carry out the last few rituals of summer, for they felt that now the final day, the final night had come. As the day grew late they realized that for two or three nights now, porches had emptied early of their inhabitants. The air had a different, drier smell and Grandma was talking of hot coffee instead of iced tea; the open, white-flutter-curtained windows were closing in the great bays; cold cuts were giving way to steamed beef. The mosquitoes were gone from the porch, and surely when they abandoned the conflict the war with Time was really done, there was nothing for it but that humans also forsake the battleground.

Now Tom and Douglas and Grandfather stood, as they had stood three months, or was it three long centuries ago, on this front porch which creaked like a ship slumbering at night in growing swells, and they sniffed the air. Inside, the boys' bones felt like chalk and ivory instead of green mint sticks and licorice whips as earlier in the year.

But the new cold touched Grandfather's skeleton first, like a raw hand chording the yellow bass piano keys in the dining room.

As the compass turns, so turned Grandfather, north.

'I guess,' he said, deliberating, 'we won't be coming out here anymore.'

And the three of them clanked the chains shaken down from the porch-ceiling eyelets and carried the swing like a weathered bier around to the garage, followed by a blowing of the first dried leaves. Inside, they heard Grandma poking up a fire in the library. The windows shook with a sudden gust of wind.

Douglas, spending a last night in the cupola tower above Grandma and Grandpa, wrote in his tablet:

'Everything runs backward now. Like matinee films sometimes, where people jump out of water onto diving boards. Come September you push down the windows you pushed up, take off the sneakers you put on, pull on the hard shoes you threw away last June. People run in the house now like birds jumping back inside clocks. One minute, porches loaded, everyone gabbing thirty to a dozen. Next minute, doors slam, talk stops, and leaves fall off trees like crazy.'

He looked from the high window at the land where the crickets were strewn like dried figs in the creek beds, at a sky where birds would wheel south now through the cry of autumn loons and where trees would go up in a great fine burning of color on the steely clouds. Way out in the country tonight he could smell the pumpkins ripening toward the knife and the triangle eye and the singeing candle. Here in town the first few scarves of smoke unwound from chimneys and the faint faraway quaking of iron was the rush of black hard rivers of coal down chutes, building high dark mounds in cellar bins.

But it was late and getting later.

Douglas in the high cupola above the town, moved his hand.

'Everyone, clothes off!'

He waited. The wind blew, icing the windowpane.

'Brush teeth.'

He waited again.

'Now,' he said at last, 'out with the lights!'

He blinked. And the town winked out its lights, sleepily, here, there, as the courthouse clock struck ten, ten-thirty, eleven, and drowsy midnight.

'The last ones now... there... there...'

He lay in his bed and the town slept around him and the ravine was dark and the lake was moving quietly on its shore and everyone, his family, his friends, the old people and the young, slept on one street or another, in one house or another, or slept in the far country churchyards.

He shut his eyes.

June dawns, July noons, August evenings over, finished, done, and gone forever with only the sense of it all left here in his head. Now, a whole autumn, a white winter, a cool and greening spring to figure sums and totals of summer past. And if he should forget, the dandelion wine stood in the cellar, numbered huge for each and every day. He would go there often, stare straight into the sun until he could stare no more, then close his eyes and consider the burned spots, the fleeting scars left dancing on his warm eyelids; arranging, rearranging each fire and reflection until the pattern was clear...

So thinking, he slept.

And, sleeping, put an end to Summer, 1928.

meaning · memory · time

'The Scarf'

JOYCE CAROL OATES

◆

⧗ 15 minutes

This is a story about the passing of time, and
the changing roles of parents and children.

◆

A turquoise silk scarf, elegantly long, and narrow; so deli-
cately threaded with pale gold and silver butterflies, you
might lose yourself in a dream contemplating it, imagining you're gazing into another dimension or another time
in which the heraldic butterflies are living creatures with
slow, pulsing wings.

*

Eleven years old, I was searching for a birthday present
for my mother. *Mom* she was to me though often in weak
moments I'd hear my voice cry *Mommy*.

It was a windy grit-borne Saturday in late March, a
week before Easter, and cold. Searching through the
stores of downtown Strykersville. Not Woolworth's, not
Rexall's Drugs, not Norban's Discounts where a gang of

girls might prowl after school but the 'better' women's stores where few of us went except with our mothers, and rarely even then.

Saved jealously, in secret, for many months in a bunched-up white sock in my bureau drawer was eight dollars and sixty-five cents. Now in my jacket pocket, the bills carefully folded. This sum was sufficient, I believed, for a really nice, really special present for my mother. I was excited, nervous; already I could see the surprised pleasure in my mother's eyes as she unwrapped the box, and this was to be my reward. For there was a delicious way Mom had of squinching up her face, which was an unlined, pretty face, a young-woman face still (my parents' ages were mysteries to me I would not have dared to penetrate but clearly they were 'young' compared with most of my friends' parents – in their early thirties) and saying, in her warm whispery voice, as if this were a secret between us, 'Oh, honey, what have you done—!'

I wanted to strike that match bringing out a warm startled glow in my mother's face, that glistening in her eyes.

I wanted to present my mother with, not a mere store-bought item, but a love offering. A talisman against harm. The perfect gift that was a spell against hurt, fear, aloneness; sorrow, illness, age and death and oblivion. The gift that says, *I love you, you are life to me.*

[...]

At last I found myself amid glittery glass display cases and racks of beautiful leather goods hanging like the slain carcasses of animals. A well-worn parquet floor creaked incriminatingly beneath my feet. How had I dared enter Kenilworth's Ladies Fashions, where mother never shopped? What gusty wind had propelled me inside, like a taunting hand on the flat of my back? The lady salesclerk, tight-corseted with a scratchy steel-wool bun at the nape of her neck and smacking-red downturned mouth, eyed my every movement up and down the dazzling aisles. 'May I assist you, miss?' this lady asked in a cold, doubtful voice. I murmured I was just looking. 'Did you come to look, miss, or to buy?' My face pounded with blood as if I'd been turned upside-down. This woman didn't trust me! [...]

In a weak voice I said, 'It's for my mother – a birthday present. How much is – this?' I'd been staring at a display of scarves. The price tags on certain of the items of merchandise – the wallets, the handbags, even gloves and handkerchiefs – were so absurdly high, my eye took them in even as my brain repelled them, as information bits not to be assimilated. Scarves, I seemed to believe, would be more reasonably priced. And what beautiful scarves were on display – I stared almost without comprehension at these lovely colors, these exquisite fabrics and designs. For these were not coarse, practical, cottony-flannel scarves like the kind I wore most of the winter, that tied tightly beneath the chin; scarves that kept one's hair from whipping into snarls, kept ears and neck warm; scarves that looked, at their frequent worst, not unlike bandages wrapped around the head. These scarves were works of art. [...] Blindly I pointed at – I didn't dare touch – the most beautiful of the scarves, turquoise, a fine delicate silk patterned with small gold and silver figures I couldn't quite decipher. Through her pinched-looking bifocals the salesclerk peered at me, saying, in a voice of reproach, '*That* scarf is pure silk, from China. *That* scarf is—' Pausing then to consider me as if for the first time. Maybe she felt in the air the tremor and heat of my blood. Maybe it was simple pity. This utterly mysterious transaction, one of those unfathomable and incalculable events that mark at rare intervals the inner curve of our lives, gratuitous moments of grace. In a lowered, more kindly voice, though with an edge of adult annoyance, the salesclerk said, 'It's ten dollars. Plus tax.'

Ten dollars. Like a child in an enchantment I began numbly to remove my savings from my pocket, six wrinkled dollars and nickels, dimes, a single quarter, and numerous pennies, counting them with frowning earnestness as if I hadn't any idea what they might add up to. The sharp-eyed salesclerk said irritably, '—I mean eight dollars. It's been marked down to eight dollars for our Easter sale.' Eight dollars! I said, stammering, 'I – I'll take it. Thank you.' Relief so flooded me I might have fainted. I was smiling, triumphant. I couldn't believe my good luck even as, with childish egotism, I never paused to doubt it.

Eagerly I handed over my money to the salesclerk, who rang up the purchase with that curious prickly air of impatience, as if I'd embarrassed her; as if I were not an intruder in Kenilworth's after all, but a child-relative of hers she did not wish to acknowledge. As she briskly wrapped the boxed scarf in glossy pink paper stamped with HAPPY BIRTHDAY! I dared raise my eyes and saw with a mild shock that the woman wasn't so old as I'd thought – not much older than my mother. Her hair was a thin, graying brown caught in an angry-looking bun, her face was heavily made-up yet not pretty, her bright lipstick-mouth downturned. When she handed me the gift-wrapped box in a Kenilworth's silver-striped bag she said, frowning at me through her eyeglasses, 'It's ready to give to your mother. The price tag is off.'

*

Mother insists *But I have no more use for this, dear. Please take it.* Rummaging through closets, bureau drawers of the old house soon to be sold to strangers. In her calm melodic voice that belies the shakiness of her hands, saying, *If – later – something happens to me – I don't want it to be lost.*

Each visit back home, Mother has more to give me. Things once precious out of the ever-more remote, receding past. What is the secret meaning of such gift-giving by a woman of eighy-three, don't inquire.

Mother speaks often, vaguely, of *lost.* She fears papers being lost – insurance policies, medical records. *Lost* is a bottomless ravine into which you might fall, and fall. Into which her several sisters and brothers have disappeared one by one, and a number of her friends. And Father – has it already been a year? So that, for the remainder of her life, Mother's life grown mysterious to her as a dream that continues ceaselessly without defining itself, without the rude interruption of lucidity, she will wake in the morning wondering where had Dad gone? She reaches out and there's no one beside her, so she tells herself, He's in the bathroom. And, almost, she can hear him in there.

Later she thinks, He must be outside. And, almost, she can hear the lawn mower. Or she thinks, He's taken the car. And gone – where?

'Here! Here it is.'

At the bottom of a drawer in a bedroom bureau Mother has found what she's been searching for with such concentration. This afternoon she has pressed upon me a square-cut amethyst in an antique setting, a ring once belonging to her mother-in-law, and a handwoven potholder only just perceptibly marred by scorching. And now she opens a long flat box, and there it is, amid tissue paper: the silk turquoise scarf with its pale heraldic butterflies.

For a moment, I can't speak. I've gone entirely numb.

Fifty years. Can it have been – fifty years.

Says Mother, proudly, 'Your father gave it to me. When we were just married. It was my favorite scarf but you can see – it was too pretty to wear, and too thin. So I put it away.'

'But you did wear it, Mother. I remember.'

'Did I?'

'With that beige silk suit you had, for Audrey's wedding? And – well – a few other times.' I can see in Mother's face that expression of veiled alarm. Any suggestion of her memory failing frightens her; she's seen, at close range, the ravages of age in others.

Mother says quickly, 'Please take it, dear. It would make me happy if you did.'

'But, Mother—'

'I don't have any use for it, and I don't want it to get *lost*.'

Her voice rises just perceptibly, somewhere between a plea and a command.

Staring, I lift the turquoise scarf from the box. Admiring. In fact its label is French, not Chinese. In fact the turquoise isn't so vivid as I remember[...]

Fifty years. My mother's thirty-third birthday. She'd opened my present to her nervously: the luxurious wrappings with ribbons and bows, the embossed silver KENILWORTH'S on the box must have alarmed her. Taking the scarf out of the box, Mother had been speechless for a long moment before saying, 'Oh, honey it's – *beautiful*. How did you—' But her voice trailed off. As if words failed her. Or with her subtle sense of tact she believed it would be rude to make such an inquiry even of an eleven-year-old daughter.

That talisman that says *I love you. You are life to me*.

This luminous silky scarf imprinted with butterflies like ancient heraldic coins. The kind of imported, expensive scarf women are wearing today, flung casually over their shoulders. I ask Mother if she's absolutely certain she wants to give away the scarf though I know the answer; for Mother has come to an age when she knows exactly what she wants and what she doesn't want, what she needs and doesn't need. These encumbrances of life, that bind one to life.

In reply Mother loops the scarf around my neck, at first lightly tying the ends, then untying them, beside me at the mirror.

'Darling, see? It's beautiful on *you*.'

beauty · meaning · memory · time

From *The Life and Letters of Lewis Carroll*

LEWIS CARROLL

◆———

⧖ 4 minutes

In a letter to Isabel Standen, a young friend
of his, the author of *Alice's Adventures in
Wonderland* has some wise advice to impart on
how to deal with changing conditions.

———◆

I can quite understand, and much sympathise with,
what you say of your feeling lonely, and not what you can
honestly call 'happy.' Now I am going to give you a bit of
philosophy about that – my own experience is that every
new form of life we try is, just at first, irksome rather than
pleasant. My first day or two at the sea is a little depress-
ing; I miss the Christ Church interests, and haven't taken
up the threads of interest here; and, just in the same way,
my first day or two, when I get back to Christ Church, I
miss the seaside pleasures, and feel with unusual clearness the bothers of business-routine. In all such cases, the
true philosophy, I believe, is 'wait a bit.' Our mental nerves
seem to be so adjusted that we feel first and most keenly,
the discomforts of any new form of life; but, after a bit, we

get used to them, and cease to notice them; and then we have time to realise the enjoyable features, which at first we were too much worried to be conscious of.

Suppose you hurt your arm, and had to wear it in a sling for a month. For the first two or three days the discomfort of the bandage, the pressure of the sling on the neck and shoulder, the being unable to use the arm, would be a constant worry. You would feel as if all comfort in life were gone; after a couple of days you would be used to the new sensations, after a week you perhaps wouldn't notice them at all; and life would seem just as comfortable as ever.

So my advice is, don't think about loneliness, or happiness, or unhappiness, for a week or two. Then 'take stock' again, and compare your feelings with what they were two weeks previously. If they have changed, even a little, for the better you are on the right track; if not, we may begin to suspect the life does not suit you. But what I want specially to urge is that there's no use in comparing one's feelings between one day and the next; you must allow a reasonable interval, for the direction of change to show itself.

Sit on the beach, and watch the waves for a few seconds; you say 'the tide is coming in'; watch half a dozen successive waves, and you may say 'the last is the lowest; it is going out.' Wait a quarter of an hour, and compare its average place with what it was at first, and you will say 'No, it is coming in after all.'

With love, I am always affectionately yours...

calm · resilience · happiness

'The Oak in my Garden'

FRANCESCO DIMITRI

◆

⧗ 12 minutes

There is an oak, and there is a young family,
and there are things which might or
might not come to pass...

◆

I cannot carve my sweetheart's initials on the oak in
my garden, nor can I climb it on a summer afternoon. I
cannot hang a hammock on it and I cannot sit in its shade,
with ice-cold lemonade and a book. This oak is far too
small for that.

The oak in my garden barely reaches halfway up my
shin: young as she is, she can't travel all the way up to my
knee. In winter I need to be careful not to stamp on her,
not to mistake her for a dead branch sticking out from the
earth. When the oak looks up at me, she must feel I am
a giant: I could kill her on a whim. And yet I can see that
she is not afraid of me. Being an oak, she is brave, almost
foolhardy.

This oak was born after my wife and I moved into this

house. We didn't buy her in a shop. She came out of an acorn – buried, I would guess, by one of the grey squirrels that hang around our neighbourhood. Why did the squirrel not come back for it? I couldn't say, but food is plentiful around here, and I imagine that squirrels can afford to be careless with their acorns. But was it carelessness, I wonder? Or perhaps the squirrel met its end soon after burying the acorn? A car, a cat, a misjudged jump, or simply old age

Be that as it may, the squirrel made the oak. In fifty years from now it will be surprising to think of that – but only if the oak survives that long, if she has the chance to transform herself into a towering marvel with deep roots, thick bark, and a green crown of foliage around her head. For today the oak is still comfortably squirrel-sized. A mere acorn is fatter than her trunk; and from that trunk only a forlorn offshoot pokes out, hesitantly, as if not sure that poking out was the clever thing to do.

The oak grows – slowly, as oaks do – in the strip of bare earth between the lawn and the fence. She is fragile, easy to kill, and she keeps out of the way of us giants. I look at her as little as I can, for I know, as she knows, that her future is set to be grim.

The first time I noticed her, I was having breakfast on the patio with my wife and a friend. It was late Spring, and the oak had proudly managed not one, but two green leaves. Our friend noticed them, and nodded at them, and said that we should root it up. You can't keep an oak in a city garden.

He was right, of course. This oak is like a tiger cub:

manageable while she stays small, but ultimately not cut out for the tame amusements we have to offer. Though she is harmless now, cute in a defenceless sort of way, she has the sap of the Queen of the Woods running through her trunk, beating to the rhythm of her roots. Her spirit is strong, stronger than mine, and left to herself, she will grow – although slowly, as oaks do.

This garden is no place for towering marvels. Year after year, this oak will become bigger, and new offshoots will band together with the one I see now, a small group of friends at first, and then an army. The oak will become taller than me, and mightier. Her roots will reach deep underground, and will declare war on the foundations of my house, and though the roots might lose a few battles, roots always win in the end. The oak will become too proud for the fence she is growing so close to, and she will want to bring it down. She will become too big for the herbaceous border, and she will fatten herself on the precious space she now shares with violets and roses and daffodils. She will eat up the fence, she will eat up the border, she will eat up the lawn, and the very basis of the little dwelling my wife and I call our home, reclaiming her rightful heritage, her crown of leaves. So yes, I should get rid of her.

But not just yet.

This oak was small last year, and she is small this year, and she will be small for years to come. My wife and I are not planning to live in this house for ever: by the time the oak has grown to be tall and mighty, we shall be long gone. And maybe we will leave her here, and hope the new owners of the garden (not of the oak, because nobody can ever own an oak) will let her enjoy a few more springs. Or maybe we will take her with us when we depart, a living memory of this particular moment of our life, and when we have the bigger garden we sometimes talk of, there might be room for her there too. Wouldn't it be cruel to kill her now, small as she is?

The oak is aware that the cards are stacked against her. If she is permitted to grow, a time will come when she is too big and too powerful and has to be cut down. And even if we took her with us to a new home, the journey would be dangerous, and it is far from certain that she would survive it. So for all the potential for royalty that runs fierce in her sap, it is unlikely that the oak will ever live to realise it. Her hopes will be crushed, and she will end her days uprooted and forgotten in a metropolitan dump.

She knows that, and she doesn't care. She is much too wise. She looks at me, defiant, and if only I knew how to talk to spirits, I would hear her saying, this is what I am, a thing of the wild, able to grow in the deep of the woods as much as in your neat garden, built by squirrels and the secret workings of the earth, and you might kill me, but you can't bend me: you have no real power over me. You could destroy me right now, without breaking sweat, but even so, I am much stronger than you, because you are afraid of the future and I am not, and my kind will reign over this world long after your kind is past and gone.

And I know she is right, and I let her be, for now. One day I will have to consider the problem she poses; I will have to ponder the balance between the call of the wild and the need to protect fences, foundations, and herbaceous borders.

One day – but not just yet.

◖

anxiety · hope · married life · potential

'The Woman's Rose'

OLIVE SCHREINER

◆

⏳ 12 minutes

A small gift can change a relationship, and
become a cherished memory in years to come.

◆

I have an old, brown carved box; the lid is broken and tied
with a string. In it I keep little squares of paper, with hair
inside, and a little picture which hung over my brother's
bed when we were children, and other things as small. I
have in it a rose. Other women also have such boxes where
they keep such trifles, but no one has my rose.

When my eye is dim, and my heart grows faint, and my
faith in woman flickers, [...] the scent of that dead rose,
withered for twelve years, comes back to me. I know there
will be spring; as surely as the birds know it when they see
above the snow two tiny, quivering green leaves. Spring
cannot fail us.

There were other flowers in the box once; a bunch of
white acacia flowers, gathered by the strong hand of a

man, as we passed down a village street on a sultry afternoon, when it had rained, and the drops fell on us from the leaves of the acacia trees. The flowers were damp; they made mildew marks on the paper I folded them in. After many years I threw them away. There is nothing of them left in the box now, but a faint, strong smell of dried acacia, that recalls that sultry summer afternoon; but the rose is in the box still.

It is many years ago now; I was a girl of fifteen, and I went to visit in a small up-country town. It was young in those days, and two days' journey from the nearest village; the population consisted mainly of men. A few were married, and had their wives and children, but most were single. There was only one young girl there when I came. She was about seventeen, fair, and rather fully-fleshed; she had large dreamy blue eyes, and wavy light hair; full, rather heavy lips, until she smiled; then her face broke into dimples, and all her white teeth shone. The hotel-keeper may have had a daughter, and the farmer in the outskirts had two, but we never saw them. She reigned alone. All the men worshipped her. She was the only woman they had to think of. They talked of her on the 'stoep,' at the market, at the hotel; they watched for her at street corners; they hated the man she bowed to or walked with down the street. They brought flowers to the front door; they offered her their horses; they begged her to marry them when they dared. Partly, there was something noble and heroic in this devotion of men to the best woman they knew; partly there was something natural in it, that these men, shut off from the world, should pour at the feet of one woman the worship that otherwise would have been given to twenty; and partly there was something mean in their envy of one another. If she had raised her little finger, I suppose, she might have married any one out of twenty of them.

Then I came. I do not think I was prettier; I do not think I was so pretty as she was. I was certainly not as handsome. But I was vital, and I was new, and she was old – they all forsook her and followed me. They worshipped me. It was to my door that the flowers came; it was I had twenty horses offered me when I could only ride one; it was for me they waited at street corners; it was what I said and did that they talked of. Partly I liked it. I had lived alone all my life; no one ever had told me I was beautiful and a woman. I believed them. I did not know it was simply a fashion, which one man had set and the rest followed unreasoningly. I liked them to ask me to marry them, and to say, No. I despised them. The mother heart had not swelled in me yet; I did not know all men were my children, as the large woman knows when her heart is grown. I was too small to be tender. I liked my power. I was like a child with a new whip, which it goes about cracking everywhere, not caring against what. I could not wind it up and put it away. Men were curious creatures, who liked me, I could never tell why. Only one thing took from my pleasure; I could not bear that they had deserted her for me. I liked her great dreamy blue eyes, I liked her slow walk and drawl; when I saw her sitting among men, she seemed to me much too good to be among them; I would have given all their compliments if she would once have smiled at me as she smiled at them, with all her face breaking into radiance, with her dimples and flashing teeth. But I knew it never could be; I felt sure she hated me; that she wished I was dead; that she wished I had never come to the village. She did not know, when we went out riding, and a man who had always ridden beside her came to ride beside me, that I sent him away; that once when a man thought to win my favour by ridiculing her slow drawl before me I turned on him so fiercely that he never dared come before me again. I knew she knew that at the hotel men had made a bet as to which was the prettier, she or I, and had asked each man who came in, and that the one who had staked on me won. I hated them for it, but I would not let her see that I cared about what she felt towards me.

She and I never spoke to each other.

If we met in the village street we bowed and passed on; when we shook hands we did so silently, and did not look at each other. But I thought she felt my presence in a room just as I felt hers.

At last the time for my going came. I was to leave the next day. Someone I knew gave a party in my honour, to which all the village was invited.

It was midwinter; there was nothing in the gardens but a few dahlias and chrysanthemums, and I suppose that for two hundred miles round there was not a rose to be bought for love or money. Only in the garden of a friend of mine, in a sunny corner between the oven and the brick wall, there was a rose tree growing which had on it one bud. It was white, and it had been promised to the fair haired girl to wear at the party.

The evening came; when I arrived and went to the waiting-room, to take off my mantle, I found the girl there already. She was dressed in pure white, with her great white arms and shoulders showing, and her bright hair glittering in the candle-light, and the white rose fastened at her breast. She looked like a queen. I said 'Good evening,' and turned away quickly to the glass to arrange my old black scarf across my old black dress.

Then I felt a hand touch my hair.

'Stand still,' she said.

I looked in the glass. She had taken the white rose from her breast, and was fastening it in my hair.

'How nice dark hair is; it sets off flowers so.' She stepped back and looked at me. 'It looks much better there!'

I turned round.

'You are so beautiful to me,' I said.

'Y-e-s,' she said, with her slow Colonial drawl; 'I'm so glad.'

We stood looking at each other.

Then they came in and swept us away to dance. All the evening we did not come near to each other. Only once, as she passed, she smiled at me.

The next morning I left the town.

I never saw her again.

Years afterwards I heard she had married and gone to America; it may or may not be so – but the rose – the rose is in the box still! When my faith in woman grows dim, and it seems that for want of love and magnanimity she can play no part in any future heaven; then the scent of that small withered thing comes back: spring cannot fail us.

▶

companionship · hope · learning

Dust Tracks on a Road

ZORA NEALE HURSTON

———◆———

⏳ 4 minutes

Zora Neale Hurston was an African-American writer
whose work fell into obscurity after her death in
1960. Here, in her autobiography, she remembers
when, as a little girl, she started having visions
about her future, and all that it would entail.

———◆———

I do not know when the visions began. Certainly I was
not more than seven years old, but I remember the first
coming very distinctly. My brother, Joel, and I had made
a hen take an egg back and been caught as we turned
the hen loose. We knew we were in for it and decided to
scatter until things cooled off a bit. He hid out in the barn,
but I combined secretion with pleasure, and ran clear off
the place. Mr Linsay's house was vacant at the time. He
was a neighbour who was off working somewhere. I had
not thought of stopping there when I set out, but I saw a
big raisin lying on the porch and stopped to eat it. There
was some cool shade on the porch, so I sat down, and

soon I was asleep in a strange way. Like clearcut stere-
opticon slides, I saw twelve scenes flash before me, each
one held until I had seen it well in every detail, and then
be replaced by another. There was no continuity as in an
average dream. Just disconnected scene after scene with
blank spaces in between. I knew that they were all true, a
preview of things to come, and my soul writhed in agony
and shrunk away. But I knew that there was no shrinking.
These things had to be. I did not wake up when the last
one flickered and vanished. I merely sat up and saw the
Methodist Church, the line of moss-draped oaks, and our
strawberry patch stretching off to the left.

So when I left the porch, I left a great deal behind me.
I was weighed down with a power I did not want. I had
knowledge before its time. I knew my fate. I knew that
I would be an orphan and homeless. I knew that while I
was still helpless, that the comforting circle of my family
would be broken, and that I would have to wander cold
and friendless until I had served my time. I would stand
beside a dark pool of water and see a huge fish move slowly
away at a time when I would be somehow in the depth of
despair. I would hurry to catch a train, with doubts and
fears driving me and seek solace in a place and fail to find
it when I arrived, then cross many tracks to board the
train again. I knew that a house, a shot-gun built house
that needed a new coat of white paint, held torture for
me, but I must go. I saw deep love betrayed, but I must
feel and know it. There was no turning back. And last of
all, I would come to a big house. Two women waited there
for me. I could not see their faces, but I knew one to be

young and one to be old. One of them was arranging some queer-shaped flowers such as I had never seen. When I had come to these women, then I would be at the end of my pilgrimage, but not the end of my life. Then I would know peace and love and what goes with those things, and not before.

■▶

anxiety · hope · resilience · time · potential

A Field Guide to Getting Lost

REBECCA SOLNIT

◆

⏳ 3 minutes

Change can be frightening, because it moves
us from a known territory into uncharted lands.
Rebecca Solnit says you shouldn't fear the
unknown. Quite the contrary...

◆

Leave the door open for the unknown, the door into the
dark. That's where the most important things come from,
where you yourself come from, and where you will go.
Three years ago I was giving a workshop in the Rockies. A
student came in bearing a quote from what she said was
the pre-Socratic philosopher Meno. It read, 'How will
you go finding that thing the nature of which is totally
unknown to you?' I copied it down, and it has stayed
with me since. The student made big transparent photographs of swimmers underwater and hung them from the
ceiling with the light shining through them, so that to
walk among them was to have the shadows of swimmers
travel across your body in a space that itself came to seem

aquatic and mysterious. The question she carried struck me as the basic tactical question in life. The things we want are transformative, and we don't know or only think we know what is on the other side of that transformation. Love, wisdom, grace, inspiration – how do you go about finding these things that are in some ways about extending the boundaries of the self into unknown territory, about becoming someone else?

Certainly for artists of all stripes, the unknown, the idea or the form or the tale that has not yet arrived, is what must be found. It is the job of artists to open doors and invite in prophesies, the unknown, the unfamiliar; it's where their work comes from, although its arrival signals the beginning of the long disciplined process of making it their own. Scientists too, as J. Robert Oppenheimer once remarked, 'live always at the "edge of mystery" – the boundary of the unknown.' But they transform the unknown into the known, haul it in like fishermen; artists get you out into that dark sea.

Edgar Allan Poe declared, 'All experience, in matters of philosophical discovery, teaches us that, in such discovery, it is the unforeseen upon which we must calculate most largely.' Poe is consciously juxtaposing the word 'calculate', which implies a cold counting up of the facts of measurements, with the 'unforeseen,' that which cannot be measured or counted, only anticipated. How do you calculate upon the unforeseen? It seems to be an art of recognising the role of the unforeseen, of keeping your balance amid surprises, of collaborating with chance, of recognising that there are some essential mysteries in the world and thereby a limit to calculation, to plan, to control. To calculate on the unforeseen is perhaps exactly the paradoxical question that life most requires of us.

◗

anxiety · learning · potential

PLEASURE

A CLOUD OF SUSPICION hovers over the idea of pleasure. If you are doing something pleasurable, then you are not working, and if you are not working, then you are being irresponsible. Even when we disagree with this view in theory, the fabric of our culture makes it easier to lean that way in practice.

When a friend asks how we're doing, a standard answer is, 'busy', followed by a nod on our friend's part, who will hasten to say, 'me too', slightly ashamed that he had dared to doubt our busyness. You don't answer, 'I had a fantastic threesome with two friends last Sunday,' even when it is true. Having pleasure is not the done thing. We are allowed to rest, at most, because that goes to show we can pace ourselves, so that we can work better and be the pillars of our community that we aim to be. But to wallow in pleasure, for the sake of it? Good heavens, no.

Even if we wanted to, we wouldn't know where to start. Do you ever sit and think about what you enjoy, what you find exciting? We are not trained to *explore* our pleasures. Students of literature, for instance, generally learn a great deal about works that are considered to be important, but rather less about the ones they actually *like*. Only very rarely do they encounter a teacher who bothers to communicate the frisson that great writing is meant to give – or who still feels that frisson herself. I am not suggesting the discipline of academic study is pointless and that we should restrict our cultural consumption to those things we find immediately appealing. Learning to appreciate different books, different paintings and new pieces of music can open the door to new pleasures. I quite like Mozart, but I have friends who have studied music, and they get far more from a concert of his music than I can. One of the marvellous things about growing up is that we have the opportunity to widen our range of pleasures. But all too often we neglect to do so.

Nowhere is this more evident than with the twin physical pleasures of sex and food. In theory, we live in a liberal, open-minded and permissive age, and we are pretty much comfortable with any sexual act that consenting adults care to engage in together. And in culinary terms, we have access to a far wider range of foods and gastronomic experiences than was the case for our parents' generation. Yet in practice we tend to be exceedingly conservative in both areas, rarely venturing beyond the boundaries of the safe and the familiar, whether in the bedroom or at the dining-table. Then we get bored, and we convince ourselves that we are only sticking to what we know because, well, we are too busy. But pleasure requires renewal, and discovering new pleasures requires us to make ourselves slightly nervous, even ill-at-ease. The point of a comfort zone is being comfortable, not being exciting.

*

The writings in this chapter will motivate you to be *less* busy, so that you can stick with the tried and tested a little less, and explore a little more. They all deal with pleasure, mostly in its physical forms. Our society seems to believe that the pleasures of the mind are somehow 'better', more elevated, than the pleasures of the body. Some very fine writers have challenged that assumption, and I hope they will convince you to do the same.

We start with the myth of Psyche and Eros. In Eros' palace, Psyche has all the pleasure she can ask for, until she puts it all in jeopardy because she can't trust pleasure itself.

Jim Dodge opens our minds to the pleasure of walking naked in the rain.

The pleasure of cooking – a 'sorcery', as she calls it – is the subject of Joanne Harris's wonderfully sensuous piece.

Anaïs Nin writes playfully and very entertainingly about a well-endowed young man and his compulsive exhibitionism.

Jorge Amado addresses an important component of pleasure: freedom. Amado seems to imply that the reason why so many relationships fail is that freedom doesn't enter into them.

Next comes Lillian Beckwith, who celebrates the pleasures of simple food, followed by Epicurus, who summarises the ethics of his – Epicurean – philosophy in his Letter to Menoeceus.

D. H. Lawrence allows Constance Chatterley and Oliver Mellors to enjoy one of literature's most famous *cinq à sept* in the heart of an English wood. John Cleland, a verbally resourceful pornographer writing nearly two centuries before Lawrence, peers through the keyhole and describes in long, detailed and well-constructed sentences exactly what he sees.

Giacomo Leopardi, an Italian Romantic poet, makes us wonder whether pleasure exists at all. We spoil it, he says, by focusing on the pleasures we believe will come after, or those we believe came earlier. If only we could enjoy pleasure as it happens, we would be much happier.

Psyche and Eros

FRANCESCO DIMITRI

◆

⧗ 11 minutes

Psyche, in Greek, is the mind or soul, while Eros
is sensual love. This is how they met.

◆

Psyche was beautiful. So beautiful, in fact, that some of her
fellow townsfolk compared her to Aphrodite. They said
that she gave as much pleasure to the eye as the goddess
of beauty herself. Some even suggested that Psyche was,
in fact, Aphrodite. It started as a joke, but more and more
people joined in, and the joke grew into something more,
with the townsfolk paying homage at Psyche's feet, and
neglecting to visit Aphrodite's temple.

Aphrodite was not pleased.

Time went by. While Psyche's sisters married happily,
no suitor came forward for Psyche. Her father was puzzled.
Being a sensible man, he consulted the oracle, who came
up with a chilling response: Psyche was destined to marry
a monster whom nobody, mortal or god, could resist. She
was to be brought to a lonely mountain, and there the
monster would take her.

Psyche understood at once: she was cursed, for having offended Aphrodite. She could do nothing but accept her fate. So she was dressed as for a funeral, brought to the mountain in a mournful procession, and left there to confront her destiny.

She was alone on the mountain when the wind of the West came to her.

The wind tickled her playfully, lifted her gently, and carried her high up in the sky, safe from hurt, and laid her down on the soft grass of a hidden valley, at the edge of a grove.

Psyche fell asleep.

When she woke up she was still alone. No monster was there, and she felt quite safe. She set out to explore the grove. She saw majestic trees and springs as clear as her own beauty, and wild flowers whose scent made her dizzy. She glimpsed something in the distance, a flash of white and gold in the trees. She walked there – and found a palace.

It was made of exquisite marble and precious stones, its columns carved so finely they seemed to sway in the breeze, each doorway so elegant it was like a living thing. This had to be the palace of her future husband, though it didn't look like the lair of a monster. Be that as it may, there was no way back. Psyche walked to the entrance, and stepped inside.

'Welcome, my lady,' a voice said. 'All that you can see is yours, all yours.'

Psyche tried to locate where the voice came from, but it came from nowhere.

'There is a meal set for you,' the voice went on, 'and a bath, when you are comfortable.'

Psyche followed the voice, walking through frescoed corridors and passing by secret alcoves, to find a splendid meal: honey and figs and meat were laid out for her on a table, along with the best cheese she had ever tasted, and wine as sweet as ambrosia. As she ate, music lulled her into a state of bliss. She dined and she bathed, and then she braced herself for the night. The day had been full of pleasures, but now the monster would come.

Psyche lay in the bed, in pitch darkness, and waited, trembling with fear.

Soon enough someone came to the edge of the bed. She couldn't see him, but she could feel the bed give way under his weight. And then the unseen creature came closer, and Psyche could barely breath, as she felt his hand hovering above her skin.

The hand touched her.

It wasn't coarse and rough as she had expected, but smooth, and its touch was kind. The hands of the stranger were now undoing her clothes, eager but unhurried. Psyche reached out to the stranger, and touched his chin, which was strong and unmistakably human; she touched his neck, and caressed his shoulders, and let her hand slide down his belly, and grab his powerful erection. She was shivering with pleasure by then: the stranger knew how to kiss and how to touch, and he was biting her earlobes when she took his penis inside her, screaming, laughing, and then crying a bit.

After that, she fell asleep.

When she woke up, in the daylight, the stranger was gone.

She spent the day enjoying the pleasures of the palace. She was never more than a few steps away from a painting, a statue, the sound of music wafting through the air, or a chamber laid with food and wine. From the windows, she could take in breathtaking views of the surrounding woods.

That night her lover came back. They made love again, in ways different from yesterday, and again she found herself laughing and crying. This time he talked. 'I'll be back every night,' he said. 'But you can never see me. Is that fine with you?'

Psyche's answer was a kiss.

And so she continued for a while, basking in pleasure. Until it dawned on her that her family thought her the prisoner of a monster, that everybody thought she was trapped, unhappy, and possibly dead. So she asked her lover if she could go and visit her family. He said yes, of course, she was not a prisoner.

She went to meet her sisters, radiating with happiness. But seeing her joy didn't make them happy, no: it made them jealous. They asked her what her husband looked like, and when she couldn't answer, they told her that she shouldn't trust him. Something dodgy was surely going on.

Psyche retuned to her new home full of doubt. The pleasures of her palace weren't as intense as they used to be; and the wait for her lover was much less sweet. He came, and undressed, and undressed her; and they made love, in new ways and old ones. Psyche almost managed to lose herself in pleasure, as she had done before. But always that nagging thought: she needed to *know*. She needed to *understand*.

This time she didn't fall asleep.

She waited for him to fall asleep, and when she was sure he was, she lit a lantern, to look at him.

He was a young man, more beautiful than any work of art, more beautiful than the wild woods, and life itself. Looking at his naked body was enough to make her cry with pleasure again.

He woke up.

He looked at Psyche, hurt.

'My love...' she tried.

He stopped her. 'I'm Eros,' he said. 'Aphrodite's son.' He stood up. 'My mother sent me to curse you, but I couldn't.' He fished for his clothes, and started putting them on. 'The moment I saw you, I fell in love with you, and decided I'd give you all the pleasure I could. But you didn't trust me.'

She tried again, 'My love...'

'You didn't lose yourself,' Eros said, turning his back.

'Please,' Psyche cried.

Eros walked to the window, and jumped off, and flew away, leaving Psyche crying in the bed that used to be theirs, crying for all that she had lost.

*

This is the part of the story I wanted to tell you today, because I think there's something there, but I won't leave you with such a bitter ending. This is not how the story ends. Psyche left the palace too, and she travelled through this world and beyond, and finally gained forgiveness from both her lover and his mother: Eros and Psyche ended up married, with Aphrodite's blessing, and Psyche drank of the nectar of the Gods, and was made immortal. And Eros and Psyche had a daughter together.

They named her Pleasure.

companionship · happiness · instinct · married life · rules

Stone Junction

JIM DODGE

◆

⏳ 5 minutes

Have you ever danced naked in the rain?
Believe me, it's a fantastic experience. And
this is what happens when you try.

◆

The most memorable lesson for both Daniel and Annalee
occurred on a warm May afternoon. All three of them
were cleaning the pantry, item number nine on Annalee's
list of spring chores, when the sky suddenly darkened
with a mass of clouds. Within minutes rain began falling.
Johnny Seven Moons went to the open door, inhaled
deeply, and started stripping off his clothes. Daniel and
Annalee exchanged anxious glances.

'You going swimming?' Daniel joked.

'No,' Seven Moons said, hopping out of his pants and
tossing them aside. 'I'm going for a walk in the warm
spring rain. Join me if you like. Walking naked in warm
spring rain is one of the highest spiritual pleasures available to human creatures.'

Annalee was already wiggling out of her jeans, but Daniel had a question: 'Is it a higher pleasure than blowing up dams?'

Seven Moons shut his eyes and almost immediately opened them. 'That's a tough one, but I think they'd have to be the same. You see, if I didn't blow up dams and keep rivers where they're supposed to be, in not very long there would be no warm spring rain to walk naked in.'

It was splendid. Hands joined, Daniel in the middle, they walked naked across the flat and up the oak-studded knoll where, deliriously drenched, they sang 'Old Man River' to the clearing sky. The sun burned through minutes later. By the time they walked back to the house through the wraiths of mist lifting from the soaked grass, everything but their feet and hair had dried.

Annalee and Daniel recalled that walk with Seven Moons often, but they never talked about what had really moved them. Annalee had been so overwhelmed by the rain on her flesh that she was afraid she was going to come, to collapse in wet grass. She felt constrained. It was difficult to shift her attention away from her body and back to them, even though they brought their own sweet joy.

Daniel remembered a moment as they'd started up the knoll, when he looked at his mother, so beautiful, her skin shining with rain, and then he'd looked at Seven Moons, strong and wise and brave, feeling their large hands in his and the rain splattering on his shoulders, feeling for just a moment that the world was perfect.

They both remembered yet never mentioned what Johnny Seven Moons had said when they reached the top of the knoll. He'd tilted his head back and groaned out, 'Oh, blowing up dams is a *tremendous* responsibility, an *important* responsibility, a *grave* responsibility...' And then he'd laughed like a loon, the sound echoing distantly across the flat and then lost in the hush of rain. He squeezed Daniel's hand and grinned at Annalee. 'It's only at moments like this that I'm glad we're all going to die.'

adventure · companionship · instinct · meaning

Chocolat

JOANNE HARRIS

———◆———

⏳ 8 minutes

There is a special magic to the preparation of
food, an alchemy which not only transforms the
ingredients but also transforms *us*, as we cook.

———◆———

This is an art I can enjoy. There is a kind of sorcery in
all cooking: in the choosing of ingredients, the process
of mixing, grating, melting, infusing and flavouring,
the recipes taken from ancient books, the traditional
utensils – the pestle and mortar with which my mother
made her incense turned to a more homely purpose,
her spices and aromatics giving up their subtleties to a
baser, more sensual magic. And it is partly the transience
of it that delights me; so much loving preparation, so
much art and experience put into a pleasure which can
last only a moment, and which only a few will ever fully
appreciate. My mother always viewed my interest with
indulgent contempt. To her, food was no pleasure but a
tiresome necessity to be worried over, a tax on the price of
our freedom. I stole menus from restaurants and looked

longingly into *pâtisserie* windows. I must have been ten years old – maybe older – before I first tasted real chocolate. But still the fascination endured. I carried recipes in my head like maps. All kinds of recipes: torn from abandoned magazines in busy railway stations, wheedled from people on the road, strange marriages of my own confections. Mother with her cards, her divination directed our mad course across Europe. Cookery cards anchored us, placed landmarks on the bleak borders. Paris smells of baking bread and *croissants*; Marseille of *bouillabaisse* and grilled garlic. Berlin was *Eisbrei* with *Sauerkraut* and *Kartoffelsalat*, Rome was the ice-cream I ate without paying in a tiny restaurant beside the river. Mother had no time for landmarks. All her maps were inside, all places the same. Even then we were different. Oh, she taught me what she could. How to see to the core of things, of people, to see their thoughts, their longings. The driver who stopped to give us a lift, who drove ten kilometers out of his way to take us to Lyon, the grocers who refused payment, the policeman who turned a blind eye. Not every time, of course. Sometimes it failed for no reason we could understand. Some people are unreadable, unreachable. [...] And even when it did not, the casual intrusion disturbed me. It was all too easy. Now making chocolate is a different matter. Oh, some skill is required. A certain lightness of touch, speed, a patience my mother would never have had. But the formula remains the same every time. It is safe. Harmless. And I do not have to look into their hearts and take what I need; these are wishes which can be granted simply, for the asking.

Guy, my confectioner, has known me for a long time. We worked together after Anouk was born and he helped me to start my first business, a tiny *pâtisserie-chocolaterie* in the outskirts of Nice. Now he is based in Marseille, importing the raw chocolate liquor direct from South America and converting it to chocolate of various grade in his factory.

I only use the best. The blocks of couverture are slightly larger than house bricks, one box of each per delivery, and I use all three types: the dark, the milk and the white. It has to be tempered to bring it to its crystalline state, ensuring a hard, brittle surface and a good shine. Some confectioners buy their supplies already tempered, but I like to do it myself. There is an endless fascination in handling the raw dullish blocks of couverture, in grating them by hand – I never use electrical mixers – into the large ceramic pans, then melting, stirring, testing each painstaking step with the sugar thermometer until just the right amount of heat has been applied to make the change.

There is a kind of alchemy in the transformation of base chocolate into the wise fool's gold, a layman's magic which even my mother might have relished. As I work I clear my mind, breathing deeply. The windows are open, and the through draught would be cold if it were not for the heat of the stoves, the copper pans, the rising vapour from the melting couverture. The mingled scents of chocolate, vanilla, heated copper and cinnamon are intoxicating, powerfully suggestive; the raw and earthy tang of the Americas, the hot and resinous perfume of the rainforest. This is how I travel now, as the Aztecs did in their sacred rituals. Mexico, Venezuela, Colombia. The court of Montezuma. Cortez and Columbus. The food of the gods, bubbling and frothing in ceremonial goblets. The bitter elixir of life.

[...] a throwback to times when the world was a wider, wilder place. Before Christ – before Adonis was born in Bethlehem or Osiris sacrificed at Easter – the cocoa bean was revered. Magical properties were attributed to it. Its brew was sipped on the steps of sacrificial temples; its ecstasies were fierce and terrible.

creativity · instinct · magic · time · potential

'Manuel'

ANAÏS NIN

◆

⧗ 10 minutes

We all have our own particular ways of pursuing
pleasure. Some are stranger than others.

◆

Manuel had developed a peculiar form of enjoyment that
caused his family to repudiate him, and he lived like a
Bohemian in Montparnasse. When not obsessed with his
erotic exigencies, he was an astrologer, an extraordinary
cook, a great conversationalist and an excellent café companion. But not one of these occupations could divert his
mind from his obsession. Sooner or later Manuel had to
open his pants and exhibit his rather formidable member.

The more people there were, the better. The more
refined the party, the better. If he got among the painters
and models, he waited until everybody was a little drunk
and gay, and then he undressed himself completely. His
ascetic face, dreamy and poetic eyes and lean monklike
body were so much in dissonance with his behavior that
it startled everyone. If they turned away from him, he had

no pleasure. If they looked at him for any time at all, then he would fall into a trance, his face would become ecstatic, and soon he would be rolling on the floor in a crisis of orgasm.

Women tended to run away from him. He had to beg them to stay and resorted to all kinds of tricks. He would pose as a model and look for work in women's studios. But the condition he got into as he stood there under the eyes of the female students made the men throw him out into the street.

If he were invited to a party, he would first try to get one of the women alone somewhere in an empty room or on a balcony. Then he would take down his pants. If the woman was interested he would fall into ecstasy. If not, he would run after her, with his erection, and come back to the party and stand there, hoping to create curiosity. He was not a beautiful sight but a highly incongruous one. Since the penis did not seem to belong to the austere religious face and body, it acquired a greater prominence – as it were, an apartness.

He finally found the wife of a poor literary agent who was dying of starvation and overwork, with whom he reached the following arrangement. He would come in the morning and do all her housework for her, wash her dishes, sweep her studio, run errands, on condition that when all this was over he could exhibit himself. In this case he demanded all her attention. He wanted her to watch him unfasten his belt, unbutton his pants, pull them down. He wore no underwear. He would take out his penis and shake it like a person weighing a thing of value. She had to stand near him and watch every gesture. She had to look at his penis as she would look at food she liked.

This woman developed the art of satisfying him completely. She would become absorbed in the penis, saying, 'It's a beautiful penis you have there, the biggest I have seen in Montparnasse. It's so smooth and hard. It's beautiful.'

As she said these words, Manuel continued to shake his penis like a pot of gold under her eyes, and saliva came to his mouth. He admired it himself. As they both bent over it to admire it his pleasure would become so keen that he would close his eyes and be taken with a bodily trembling from head to foot, still holding his penis and shaking it under her face. Then the trembling would turn into undulation and he would fall on the floor and roll himself into a ball as he came, sometimes all over his own face.

Often he stood at dark corners of the streets, under an overcoat, and if a woman passed he opened his coat and shook his penis at her. But this was dangerous and the police punished such behavior rather severely. Oftener still he liked to get into an empty compartment of a train, unbutton two of the buttons, and sit back as if he were drunk or asleep, his penis showing a little through the opening. People would come in at other stations. If he were in luck it might be a woman who would sit across from him and stare at him. As he looked drunk, usually no one tried to wake him. Sometimes one of the men would rouse him angrily and tell him to button himself. Women did not protest. If a woman came in with little schoolgirls, then he was in paradise. He would have an erection, and finally the situation would become so intolerable, the woman and her little girls would leave the compartment.

One day Manuel found his twin in this form of enjoyment. He had taken his seat in a compartment, alone, and was pretending to fall asleep when a woman came in and sat opposite him. She was a rather mature prostitute as he could see from the heavily painted eyes, the thickly powdered face, the rings under her eyes, the over-curled hair, the worn-down shoes, the coquettish dress and hat.

Through half-closed eyes he observed her. She took a glance at his partly opened pants and then looked again. She too sat back and appeared to fall asleep, with her legs wide apart. When the train started she raised her skirt completely. She was naked underneath. She stretched open her legs and exposed herself while looking at Manuel's penis, which was hardening and showing through the pants and which finally protruded completely. They sat in front of each other, staring. Manuel was afraid the woman would move and try to get hold of his penis, which was not what he wanted at all. But no, she was addicted to the same passive pleasures. She knew he was looking at her sex, under the very black and bushy hair, and finally they opened their eyes and smiled at each other. He was entering his ecstatic state, but he had time to notice that she was in a state of pleasure herself. He could see the shining moisture appearing at the mouth of the sex. She moved almost imperceptibly to and fro, as if rocking herself to sleep. His body began to tremble with voluptuous pleasure. She then masturbated in front of him, smiling all the time.

Manuel married this woman, who never tried to possess him in the way of other women.

irony · instinct · luck

Gabriela, Clove and Cinnamon

JORGE AMADO

◆

⏳ 14 minutes

We can't feel any pleasure if we feel trapped.
This is how many relationships hit the rocks.

◆

'Oh, how beautiful!' exclaimed Gabriela.

Nacib placed the cage on a chair. The bird was beating against the bars.

'For you – to keep you company.'

He sat down and Gabriela curled up on the floor at his feet. She took his big hairy hand and kissed the palm of it. Nacib wondered why this gesture reminded him of the land of his fathers, the hills of Syria. Then she leaned her head against his knee and he stroked her hair. The bird calmed down. It began to sing.

'Two presents at the same time. Such a kind man!'

'Two?'

'The bird and something even nicer: you came home with it. Usually you only come at night.'

And he was going to lose her. 'The resistance of every

155

woman, even the most faithful, has its limit.' Nhô-Galo had meant, of course, that every woman had her price. Nacib's despondence showed in his face, and Gabriela, who had looked up at him as she spoke, noticed it.

'Mr Nacib is feeling sad. Didn't use to be that way. He used to be happy, smiling. Now he's sad. Why?'

What could he say? That he did not know how to hold her, to tie her to himself forever?

'I have something to say to you.'

'Yes, Mr Nacib.'

'There's something I don't like. It's bothering me.'

She was alarmed.

'Is the food bad? Didn't I iron your shirts right?'

'Nothing like that. It's something else.'

'Then what is it?'

'Your trips to the bar. I don't like them, they don't please me.'

Gabriela's eyes opened wide.

'But I go to help, and so your lunch won't get cold. That's why I go.'

'I know. But the others don't.'

'I see. I never thought about that. It's not nice for me to be in the bar, is it? The others don't like it – a cook in the bar. I didn't think about that.'

He seized the opportunity.

'Yes, that's it. Some don't care, but others complain.'

Gabriela's eyes turned sad. The sofrê's throat was about to burst, its song was heart-rending.

'What harm did I do?'

Why make her suffer so, why not tell her the truth, tell

her of his jealousy, cry out his love? Why not call her Bié, the affectionate nickname that he always gave her in his thoughts?

'Beginnin' tomorrow here's what I'll do: I'll go in the back way and just serve your lunch. Hardly anybody'll see me.'

Why not? In this way he could continue to have her near him at noon, to feel her hand, her leg, her breast. And wouldn't her half-concealment put an end to the tempting offers, the honeyed words?

'Do you like to go to the bar?'

She nodded. How she enjoyed it! – Walking in the sunlight with the pot in her hand, threading her way among the tables, hearing the remarks, feeling the eyes fixed intently upon her. But not the old men. Not the colonel's offers of furnished houses. She loved to feel herself gazed upon, played up to, desired. It was a kind of preparation for the night: it left her enveloped in an aura of desire, and in Nacib's arms she would see again all the beautiful young men – Mr Tonico, Mr Josué, Mr Ari, Mr Epaminondas (a store clerk). Could one of them have made the complaint to Nacib about her? She thought not. It was one of those ugly old men, no doubt, to spite her for not paying attention to him.

'All right, you can go. But not to wait on me at the table. You can remain seated behind the counter.'

She would have their glances, anyway, and their smiles; some would probably come to the counter to speak to her.

'I have to go back,' announced Nacib.

'So soon?'

'I shouldn't have come at all.'

Gabriela threw her arms around his legs, holding him back. He had never had her in the daytime, it had always been at night. He wanted to rise, but she held him, silent and grateful.

'Come here. Yes, right here.'

He drew her after him. It would be the first time he had possessed her in his bedroom, in his own bed, as if she were his wife and not his cook. When he had pulled off her cotton dress and her nude body lay invitingly on the bed – her shapely buttocks, her firm breasts – and when she had held his head in her hands and kissed his eyes, he asked her, for the first time:

'Tell me something: are you very fond of me?'

She laughed in tune with the bird's thrill.

'I like you too much.'

He had hurt her with that business about going to the bar. Why make her suffer, why not tell her the truth?

'Nobody complained about you going to the bar. I'm the one who doesn't want you to go. That's why I was sad. Everybody talks to you, they make fresh remarks, they hold your hand. They do everything but grab you and throw you on the floor.'

She laughed.

'It don't mean anything. I'm not interested in them.'

'You aren't? Really?'

Gabriela pulled him toward her, burying his head in her breasts. Nacib murmured: 'Bié...' And in his language of love, which was Arabic, he said while possessing her: 'From now on, you are Bié and this is your bed, here you will sleep. You are not a cook although you cook. You are the woman of this house, the rays of the sun, the light of the moon, the song of birds. Your name is Bié.'

'Is Bié a foreign name? Call me Bié, talk to me some more in that language. I like to hear it.'

When Nacib had left, she sat in the chair by the bird cage. Mr Nacib was good, she thought, and he was jealous. She laughed and stuck her finger between the wires of the cage. The frightened bird tried to escape. He was jealous – how silly! She wasn't: if he wanted to lie with another woman, he could. At first he had done so, she knew. He lay with her and with others. She didn't mind. He could go to them if he wanted to. Not to stay, just to lie with them. But Mr Nacib was jealous. What harm was there if Mr José touched her hand? Or if Mr Tonico tried to kiss the back of her neck while Nacib wasn't looking? Or if Mr Epaminondas tried to date her, or if Mr Ari gave her candy and took her by the chin? She slept with all of them every night – with them and with those who had come before, except her uncle – as she lay in Nacib's arms. First with one, then with another; most of the time with the boy Bebinho and Mr Tonico. It was so nice.

And it was so nice to go to the bar, to pass among the men. Life was good, one had only to live it. To warm oneself in the sun, take a cold bath; to eat guavas and mangoes, to chew peppercorn, to walk through the streets, to sing songs, to sleep with a young man. And to dream of another.

Bié. She liked the name. Mr Nacib was so big and he could talk a foreign language, but he called her Bié and he was jealous. Funny. She didn't want to hurt him, he was so good. She would be very careful. But when a man got jealous, almost anything could offend him. She might have to stay in the house and never hear men say things to her, or laugh with them, or see the glint she inspired in their eyes. 'Please don't ask me to, Mr Nacib, I couldn't.'

The bird was beating against the bars. How many days had it been in there? Not many, certainly, for it was not yet used to it. Who can get used to living in prison, anyway? She was fond of animals and befriended them easily. Cats, dogs, even chickens. In the country she had owned a parrot that could talk; it died of starvation in the drought. She had never wanted a bird in a cage. She felt sorry for the sofrê. She had not said so, in order not to offend Nacib. Its song was so sad, Mr Nacib was so sad. She did not want to hurt him, she would be very careful: she would say the bird had escaped.

She went to the back yard. Under the guava tree, where the cat was sleeping, she opened the cage. The bird flew out, paused on a branch, and sang for her. What a clear, happy song! Gabriela smiled. The cat woke up.

happiness · instinct · married life · rules

The Hills is Lonely

LILLIAN BECKWITH

◆

⌛ 6 minutes

The simplest food can be intensely pleasurable.
And you don't need to travel all the way to
the Mediterranean to find it.

◆

During the summer months, when milk was plentiful
and rich, Morag made butter – and such butter! In town I
would have complained that it was rancid, but though its
'ripeness' stung my throat and I might have to swallow two
or three times to every mouthful, I came to enjoy it as I
had never enjoyed butter before. Morag's butter churn was
a large sweetie jar with a hole in the lid. Through this hole
went a rod about three feet long, at the bottom of which
was a circle of wood with three or four holes in it. To make
the butter Morag would sit on the edge of her chair, the jar,
which would be about half full of cream, gripped firmly
between her knees; then she would grasp the plunger and
jerk it furiously up and down until the butter came. She
reminded me of a jockey crouched grimly on the neck of

his mount, his eyes fixed on the winning-post, while the illusion was intensified by the spatters of cream from the churn which spotted and streaked her face and hair, like the flecks of foam from a hard-ridden horse. The process sometimes lasted for hours and neighbours dropping in would obligingly take a turn at churning while Morag made tea. If she tired, my landlady would go to bed and resume her butter-making the next day or even the day after, and sometimes I would hear the 'plop! plop!' of the churn as a background to my dreams. It was a slap-dash way of butter-making – slap-dash in every sense of the word – but we nearly always got the butter, and it usually took longer to make than it did to eat!

Mushrooms in season grew abundantly on the moors and when the villagers heard of my fondness for them they persisted in bringing me all they could find. Day after day the mushrooms arrived, in milk-pails, in jam-jars, in dirty handkerchiefs and even dirtier caps. I ate mushrooms fried for breakfast; I ate them in soups; I concocted mushroom savouries; I experimented with the idea of drying them, but still I could not use all the mushrooms they so generously bestowed upon me. I was touched by the thoughtfulness of my new friends until disillusionment came with the discovery of their ineradicable belief that all mushrooms were deadly poison!

There were of course the dumplings.

There appears to be a tradition that a Scotch dumpling shall weigh at least ten pounds when cooked, no matter what size the household may be. It is fruity and spicy and is a noble sight when it is lifted from the pan in which it has been bubbling away for several hours and turned out on to the largest meat dish. Morag always used one of her woollen vests, well floured, for a dumpling cloth as this produced a pleasing lacy effect on the outside. Ten pounds of rich fruit dumpling is a formidable quantity for two women to eat their way through unaided and whenever I saw one in preparation I knew I could look forward to a prolonged bout of indigestion. No scrap of it was ever wasted. The first day we ate it in steaming wedges hot from the pan and it was wonderful; on the following days we sliced it cold with a sharp knife and ate it either as cake or heated in the frying-pan for pudding. It was still good. Towards the end, when the pattern of Morag's vest began to take on a decidedly angora-like quality, we hewed the last craggy pieces, soaked them in custard and made them into a trifle. And that was the dumpling finished. I would heave a sigh of mingled regret and relief and put away my magnesia tablets – until the next time.

comfort · irony

Letter to Menoeceus

EPICURUS

———◆———

⏳ 5 minutes

Epicurus was a Greek philosopher who considered
pleasure to be the only thing that mattered in life.
Strangely enough, though, he wasn't what we
would call a *hedonist* today.

———◆———

We say that pleasure is all that matters for a blessed life.
Pleasure is our first and kindred good. It is the starting
point of every choice and every aversion, and we always
come back to it, because we judge every good thing based
on how it makes us feel.

And since pleasure is our first and natural good, we do
not choose every pleasure whatsoever, but will pass over
many pleasures when a greater annoyance ensues from
them. On the contrary, we often choose pains over pleasures when some pain will bring us, as a consequence,
a greater pleasure in the future. So while all pleasure is
good, because it is naturally akin to us, not all pleasure
should be chosen, just as all pain is an evil, and yet not all

pain is to be shunned. It is by considering both pain and pleasure, and by looking at the conveniences and inconveniences, that we have to make our choices. Sometimes we treat the good as an evil, and the evil, on the contrary, as a good.

Again, we regard self-sufficiency as a great good, not because we should always live with very little, but because we should be contented with little if we have not much, being honestly persuaded that those who need luxury less are those who enjoy it more, and that whatever is natural, is easy to attain, and only the vain and worthless things are hard to win. Plain fare gives as much pleasure as a costly diet, once you remove the pain of desiring the costly diet, while bread and water confer the highest possible pleasure when they are brought to hungry lips. To habituate ourselves to a simple and inexpensive diet, supplies all that we need for health, and enables us to meet the necessary requirements of life without shrinking. It also places us in a better condition at the times when we do approach costly fare; and it renders us fearless of fortune.

When we say, then, that pleasure is all that matters, we do not mean the pleasures of the prodigal, or the pleasures of unbridled sensuality, as someone, through ignorance, prejudice, or wilful misrepresentation, says we do. By pleasure we mean the absence of pain in the body and of trouble in the soul. A pleasant life does not come from an unbroken succession of drinking-bouts and revelry, or sexual lust, or the enjoyment of fish and other delicacies of a luxurious table; it comes from sober reasoning, searching out the reasons for every choice and every act of avoidance we make, and banishing those beliefs through which the greatest tumults take possession of the soul. Of all this, the beginning and the greatest good is wisdom. Therefore wisdom is even more precious than philosophy; all the other virtues spring from it, because it teaches that we cannot live pleasantly without living wisely, honourably, and justly; nor can we live wisely, honourably, and justly without living pleasantly. The virtues grow along with a pleasant life, and a pleasant life is inseparable from them.

self-knowledge · instinct

Lady Chatterley's Lover

D. H. LAWRENCE

◆

⏳ 12 minutes

Like Pysche (see page 137), Constance
Chatterley discovers the true wonder of
sexual love in the greenwood.

◆

Connie climbed the fence into the narrow path between
the dense, bristling young firs. Mrs Flint went running
back across the pasture, in a sun-bonnet, because she
was really a schoolteacher. Constance didn't like this
dense new part of the wood; it seemed gruesome and
choking. She hurried on with her head down, thinking
of the Flints' baby. It was a dear little thing, but it would
be a bit bow-legged like its father. It showed already, but
perhaps it would grow out of it. How warm and fulfilling
somehow to have a baby, and how Mrs Flint had showed
it off! She had something anyhow that Connie hadn't got,
and apparently couldn't have. Yes, Mrs Flint had flaunted
her motherhood. And Connie had been just a bit, just a
little bit jealous. She couldn't help it.

She started out of her muse, and gave a little cry of fear. A man was there.

It was the keeper. He stood in the path like Balaam's ass, barring her way.

'How's this?' he said in surprise.

'How did you come?' she panted.

'How did you? Have you been to the hut?'

'No! No! I went to Marehay.'

He looked at her curiously, searchingly, and she hung her head a little guiltily.

'And were you going to the hut now?' he asked rather sternly. 'No! I mustn't. I stayed at Marehay. No one knows where I am. I'm late. I've got to run.'

'Giving me the slip, like?' he said, with a faint ironic smile.

'No! No. Not that. Only...'

'Why, what else?' he said. And he stepped up to her and put his arms around her. She felt the front of his body terribly near to her, and alive.

'Oh, not now, not now,' she cried, trying to push him away.

'Why not? It's only six o'clock. You've got half an hour. Nay! Nay! I want you.'

He held her fast and she felt his urgency. Her old instinct was to fight for her freedom. But something else in her was strange and inert and heavy. His body was urgent against her, and she hadn't the heart any more to fight.

He looked around.

'Come... come here! Through here,' he said, looking

penetratingly into the dense fir-trees, that were young and not more than half-grown.

He looked back at her. She saw his eyes, tense and brilliant, fierce, not loving. But her will had left her. A strange weight was on her limbs. She was giving way. She was giving up.

He led her through the wall of prickly trees, that were difficult to come through, to a place where was a little space and a pile of dead boughs. He threw one or two dry ones down, put his coat and waistcoat over them, and she had to lie down there under the boughs of the tree, like an animal, while he waited, standing there in his shirt and breeches, watching her with haunted eyes. But still he was provident – he made her lie properly, properly. Yet he broke the band of her underclothes, for she did not help him, only lay inert.

He too had bared the front part of his body and she felt his naked flesh against her as he came into her. For a moment he was still inside her, turgid there and quivering. Then as he began to move, in the sudden helpless orgasm, there awoke in her new strange thrills rippling inside her. Rippling, rippling, rippling, like a flapping overlapping of soft flames, soft as feathers, running to points of brilliance, exquisite, exquisite and melting her all molten inside. It was like bells rippling up and up to a culmination. She lay unconscious of the wild little cries she uttered at the last. But it was over too soon, too soon, and she could no longer force her own conclusion with her own activity. This was different, different. She could do nothing. She could no longer harden and grip for her own satisfaction upon him. She could only wait, wait and moan in spirit as she felt him withdrawing, withdrawing and contracting, coming to the terrible moment when he would slip out of her and be gone. Whilst all her womb was open and soft, and softly clamouring, like a sea-anemone under the tide, clamouring for him to come in again and make a fulfilment for her. She clung to him unconscious in passion, and he never quite slipped from her, and she felt the soft bud of him within her stirring, and strange rhythms flushing up into her with a strange rhythmic growing motion, swelling and swelling till it filled all her cleaving consciousness, and then began again the unspeakable motion that was not really motion, but pure deepening whirlpools of sensation swirling deeper and deeper through all her tissue and consciousness, till she was one perfect concentric fluid of feeling, and she lay there crying in unconscious inarticulate cries. The voice out of the uttermost night, the life! The man heard it beneath him with a kind of awe, as his life sprang out into her. And as it subsided, he subsided too and lay utterly still, unknowing, while her grip on him slowly relaxed, and she lay inert. And they lay and knew nothing, not even of each other, both lost. Till at last he began to rouse and become aware of his defenceless nakedness, and she was aware that his body was loosening its clasp on her. He was coming apart; but in her breast she felt she could not bear him to leave her uncovered. He must cover her now for ever.

But he drew away at last, and kissed her and covered her over, and began to cover himself. She lay looking up to the boughs of the tree, unable as yet to move. He stood and fastened up his breeches, looking round. All was dense and silent, save for the awed dog that lay with its paws against its nose. He sat down again on the brushwood and took Connie's hand in silence.

She turned and looked at him. 'We came off together that time,' he said.

She did not answer.

'It's good when it's like that. Most folks live their lives through and they never know it,' he said, speaking rather dreamily.

She looked into his brooding face.

'Do they?' she said. 'Are you glad?'

He looked back into her eyes. 'Glad,' he said, 'ay, but never mind.' He did not want her to talk. And he bent over her and kissed her, and she felt, so he must kiss her for ever.

At last she sat up.

'Don't people often come off together?' she asked with naive curiosity.

'A good many of them never. You can see by the raw look of them.' He spoke unwittingly, regretting he had begun.

'Have you come off like that with other women?'

He looked at her amused.

'I don't know,' he said, 'I don't know.'

❧

companionship · desire · instinct · rules

Pleasure · 171

Fanny Hill: or, Memoirs of a Woman of Pleasure

JOHN CLELAND

◆

⏳ 15 minutes

John Cleland's *Fanny Hill*, a pornographic novel
written in the 1740s, was, like *Lady Chatterley's
Lover*, the subject of an obscenity trial when it was
republished in the early 1960s. *Fanny Hill: or, Memoirs
of a Woman of Pleasure* is verbally ingenious, ironic –
and wildly filthy. Here, two of the protagonists
discover the pleasures of voyeurism.

◆

At five in the evening next day, Phoebe, punctual to her
promise, came to me as I sat alone in my own room, and
beckoned me to follow her.

We went down the back stairs very softly, and opening
the door of a dark closet, where there was some old furniture kept, and some cases of liquor, she drew me in
after her, and fastened the door upon us. We had no light
but what came through a long crevice in the partition
between ours and the light closet, where the scene of

action lay; so that sitting on those low cases, we could, with the greatest ease, as well as clearness, see all objects (ourselves unseen), only by applying our eyes close to the crevice, where the moulding of a panel had warped, or started a little on the other side.

The young gentleman was the first person I saw, with his back directly towards me, looking at a print. Polly was not yet come: in less than a minute though, the door opened, and she came in; and at the noise the door made he turned about, and came to meet her, with an air of the greatest tenderness and satisfaction.

After saluting her, he led her to a couch that fronted us, where they both sat down, and the young Genoese helped her to a glass of wine, with some Naples biscuits on a salver.

Presently, when they had exchanged a few kisses, and questions in broken English on one side, he began to unbutton, and, in fine, stript into his shirt.

As if this had been the signal agreed on for pulling off all their clothes, a scheme which the heat of the season perfectly favoured, Polly began to draw her pins, and as she had no stays to unlace, she was in a trice, with her gallant's officious assistance, undressed to all but her shift.

When he saw this, his breeches were immediately loosened, waist and knee bands, and slipped over his ankles, clean off; his shirt collar was unbuttoned too: then, first giving Polly an encouraging kiss, he stole, as it were, the shift off the girl, who being, I suppose, broke and familiarised to this humour, blushed indeed, but less than I did at the apparition of her, now standing stark naked, just as she came out of the hands of pure nature, with her black hair loose and a-float down her dazzling white neck and shoulders, whilst the deepened carnation of her cheeks went off gradually into the hue of glazed snow: for such were the blended tints, and polish of her skin.

This girl could not be above eighteen: her face regular and sweet featured, her shape exquisite; nor could I help envying her two ripe enchanting breasts, finely plumped out in flesh, but withal so round, so firm, that they sustained themselves, in scorn of any stay: then their nipples, pointing different ways, marked their pleasing separation; beneath them lay the delicious tract of the belly, which terminated in a parting or rift scarce discernable, that modesty seemed to retire downward, and seek shelter between two plump fleshy thighs: the curling hair that overspread its delightful front, clothed it with the richest sable fur in the universe: in short, she was evidently a subject for the painters to court her, sitting to them for a pattern of female beauty, in all the true pride and pomp of nakedness.

The young Italian (still in his shirt) stood gazing and transported at the sight of beauties that might have fired a dying hermit; his eager eyes devoured her, as she shifted attitudes at his discretion: neither were his hands excluded their share of the high feast, but wandered, on the hunt of pleasure, over every part and inch of her body, so qualified to afford the most exquisite sense of it.

In the mean time, one could not help observing the swell of his shirt before, that bolstered out, and pointed out the condition of things behind the curtain: but he soon removed it, by slipping his shirt over his head; and now, as to nakedness, they had nothing to reproach one another.

The young gentleman, by Phoebe's guess, was about two and twenty; tall and well limbed. His body was finely formed, and of a most vigorous make, square shouldered, and broad chested: his face was not remarkable in any way, but for a nose inclining to the Roman, eyes large, black, and sparkling, and a ruddiness in his cheeks that was the more a grace, for his complexion was of the brownest, not of that dusky dun colour which excludes the idea of freshness, but of that clear, olive gloss, which glowing with life, dazzles perhaps less than fairness, and yet pleases more, when it pleases at all. His hair being too short to tie fell no lower than his neck, in short easy curls; and he had a few sprigs about his paps, that garnished his chest in a style of strength and manliness. Then his grand movement, which seemed to rise out of a thicket of curling hair, that spread from the root all over his thighs and belly up to the navel, stood stiff and upright, but of a size to frighten me, by sympathy for the small tender part, which was the object of its fury, and which now lay exposed to my fairest view: for he had, immediately on stripping off his shirt, gently pushed her down on the couch, which stood conveniently to break her willing fall. Her thighs were spread out to their utmost extention, and discovered between them the mark of the sex, the red-centered cleft of flesh, whose lips vermillioning inwards, expressed a small ruby line in sweet miniature, such as Guido's touch or colouring: could never attain to the life or delicacy of.

Phoebe, at this, gave me a gentle jog, to prepare me for a whispered question: 'Whether I thought my little maiden-head was much less?' But my attention was too much engrossed, too much enwrapped with all I saw, to be able to give her any answer.

By this time the young gentleman had changed her posture from lying breadth to length-wise on the coach: but her thighs were still spread, and the mark lay fair for him, who now kneeling between them, displayed to us a side view of that fierce erect machine of his, which threatened no less than splitting the tender victim [...]. He looked upon his weapon himself with some pleasure, and guiding it with his hand to the inviting slit, drew aside the lips, and lodged it (after some thrusts, which Polly seemed even to assist) about half way; but there it stuck, I suppose from its growing thickness: he draws it again, and just wetting it with spittle, re-enters, and with ease sheathed it now up to the hilt, at which Polly gave a deep sigh, which was quite another tone than one of pain; he thrusts, she heaves, at first gently, and in a regular cadence; but presently the transport began to be too violent to observe any order or measure; their motions were too rapid, their kisses too fierce and fervent for nature to support such fury long: both seemed to me out of themselves: their eyes darted fires: 'Oh!... oh!... I can't bear it... It is too much... I die... I am a-going...' were Polly's expressions of extasy: his joys were more silent: but soon broken murmurs, sighs heart-fetched, and at length a dispatching thrust, as if he would have forced himself up her body, and then the motionless languor of all his limbs, all shewed that the die-away moment was come upon him; which she gave signs of joining with, by the wild throwing of her hands about, closing her eyes, and giving a deep sob, in which she seemed to expire in an agony of bliss.

[...]

For my part, I will not pretend to describe what I felt over me during this scene; but from that instant, adieu all fears of what man can do unto me; they were now changed into such ardent desires, such ungovernable longings, that I could have pulled the first of that sex that should present itself, by the sleeve, and offered him the bauble, which I now imagined the loss of would be a gain I could not too soon procure myself.

Phoebe, who had more experience, and to whom such sights were not so new, could not however be unmoved at so warm a scene; and drawing me away softly from the peeping hole, for fear of being overheard, guided me as near the door as possible; all passive and obedient to her least signals.

Here was no room either to sit or lie, but making me stand with my back towards the door, she lifted up my petticoats, and with her busy fingers fell to visit and explore that part of me, where now the heat, and irritations were so violent, that I was perfectly sick and ready to die with desire; that the bare touch of her finger, in that critical place, had the effect of a fire to a train, and her hand instantly made her sensible to what a pitch I was wound up, and melted by the sight she had thus procured me: satisfied then with her success, in allaying a heat that would have made me impatient of seeing the continuation of transactions between our amorous couple, she brought me again to the crevice, so favourable to our curiosity.

◗

adventure · irony · learning

'Dialogue of Torquato Tasso and his familiar genius'

from *Operette morali*

GIACOMO LEOPARDI

◆

⏳ 3 minutes

In this dialogue, Italian Romantic poet Giacomo Leopardi argues that in order to feel real pleasure, we must be mindfully present in the moment.

◆

GENIUS: [...] What is pleasure?

TASSO: I didn't have enough of it to form an opinion.

GENIUS: Nobody did. We know pleasure only in theory: pleasure is a matter of speculation, not a reality. A desire, not a fact. It is an emotion people consider and never experience; or, to put it better, it is an idea more than a feeling.

Can you see that? In the very moment when you feel happy, even if it is on account of something you have desired for a long time, and for which you struggled and toiled extraordinarily hard, even then, you are not satisfied, and you are waiting for a bigger happiness, a more authentic happiness which will give you true pleasure. You keep thinking of that future time almost continuously. But when the moment finally arrives, it doesn't give you the pleasure you were hoping for, and by then, all you have is the blind hope that you will find a better and fuller delight on another occasion, and the comfort of telling yourself that you have been happy at some point in the past. You say the same thing to the others too, in order to look good, and to persuade yourself.

Those who accept to keep on living do that only in name of their dreams; that is, their belief that they were happy, or they will be. Both are fanciful and false.

TASSO: And couldn't people believe they are happy right now, in the present?

GENIUS: If they were able to do that, they would be happy indeed. But tell me if you remember saying, at any moment in your life, in all sincerity and with full awareness, *I am happy*. Rather you said and say every day, *I was happy*. And a few times you say, but with less conviction, *I will be happy*. That way pleasure is always past or future, but never present.

◗▬

happiness · potential · regret

WORK

Every time I turn on the radio on Saturday morning and hear the presenter say, with apparent relief, 'It's the weekend at last', I die a little inside. By waiting for the weekend as our earthly salvation, we waste five days out of seven.

Ideally, work should not be the opposite of leisure. Work should be something that pays our bills, sure, but also fulfils us in a more profound way. We need *meaning* as much as we need food: in order to be happy, we need to feel we are making something of our life and of ourselves. Given that we are going to devote a massive proportion of our lives to our work, surely that work should constitute a hugely significant source of meaning in our lives?

Too often, however, work is nothing but a means to an end. And this is not only true in the obvious cases – it must be difficult, for instance, to find meaning when you are stacking shelves in a supermarket. But even well-paid and intellectually demanding jobs do not necessarily give us scope to learn and develop as human beings (I know some deeply frustrated City lawyers). And nor does the choice of a creative profession ensure a career of unalloyed fulfilment: singers, authors and artists can be as dissatisfied as everybody else. And don't deceive yourself that the trick is to hit the jackpot and never have to work a day in your life again. Lying on a tropical beach is fine in the short term, but you would end up dying of boredom. As human beings, we have a natural impulse to work, to keep ourselves busy.

Work is a paradox – we need it, and when we have it, we often want to get rid of it.

Even when we move to a job that fits our talents better than than the last one, there are bound to be aspects of the new job that won't make us jump for joy. There are no hard-and-fast solutions: it is a matter of making constant small adjustments. More than obsessing about the result, we should learn to enjoy the process.

*

The writings in this section will help you to articulate some of the difficulties related to work, and point you in the direction of some possible solutions, and yes, help you to enjoy the process. You can use them to support a friend who has embarked on a new career path, or who is going through a professional crisis, or to offer guidance to a younger person who still has to choose which path to take.

We start with the myth of Pygmalion, a sculptor who was so good, and so much in love with his work, that he convinced the goddess Aphrodite to breathe the breath of life into one of his statues.

We then move on to Joe R. Lansdale, who shows his two most famous characters, Hap and Leonard, struggling with a mind-numbingly boring job; while George

Orwell describes the underbelly of a luxury restaurant. Both of these pieces are acutely observed, and they are both very funny, in different ways.

Virginia Woolf tackles head-on the sexist assumptions that a patriarchal society makes about 'professions for women'.

Writing more than half a century before Woolf, Anthony Trollope outlines his routine as a writer, thereby revealing that creative work is still work.

H. G. Wells describes the induction programme from hell.

When we worry about work, we often worry about money too. Elizabeth Gaskell gently teases us about such worries, making light of them.

John Fante tells the story of someone who, after a string of failed jobs, eventually finds his true *métier*.

Pygmalion

FRANCESCO DIMITRI

⏳ 7 minutes

The myth of Pygmalion has been interpreted
in different ways. The way I see it, it is about
bringing enthusiasm to one's work.

Pygmalion of Cyprus was not a lot of fun to be with. He
didn't get on with any woman (or man) he met, because
no one could live up to his high standards: he didn't care
for loose morals, and so he didn't care for modern people.
You could say he was a bit stuck-up – and yet you wouldn't
say that if you looked at his statues.

You see, with a chisel in his hand, Pygmalion became
another person: as he shaped hard matter, he shaped
himself too, the holier-than-thou loner turning into a
sympathetic observer of the human condition. He was at
his best when he was working, and his work had a warmth
and a charm that you would never suspect Pygmalion
capable of.

At one point Pygmalion came into possession of an

especially fine lot of ivory. Such fine ivory surely deserved to become the best sculpture he had ever produced, to be transformed into an ideal of beauty and perfection and all things good. He didn't doubt for one moment what his subject would be: the woman he never met, the woman who, alas, only existed in his head.

Day and night Pygmalion worked, and night and day, chiselling wide hips and shapely breasts, witty lips and clever eyes, skin as smooth as ice, an eyebrow slightly lifted, a general air of intelligence. When he was done, after I don't know how many weeks of toil, Pygmalion set down his chisel, wiped his brow, and stared.

She was beautiful.

I know what you are thinking: that Pygmalion was conceited and vain, as haughty in his work as he was in his morals. But no, that wasn't the case. He knew he was a good sculptor, yes, and he was proud of that, but more to the point, he appreciated beauty, and the beauty of that statue was unrivalled. The pleasure Pygmalion took from it wasn't about him, it was about the quality of the work itself. So intense was that beauty that it seemed to reveal a soul waiting to hatch from under the stone.

Pygmalion got close to the statue, and kissed its lips.

But there was no soul there, of course, and no skin; only cold ivory, an illusion of softness. Pygmalion stepped back and bowed his head. The sheer beauty of the statue had stirred something inside him. He was still alone, and not at peace anymore.

He only needed to sleep, he thought, and everything would go back to normal.

But sleep didn't help. On the next day Pygmalion kissed the statue again, and caressed her thighs, and whispered silly words in her ivory ears. He gave her gifts of beautiful shells, and draped her in expensive dresses, in sensuous silk and exotic jewellery. Such beauty had to be cherished.

The day of a grand feast came, a feast for Aphrodite, who was born from sea foam on Cyprus' shore. Lonely, despondent, Pygmalion went to the goddess's shrine, ignoring the partying that was going on around him, the people and their happiness. He gave his offering to the goddess, and prayed, for the first time in his life, that he might find love. He realised with horror that he was going to ask the goddess to give him *the statue's love*. Ashamed, he managed to change his prayer before it left his lips, and asked instead for the love of someone who resembled the statue.

But the gods know what we want; sometimes better than we do.

And Aphrodite was listening, and it was her festival, and she loved nothing better than to see a proud and haughty individual rendered powerless by the grip of an intense passion. For the emotion that Pygmalion felt for his creation was indeed nothing short of a passion, the blinding sexual passion that was sacred to Aphrodite – and still is. The goddess smiled, and said, *So be it*.

When Pygmalion came back home, he was still burning with shame for what he had almost asked Aphrodite to give him. He looked at the statue; it was all her fault. And yet he couldn't bear to blame her. Hating himself, hating his weakness, he went close to her, and kissed her ivory lips once more. He lingered there longer than he had ever done.

But her lips weren't ivory any more.

Pygmalion placed his hand on her chest; and it was soft, and it was warm, and its flesh was pliant to his touch. And Pygmalion kissed her once more, and warm lips kissed him back, and a tongue, and the breath of a living being melted into his own.

Pygmalion gave thanks to Aphrodite as he kissed his love.

desire · learning · happiness · potential

Captains Outrageous

JOE R. LANSDALE

◆

⏳ 8 minutes

All of us have experienced the misery of
a really boring and unfulfilling job.

◆

I made a last round and met Leonard in the break room.
He had his security cap cocked at a jaunty angle and
was standing in front of the soda machine, counting out
change.

When I came in he said, without looking up, 'You got
a quarter?'

I gave him a quarter.

'Any chickens try to break out?' I asked.

'Nope. None tried to break in either. How about on
your side? Any trouble?' Leonard pushed the button on
the soda machine and a Dr Pepper dropped out.

'No chicken problems. I saw a suspicious wood rat out
by the trees, but he didn't want any part of me.'

'Well, I can see that.'

I went over and made myself a cup of free decaf because

I'd just given Leonard my last quarter. I put lots of free creamer in it. The coffee at the chicken plant needs lots of creamer so it doesn't taste like something dead.

I stirred the coffee in the Styrofoam cup with a plastic swizzle stick and sipped it. It still tasted like something dead, only with creamer in it. I dropped the full cup in the trash and we went out to Leonard's pickup.

We had been working at Deerstone's Chicken Processing for about six months, and it wasn't so bad. We had the three-in-the-afternoon-to-midnight shift. Mostly you just walked around and made sure there weren't any holes in the fence and nothing was out of place and you didn't see workers packing their car trunks with frozen chickens.

It beat one chicken plant I tried to get on at. They didn't want me as a security guard, but thought I'd be great out at their farm, masturbating roosters for sperm to impregnate hens. No joke. They really did that, or so they said. I tried to imagine if they had you do it with tweezers and gloves, or if you had to do it with a naked thumb and forefinger. Perhaps it was better for the chickens that way.

When you spent a lot of time walking around outside a dark building and inside where chicken slaughter was going on, you thought about all kinds of possibilities. And in the middle of the night, edging on toward the big twelve, a lot of dumb ideas seemed reasonable.

The guard job had come through an acquaintance who was quitting and said they needed two. I had to get gun-certified, way it's offered in Texas, and Leonard, who already had the certification, got the job with me. We were the last hard bastion between the chickens inside the processing plant (most of them already dead, headless, defeathered, and on hooks) and the outside world who wanted them.

Let me tell you, these chicken people aren't messing around. They're serious about their fowls. They got all kinds of processing methods they hold dear and don't want stolen.

Processing plant across town, the one wanted me to jack off chickens, lived in mortal fear of spies from Deerstone's. So fearful, in fact, Leonard and I liked to imagine they would send their own chickens over for secrets. You know, dressed in black ninja outfits, going over the fence and the wall, with metal cleats on wings and feet, climbing through ventilation shafts, ready to pluck out secret information after formidable nunchaku battles in elevators and dark places with Deerstone's own chickens.

Yes, sir, sort of made you feel proud when you went home at night, put your dark green guard suit, hat, and holstered handgun on a chair, lay down in bed, smelling of chicken, knowing you kept the world safe from meat processing thieves. That and the fact you got a decent check every two weeks and a sexy uniform to dazzle the female population.

Well, decent money depends on what you've been doing before. Bouncing sometimes paid better, but you had to hang out with a bunch of drunks in a smoky joint full of naked women, and after a while the naked women were just bothersome. You wanted them to put clothes on.

I can't explain it. It's just one of those strange things in life. You start to think you wouldn't have to bounce in the first place, throw drunks in the parking lot, if they didn't serve alcohol in there and have naked women running around shaking their tits and sticking their bush in everyone's face.

Then you realise if the place wasn't like that, you wouldn't have a job. It's a bit like being a preacher. If there wasn't any sin you'd be hosing down oil at a filling station. Which, come to think of it, in either case, bouncer or preacher, was sure to be a more honourable profession.

■▶

companionship · irony · resilience

Down and Out in Paris and London

GEORGE ORWELL

———◆———

⏳ 6 minutes

When you eat in a nice restaurant, do you ever
think about the people who work there? Do you
ever wonder who they are, and how they live? And
what goes on in the secret sanctum of the kitchen?

———◆———

My bad day was when I washed up for the dining-room. I
had not to wash the plates, which were done in the kitchen,
but only the other crockery, silver, knives and glasses; yet,
even so, it meant thirteen hours' work, and I used between
thirty and forty dishcloths during the day. [...] I worked
in a dirty, crowded little den, a pantry and scullery combined, which gave straight on the dining-room. Besides
washing up, I had to fetch the waiters' food and serve
them at table; most of them were intolerably insolent, and
I had to use my fists more than once to get common civil-
ity. The person who normally washed up was a woman,
and they made her life a misery.

It was amusing to look round the filthy little scullery

and think that only a double door was between us and the dining-room. There sat the customers in all their splendour – spotless table-cloths, bowls of flowers, mirrors and gilt cornices and painted cherubim; and here, just a few feet away, we in our disgusting filth. For it really was disgusting filth. There was no time to sweep the floor till evening, and we slithered about in a compound of soapy water, lettuce-leaves, torn paper and trampled food. A dozen waiters with their coats off, showing their sweaty armpits, sat at the table mixing salads and sticking their thumbs into the cream pots. The room had a dirty, mixed smell of food and sweat. Everywhere in the cup-boards, behind the piles of crockery, were squalid stores of food that the waiters had stolen. There were only two sinks, and no washing basin, and it was nothing unusual for a waiter to wash his face in the water in which clean crockery was rinsing. But the customers saw nothing of this. There were a coco-nut mat and a mirror outside the dining-room door, and the waiters used to preen themselves up and go in looking the picture of cleanliness.

It is an instructive sight to see a waiter going into a hotel dining-room. As he passes the door a sudden change comes over him. The set of his shoulders alters; all the dirt and hurry and irritation have dropped off in an instant. He glides over the carpet, with a solemn priest-like air. I remember our assistant maître d'hôtel, a fiery Italian, pausing at the dining-room door to address an apprentice who had broken a bottle of wine. Shaking his fist above his head he yelled (luckily the door was more or less soundproof):

'*Tu me fais* – Do you call yourself a waiter, you young bastard? You a waiter! You're not fit to scrub floors in the brothel your mother came from. *Maquereau!*'

Words failing him, he turned to the door; and as he opened it he delivered a final insult in the same manner as Squire Western in *Tom Jones*.

Then he entered the dining-room and sailed across it dish in hand, graceful as a swan. Ten seconds later he was bowing reverently to a customer. And you could not help thinking, as you saw him bow and smile, with that benign smile of the trained waiter, that the customer was put to shame by having such an aristocrat to serve him.

This washing up was a thoroughly odious job – not hard, but boring and silly beyond words. It is dreadful to think that some people spend their whole decades at such occupations. The woman whom I replaced was quite sixty years old, and she stood at the sink thirteen hours a day, six days a week, the year round; she was, in addition, horribly bullied by the waiters. She gave out that she had once been an actress – actually, I imagine, a prostitute; most prostitutes end as charwomen. It was strange to see that in spite of her age and her life she still wore a bright blonde wig, and darkened her eyes and painted her face like a girl of twenty. So apparently even a seventy-eight-hour week can leave one with some vitality.

resilience · irony

'Professions for Women'

VIRGINIA WOOLF

◆

⌛ 14 minutes

The novelist Virginia Woolf had to fight an enemy
who still haunts our offices and workplaces.
She calls it the 'Angel in the House'.

◆

You have only got to figure to yourselves a girl in a bedroom with a pen in her hand. She had only to move that pen from left to right – from ten o'clock to one. Then it occurred to her to do what is simple and cheap enough after all – to slip a few of those pages into an envelope, fix a penny stamp in the corner, and drop the envelope into the red box at the corner. It was thus that I became a journalist; and my effort was rewarded on the first day of the following month – a very glorious day it was for me – by a letter from an editor containing a cheque for one pound ten shillings and sixpence. [...] instead of spending that sum upon bread and butter, rent, shoes and stockings, or butcher's bills, I went out and bought a cat – a beautiful cat, a Persian cat, which very soon involved me in bitter disputes with my neighbours.

What could be easier than to write articles and to buy Persian cats with the profits? But wait a moment. Articles have to be about something. Mine, I seem to remember, was about a novel by a famous man. And while I was writing this review, I discovered that if I were going to review books I should need to do battle with a certain phantom. And the phantom was a woman, and when I came to know her better I called her after the heroine of a famous poem, The Angel in the House. It was she who used to come between me and my paper when I was writing reviews. It was she who bothered me and wasted my time and so tormented me that at last I killed her. You who come of a younger and happier generation may not have heard of her – you may not know what I mean by the Angel in the House. I will describe her as shortly as I can. She was intensely sympathetic. She was immensely charming. She was utterly unselfish. She excelled in the difficult arts of family life. She sacrificed herself daily. If there was chicken, she took the leg; if there was a draught she sat in it – in short she was so constituted that she never had a mind or a wish of her own, but preferred to sympathize always with the minds and wishes of others. Above all – I need not say it – she was pure. Her purity was supposed to be her chief beauty – her blushes, her great grace. In those days [...] every house had its Angel. And when I came to write I encountered her with the very first words. The shadow of her wings fell on my page; I heard the rustling of her skirts in the room. Directly, that is to say, I took my pen in my hand to review that novel by a famous man, she slipped behind me and whispered:

'My dear, you are a young woman. You are writing about a book that has been written by a man. Be sympathetic; be tender; flatter; deceive; use all the arts and wiles of our sex. Never let anybody guess that you have a mind of your own. Above all, be pure.' And she made as if to guide my pen. [...] I turned upon her and caught her by the throat. I did my best to kill her. My excuse, if I were to be had up in a court of law, would be that I acted in self-defence. Had I not killed her she would have killed me. She would have plucked the heart out of my writing. For, as I found, directly I put pen to paper, you cannot review even a novel without having a mind of your own, without expressing what you think to be the truth about human relations, morality, sex. And all these questions, according to the Angel of the House, cannot be dealt with freely and openly by women; they must charm, they must conciliate, they must – to put it bluntly – tell lies if they are to succeed. Thus, whenever I felt the shadow of her wing or the radiance of her halo upon my page, I took up the inkpot and flung it at her. She died hard. Her fictitious nature was of great assistance to her. It is far harder to kill a phantom than a reality. She was always creeping back when I thought I had despatched her. Though I flatter myself that I killed her in the end, the struggle was severe; it took much time that had better have been spent upon learning Greek grammar; or in roaming the world in search of adventures. But it was a real experience; it was an experience that was bound to befall all women writers at that time. Killing the Angel in the House was part of the occupation of a woman writer.

But to continue my story. The Angel was dead; what then remained? You may say that what remained was a simple and common object – a young woman in a bedroom with an inkpot. In other words, now that she had rid herself of falsehood, that young woman had only to be herself. Ah, but what is 'herself'? I mean, what is a woman? I assure you, I do not know. I do not believe that you know. I do not believe that anybody can know until she has expressed herself in all the arts and professions open to human skill. That indeed is one of the reasons why I have come here out of respect for you, who are in process of showing us by your experiments what a woman is, who are in process Of providing us, by your failures and successes, with that extremely important piece of information.

But to continue the story of my professional experiences. I made one pound ten and six by my first review; and I bought a Persian cat with the proceeds. Then I grew ambitious. A Persian cat is all very well, I said; but a Persian cat is not enough. I must have a motor car. And it was thus that I became a novelist – for it is a very strange thing that people will give you a motor car if you will tell them a story. It is a still stranger thing that there is nothing so delightful in the world as telling stories. It is far pleasanter than writing reviews of famous novels. And yet [...] I must tell you about a very strange experience that befell me as a novelist. [...] I want you to imagine me writing a novel in a state of trance. I want you to figure to yourselves a girl sitting with a pen in her hand, which for minutes, and indeed for hours, she never dips into the inkpot. The image that comes to my mind when I think of this girl is the image of a fisherman lying sunk in dreams on the verge of a deep lake with a rod held out over the water. She was letting her imagination sweep unchecked round every rock and cranny of the world that lies submerged in the depths of our unconscious being. Now came the experience, the experience that I believe to be far commoner with women writers than with men. The line raced through the girl's fingers. Her imagination had rushed away. It had sought the pools, the depths, the dark places where the largest fish slumber. And then there was a smash. There was an explosion. There was foam and confusion. The imagination had dashed itself against something hard. The girl was roused from her dream. She was indeed in a state of the most acute and difficult distress. To speak without figure she had thought of something, something about the body, about the passions which it was unfitting for her as a woman to say. Men, her reason told her, would be shocked. The consciousness of – what men will say of a woman who speaks the truth about her passions had roused her from her artist's state of unconsciousness. She could write no more. The trance was over. Her imagination could work no longer. [...]

These then were two very genuine experiences of my own. These were two of the adventures of my professional life. The first – killing the Angel in the House – I think I solved. She died. But the second, telling the truth about my own experiences as a body, I do not think I solved. I doubt that any woman has solved it yet. The obstacles against her are still immensely powerful – and yet they are very difficult to define. [...] Outwardly, what obstacles are there for a woman rather than for a man? Inwardly, I think, the case is very different; she has still many ghosts to fight, many prejudices to overcome. Indeed it will be a long time still, I think, before a woman can sit down to write a book without finding a phantom to be slain, a rock to be dashed against.

[...] Even when the path is nominally open – when there is nothing to prevent a woman from being a doctor, a lawyer, a civil servant – there are many phantoms and obstacles, as I believe, looming in her way. [...] You have won rooms of your own in the house hitherto exclusively owned by men. You are able, though not without great labour and effort, to pay the rent. [...] But this freedom is only a beginning – the room is your own, but it is still bare. It has to be furnished; it has to be decorated; it has to be shared. How are you going to furnish it, how are you going to decorate it? With whom are you going to share it, and upon what terms? These, I think are questions of the utmost importance and interest. [...] Willingly would I stay and discuss those questions and answers – but not tonight. My time is up; and I must cease.

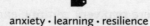

anxiety · learning · resilience

Autobiography

ANTHONY TROLLOPE

◆

⏳ 5 minutes

Here the novelist Anthony Trollope describes his
writing routine. Do you believe a writer's life is all
about waiting for the Muse to bring inspiration?
Trollope didn't think so.

◆

The work that I did during the twelve years that I remained
there, from 1859 to 1871, was certainly very great. I feel
confident that in amount no other writer contributed so
much during that time to English literature. Over and
above my novels, I wrote political articles, critical, social,
and sporting articles, for periodicals, without number.
I did the work of a surveyor of the General Post Office,
and so did it as to give the authorities of the department
no slightest pretext for fault-finding. I hunted always at
least twice a week. I was frequent in the whist-room at
the Garrick. I lived much in society in London, and was
made happy by the presence of many friends at Waltham
Cross. In addition to this we always spent six weeks at

least out of England. Few men, I think, ever lived a fuller life. And I attribute the power of doing this altogether to the virtue of early hours. It was my practice to be at my table every morning at 5.30 a.m.; and it was also my practice to allow myself no mercy. An old groom, whose business it was to call me, and to whom I paid £5 a year extra for the duty, allowed himself no mercy. During all those years at Waltham Cross he was never once late with the coffee which it was his duty to bring me. I do not know that I ought not to feel that I owe more to him than to any one else for the success I have had. By beginning at that hour I could complete my literary work before I dressed for breakfast.

All those I think who have lived as literary men – working daily as literary labourers – will agree with me that three hours a day will produce as much as a man ought to write. But then he should so have trained himself that he shall be able to work continuously during those three hours – so have tutored his mind that it shall not be necessary for him to sit nibbling his pen, and gazing at the wall before him, till he shall have found the words with which he wants to express his ideas. It had at this time become my custom – and it still is my custom, though of late I have become a little lenient to myself – to write with my watch before me, and to require from myself 250 words every quarter of an hour. I have found that the 250 words have been forthcoming as regularly as my watch went. But my three hours were not devoted entirely to writing. I always began my task by reading the work of the day before, an operation which would take me half an hour, and which consisted chiefly in weighing with my ear the sound of the words and phrases. I would strongly recommend this practice to all tyros in writing. That their work should be read after it has been written is a matter of course – that it should be read twice at least before it goes to the printers, I take to be a matter of course. But by reading what he has last written, just before he recommences his task, the writer will catch the tone and spirit of what he is then saying, and will avoid the fault of seeming to be unlike himself. This division of time allowed me to produce over ten pages of an ordinary novel volume a day, and if kept up through ten months, would have given as its results three novels of three volumes each in the year [...].

creativity · rules

Kipps

H. G. WELLS

◆

⧖ **10 minutes**

On his first day at work, the fourteen-year-old
Kipps is inducted into the strange ways of
the 'Folkestone Drapery Bazaar'.

◆

When Kipps left New Romney, with a small yellow tin
box, a still smaller portmanteau, a new umbrella, and
a keepsake half-sixpence, to become a draper, he was a
youngster of fourteen, thin, with whimsical drakes' tails
at the poll of his head, smallish features, and eyes that
were sometimes very light and sometimes very dark, gifts
those of his birth; and by the nature of his training he
was indistinct in his speech, confused in his mind, and
retreating in his manners. Inexorable fate had appointed him to serve his country in commerce, and the same
national bias towards private enterprise and leaving
bad alone, which entrusted his general education to
Mr. Woodrow, now indentured him firmly into the hands
of Mr Shalford, of the Folkestone Drapery Bazaar. [...]

He was an irascible, energetic little man, with hairy hands, for the most part under his coat tails, a long, shiny, bald head, a pointed, aquiline nose a little askew, and a neatly trimmed beard. He walked lightly and with a confident jerk, and he was given to humming. He had added to exceptional business 'push,' bankruptcy under the old dispensation, and judicious matrimony. His establishment was now one of the most considerable in Folkestone, and he insisted on every inch of frontage by alternate stripes of green and yellow down the houses over the shops. His shops were numbered 3, 5 and 7 on the street, and on his billheads 3 to 7. He encountered the abashed and awe-stricken Kipps with the praises of his system and himself. He spread himself out behind his desk with a grip on the lapel of his coat and made Kipps a sort of speech. 'We expect y'r to work, y'r know, and we expect y'r to study our interests,' explained Mr Shalford in the regal and commercial plural. 'Our system here is the best system y'r could have. I made it, and I ought to know. I began at the very bottom of the ladder when I was fourteen, and there isn't a step in it I don't know. Not a step. Mr Booch in the desk will give y'r the card of rules and fines. Jest wait a minute.' He pretended to be busy with some dusty memoranda under a paper-weight, while Kipps stood in a sort of paralysis of awe regarding his new master's oval baldness. 'Two thous'n three forty-seven pounds,' whispered Mr Shalford audibly, feigning forgetfulness of Kipps. Clearly a place of great transactions!

Mr Shalford rose, and handing Kipps a blotting-pad and an inkpot to carry – mere symbols of servitude, for he made no use of them – emerged into a counting-house where three clerks had been feverishly busy ever since his door handle had turned. 'Booch,' said Mr Shalford, ''ave y'r copy of the rules?' and a down-trodden, shabby little old man with a ruler in one hand and a quill pen in his mouth, silently held out a small book with green and yellow covers, mainly devoted, as Kipps presently discovered, to a voracious system of fines. He became acutely aware that his hands were full, and that everybody was staring at him. He hesitated a moment before putting the inkpot down to free a hand.

'Mustn't fumble like that,' said Mr Shalford as Kipps pocketed the rules. 'Won't do here. Come along, come along,' and he cocked his coat tails high, as a lady might hold up her dress, and led the way into the shop.

A vast interminable place it seemed to Kipps, with unending shining counters and innumerable faultlessly dressed young men and presently Houri-like young women staring at him. Here there was a long vista of gloves dangling from overhead rods, there ribbons and baby-linen. A short young lady in black mittens was making out the account of a customer, and was clearly confused in her addition by Shalford's eagle eye.

A thickset young man with a bald head and a round, very wise face, who was profoundly absorbed in adjusting all the empty chairs down the counter to absolutely equal distances, awoke out of his preoccupation and answered respectfully to a few Napoleonic and quite unnecessary remarks from his employer. Kipps was told that this young man's name was Mr Buggins, and that he was to do whatever Mr Buggins told him to do.

They came round a corner into a new smell, which was destined to be the smell of Kipps' life for many years, the vague, distinctive smell of Manchester goods. A fat man with a large nose jumped – actually jumped – at their appearance, and began to fold a pattern of damask in front of him exactly like an automaton that is suddenly set going.

'Carshot, see to this boy tomorrow,' said the master. 'See he don't fumble. Smart'n 'im up.'

'Yussir,' said Carshot fatly, glanced at Kipps, and resumed his pattern-folding with extreme zeal.

'Whatever Mr Carshot says y'r to do, ye do,' said Mr Shalford, trotting onward; and Carshot blew out his face with an appearance of relief.

They crossed a large room full of the strangest things Kipps had ever seen. Ladylike figures, surmounted by black wooden knobs in the place of the refined heads one might have reasonably expected, stood about with a life-like air of conscious fashion.

'Costume room,' said Shalford.

Two voices engaged in some sort of argument – 'I can assure you, Miss Mergle, you are entirely mistaken – entirely, in supposing I should do anything so unwoman-ly,' – sank abruptly, and they discovered two young ladies, taller and fairer than any of the other young ladies, and with black trains to their dresses, who were engaged in writing at a little table. Whatever they told him to do, Kipps gathered he was to do. He was also, he understood, to do whatever Carshot and Booch told him to do. And there were also Buggins and Mr Shalford. And not to forget or fumble!

They descended into a cellar called 'The Warehouse', and Kipps had an optical illusion of errand boys fighting. Some aerial voice said, 'Teddy!' and the illusion passed. He looked again, and saw quite clearly that they were packing parcels and always would be, and that the last thing in the world that they would or could possibly do was to fight. Yet he gathered from the remarks Mr Shalford addressed to their busy backs that they had been fighting – no doubt at some past period of their lives.

Emerging in the shop again among a litter of toys and what are called 'fancy articles,' Shalford withdrew a hand from beneath his coat tails to indicate an overhead change-carrier. He entered into elaborate calculations to show how many minutes in one year were saved thereby, and lost himself among the figures. 'Seven tums eight seven nine – was it? Or seven eight nine? Now, now! Why, when I was a boy your age I c'd do a sum like that as soon as hear it. We'll soon get y'r into better shape than that. Make you Fishent. Well, y'r must take my word, it comes to pounds and pounds saved in the year – pounds and pounds. System! System everywhere. Fishency.' He went on murmuring 'Fishency' and 'System' at intervals for some time.

irony · learning

Cranford

ELIZABETH GASKELL

———◆———

⏳ **5 minutes**

You might be worried about your finances, maybe even
slightly ashamed that you don't earn more money.
Just so you know: everybody else feels the same.

———◆———

I imagine that a few of the gentlefolks of Cranford were
poor, and had some difficulty in making both ends meet;
but they were like the Spartans, and concealed their smart
under a smiling face. We none of us spoke of money,
because that subject savoured of commerce and trade,
and though some might be poor, we were all aristocratic.
The Cranfordians had that kindly *esprit de corps* which
made them overlook all deficiencies in success when some
among them tried to conceal their poverty. When Mrs
Forrester, for instance, gave a party in her baby-house of
a dwelling, and the little maiden disturbed the ladies on
the sofa by a request that she might get the tea-tray out
from underneath, everyone took this novel proceeding as
the most natural thing in the world, and talked on about

household forms and ceremonies as if we all believed that our hostess had a regular servants' hall, second table, with housekeeper and steward, instead of the one little charity-school maiden, whose short ruddy arms could never have been strong enough to carry the tray upstairs, if she had not been assisted in private by her mistress, who now sat in state, pretending not to know what cakes were sent up, though she knew, and we knew, and she knew that we knew, and we knew that she knew that we knew, she had been busy all the morning making tea-bread and sponge-cakes.

There were one or two consequences arising from this general but unacknowledged poverty, and this very much acknowledged gentility, which were not amiss, and which might be introduced into many circles of society to their great improvement. For instance, the inhabitants of Cranford kept early hours, and clattered home in their pattens, under the guidance of a lantern-bearer, about nine o'clock at night; and the whole town was abed and asleep by half-past ten. Moreover, it was considered 'vulgar' (a tremendous word in Cranford) to give anything expensive, in the way of eatable or drinkable, at the evening enter-tainments. Wafer bread-and-butter and sponge-biscuits were all that the Honourable Mrs Jamieson gave; and she was sister-in-law to the late Earl of Glenmire, although she did practise such 'elegant economy.'

'Elegant economy!' How naturally one falls back into the phraseology of Cranford! There, economy was always 'elegant,' and money-spending always 'vulgar and ostenta-tious' [...]. I never shall forget the dismay felt when a certain

Captain Brown came to live at Cranford, and openly spoke about his being poor – not in a whisper to an intimate friend, the doors and windows being previously closed, but in the public street! in a loud military voice! alleging his poverty as a reason for not taking a particular house. The ladies of Cranford were already rather moaning over the invasion of their territories by a man and a gentleman. He was a half-pay captain, and had obtained some situation on a neighbouring railroad, which had been vehemently petitioned against by the little town; and if, in addition to his masculine gender, and his connection with the obnoxious railroad, he was so brazen as to talk of being poor – why, then, indeed, he must be sent to Coventry. Death was as true and as common as poverty; yet people never spoke about that, loud out in the streets. It was a word not to be mentioned to ears polite. We had tacitly agreed to ignore that any with whom we associated on terms of visiting equality could ever be prevented by poverty from doing anything that they wished. If we walked to or from a party, it was because the night was so fine, or the air so refreshing, not because sedan-chairs were expensive. If we wore prints, instead of summer silks, it was because we preferred a washing material; and so on, till we blinded ourselves to the vulgar fact that we were, all of us, people of very moderate means. Of course, then, we did not know what to make of a man who could speak of poverty as if it was not a disgrace.

anxiety · irony

The Brotherhood of the Grape

JOHN FANTE

⏳ 12 minutes

Sometimes you find the right job for you because
you're very good at it. And sometimes you find it
because you're no good at anything else.

I was a failure at the Tokyo Fish Company. A disgrace to
myself. I could not pack it. The work was too much for
me. At eighteen, in my last year of high school, my weight
had been 160 pounds, not a big man but a solid, stumpy
man with hard muscles and strong legs, a tough halfback,
a swift baseball player. In the cannery it was another kind
of game. The wiry Filipinos, the tireless Mexicans, made
a counterfeit of me and I was ashamed, lashing myself in
futility. They hoisted 100-pound sacks of rock salt with
ease while I staggered with a blue face and let them slip
from my grasp. They shoveled crushed ice by the hour
while I rested, out of breath. My boss, Julio, observed
quietly and said nothing. The other men saw it too, and
pretended not to see it. They were waiting out the ordeal,

waiting for me to throw in the towel. Even Coletti began to appear, watching the work from a doorway, looking for a moment and then walking away. A day came when we had to clear tons of ice from the hold of a half-sunk tuna clipper. In hip boots we slushed in ice water for two days. I stopped to rest on a pile of sacks and fell asleep. Julio wakened me. The job had been finished, the ice cleared away. I was cold and shivering. Coletti wanted to see me.

'You're fired,' he said, handing me a paycheck.

I had been with the Tokyo Fish Company for two weeks and two days. The check was in full payment for the third week.

'A little bonus,' Coletti said.

What now? A man who could not even shovel fish fertilizer, where did I fit in the world? I remembered another lifetime, the holy hours with Dostoyevsky, and I knew I could never be that way again. A janitor, maybe? A little tobacco shop? A bellhop? My grandfather, my father's father. He had been an intolerant knife-sharpener in Abruzzi. Was that my destiny too? Suddenly I wanted to go home, to my father's house, to my mother's arms, to her minestrone, to my old bed, to lie there the rest of my life. But it was impossible. How could I face them? I had written a few letters home those first days – all fabrications, all lies. I could never confront them now.

It was good timing. I arrived in San Elmo three hours after flu hit me. My mother turned from the kitchen sink to find me in the doorway.

'Henry! My God, what happened?'

She put me to bed. She brought hot soup. She called

Dr Maselli. He left antibiotics. I wakened and my father looked down at me.

'How do you feel?'

'Great,' I said.

'How long you gonna stay?'

'Long as I can.'

'You wanna work for me?'

'Not right this moment.'

'Sleep. We'll talk later.'

I ate and slept. Sometimes I slept and ate. Then my colon tightened. My mother brought me an enema bag. The potion didn't work. She brought another. I locked the bathroom door and applied it. Success! It roared from me. On the other side of the door my mother applauded. 'Thank God, oh, thank God!'

It was as if the purge had burst away all that troubled me – the poisons of the body, the abominations of the soul. In the morning I felt clean and pure. I set up a bridge table by the window and started to write.

I wrote in longhand, on lined paper in a grade school tablet, for of typewriters I knew nothing nor cared. My penmanship sufficed, for neat it was, painstaking and clean. In two days it was done: a short story about the Tokyo Fish Company, the boys and girls who worked there, and of a love affair between my boss Jose and a Mexican girl. When it was done I paused to see what I had wrought. No, it was not Fyodor Dostoyevsky. I didn't know what it was. A pastiche. It was Jack London, Raymond Chandler, James M. Cain, Hemingway, Steinbeck and Scott Fitzgerald. It even showed traces of Henry Molise. A marvel, a thing of beauty. What to do with it? Where could I realize the most money? *The Saturday Evening Post*, of course. I sent it off, tablet and all.

It was returned so quickly I wondered if it had ever left town and gone all the way to Philadelphia and back. I smiled at the rejection slip. It didn't matter. I had another story ready to mail. The new one went off to *The Saturday Evening Post*, the other to *Collier's*. In two months – fending off the old man with one hand and writing with the other – I completed five stories about the cannery, about Los Angeles harbour, about Filipinos and Mexicans. Not a word of appreciation from the *Post* or *Collier's*. Not a human written line acknowledging my existence. Minutely I examined every page of rejected manuscripts. Not so much as a fingerprint or smudge, not a mark. A bad time. The old man watched me as a he would an unwanted dog that had to be dealt with, a dog that ate too much and left fur on the sofa. There was a time when he growled because I read too much. Now he snarled because I wrote too much. It came down to the last valiant effort. I finished the story of Crazy Hernandez and rushed it to the *Post*. With it went my last hopes for escaping brick and stone and cement. The story sped back even faster than the others, it seemed, and I sat on the porch steps and tore open the brown envelope. There was a letter affixed to the manuscript. It read:

Dear Mr Molise:
What have you got against the typewriter? If you will type this manuscript on regular 8 ½ x 2 inch paper

I shall be glad to look at it again. The printer would never touch it in its present form. Sincerely yours,

I forced myself to walk slowly to the *San Elmo Journal*. There was this exploding heartbeat in my throat, the fear I would drop in the street with the story of Crazy Hernandez clutched in my arms. I handed it to Art Cohen, the *Journal* editor and my high school English instructor. He led me to a typewriter in the rear of the office and sat me before it. For half an hour he instructed me on the operation of a typewriter. Then I was on my own. It had taken me two days to write the Crazy Hernandez story. It took me ten days to type it without errors. What matter, ten days? When the check came I would go to San Francisco and find a room in North Beach. I would buy a typewriter, set it up before a window overlooking the bay, and write. Best of all, I wouldn't have to worry about carrying a hod, mixing mud, and mucking around in wet concrete.

What's that, Dostoyevsky? You don't approve of *The Saturday Evening Post*? Well, let me tell you something, Fyodor. I saw your journalistic pieces of 1875, and frankly, they were pretty tacky and commercial, but they brought you plenty of rubles. So let's not blush at the *Post* story. You have done worse in your time...

anxiety · irony · resilience · potential

NATURE

I GREW UP IN a small town in southern Italy, surrounded by olive trees and vineyards on all sides, just a few miles away from the sort of beaches people use as the background images on their computer desktops. My paternal grandparents were bona fide peasants, coming from a long line of peasants, and when I was little, my father, the first professional in his family, would take me to visit their small field. I grew up with a very close relationship to 'nature', but only if by 'nature' we mean countryside that people have been farming since before the founding of Rome, and beaches with more swimmers than sharks.

'Nature' is a notoriously problematic word. Take the ageless landscape of Bodmin Moor, in Cornwall. It looks wild enough, 'natural' and unchanging – but its appearance is in fact the result of centuries of human intervention. All over Europe, woodland is not left to its own devices but carefully managed. Of course spots of more or less 'wild' nature do exist, but they are rare and hard to find. Humans created the paths in the New Forest as much as they created Oxford Street. And yet we know instinctively that there is a difference between walking down a New Forest path and walking down Oxford Street:

one is 'nature', the other is not, and it would be disingenuous to say otherwise. What is it, then, that marks this difference?

I will borrow an argument that I first found in David Abram's book *The Spell of the Sensuous*: in nature we meet intelligences that are not human. The intelligence of animals, of growing plants, of an entire ecosystem which breathes and dies and reproduces – a system of which we are part, though a very special part, if nothing else because of our capacity to destroy it utterly. When you look at a city street, everything you see has a clear function, a purpose, everything serves a well-defined human need (even trees and shrubs), but when you are in 'nature', you feel that you are in the presence of a different kind of consciousness, which goes above and beyond ours (even when the landscape has been shaped by human intervention).

*

The pieces in this section are meant to help you and your friends reconnect with nature, to give you the inspiration you need to spend more time out of doors, seeking a dialogue with this different kind of consciousness. You can read them when you are at a remove from the natural world but you want to remember what it feels like. Or you could read them even when you *are* close to nature (in a wood, or by a river, or on a hillside – or in a city park) – to celebrate the moment with a friend.

The myth of Adonis shows that we *are* nature, that our bodies, our very essence, are part of the world we live in.

Rob Cowen, in his beautiful prose, reminds us that

we can find nature close to home, while John Muir's description of a storm invites us to reflect on the interconnectedness of the natural world.

Ralph Waldo Emerson writes about the importance of *seeing* nature.

Through the eyes of Dorothy Wordsworth we enjoy the view of a beautiful island in Scotland's Trossachs.

Robert Macfarlane takes us further north and west, describing a sailing expedition and its rich tapestry of sounds and feelings.

The Victorian adventurer Isabella Bird – a remarkable explorer and writer, now unfairly forgotten – describes one of nature's darker faces, an active volcano.

Chris Yates's account of a night walk in an English midsummer tells of a chance meeting with a hare – and communicates the awe that he felt on that occasion.

Amy Leach talks to us about a very different creature – the panda, and its mysterious passion for bamboo.

Adonis

FRANCESCO DIMITRI

◆

⧗ 8 minutes

We don't need to go into nature*, we don't need to
reconnect with nature. We only need to remember
that we* are *nature: our bones, our flesh, our eyes are
all made of the same substance as trees and lawns
and ponds: we are not* in *the world, but part of it.
Take the story of Adonis, for example.*

◆

He was born from a tree, in unhappy circumstances. His
mother, Myrrh, was the daughter of the king of Syria. By
some boastful words, unimportant in themselves, Myrrh
attracted the wrath of Aphrodite, who filled her with a
burning desire for her own father. Myrrh's father, of
course, would never agree to sleep with his daughter, but
Myrrh managed to fool him, and she slept with him for
twelve nights. Until the king discovered that his new lover
was his daughter, went mad with rage, and chased her, to
take the course of action that honour and piety dictated –
kill her. I know, I know. But the gods took pity on Myrrh
and changed her into a tree, the Myrrh tree.

From that tree, Adonis was born.

Aphrodite had been keeping an eye on the tree. She was not entirely sure that the woman had suffered enough; trees, after all, live very long lives. So she was there when a crack opened in the wood, and a baby rolled out of it. She was almost ready to kill the child with a kick, but then she caught a glimpse of him – and was enchanted.

Aphrodite crouched, to take a closer look at the baby, and the baby looked back. He was beautiful. In fact he was the most beautiful baby Aphrodite had ever seen. Dazzled, she scooped him up. She could not let him die, whatever the sins of his mother. She would never let beauty die.

But Aphrodite wasn't a mother, and she didn't want to be one. So she spoke to Persephone, Queen of the Underworld, and asked her to take care of little Adonis. The baby was just too charming for Persephone to say no.

And so Adonis grew up among goddesses and nymphs, between the world below and the world above, between caves and glades and dark secluded pools. He learnt to run, he learnt to hunt, to gather plants and grow them, and all those who met him were charmed by him. Soon he grew into an extremely handsome young man, nimble and strong; the sort of young man Aphrodite liked to make love to, for hours on end.

Persephone too.

The goddesses started to quarrel over Adonis. Each of them wanted him for herself. Aphrodite had found him, but Persephone had raised him. Their quarrel became a fight, and Zeus, worried that things were getting out of hand, decided to step in: Adonis, he decided, would

Nature · 225

spend one-third of the year with Persephone, one-third with Aphrodite, and one-third doing whatever he felt like doing. It was more or less the same pact he had struck for Persephone years before, when she was the object of a struggle between her mother and the Lord of the Underworld. It had worked back then, and Zeus didn't see why it shouldn't work again.

And it did work, for a while. Adonis always spent his own third of the year with Aphrodite, the goddess of sensuousness, making love in the deepest woods, on the most secluded beaches. With every day that passed he became a better hunter, and a better lover, and all was good – for a while. But all good things come to an end.

No one is sure who sent the boar. Someone says it was Ares, the god of war, who was jealous of his lover Aphrodite; others say it was Artemis, whom Adonis had slighted somehow; or Apollo, for a vendetta against Aphrodite. I suspect it might have been just bad luck. Be that as it may, a mighty boar appeared one day, and caught Adonis by surprise; and all his skills, all his courage and strength were not enough against this explosion of wildness. The boar charged Adonis, and slashed his flesh, and broke his ribs, and left him there, broken, bloodied, dying.

Aphrodite ran to her lover; she knew she couldn't save him, but she wanted to be with him as he died. And she was there, and she was crying, and she was shedding tears while he was shedding blood. For each drop of blood the mortal shed that day, the goddess shed a tear.

But then a miracle happened, fuelled by grief and love. Where Aphrodite's tears touched the soil, they didn't disappear; they quavered for a few moments, and then a rose was born from them. Where Adonis' drops of blood touched the soil, they grew up in the shape of anemones.

Adonis died, as all mortals must; Aphrodite was left with his lifeless body, surrounded now by a beautiful expanse of scented flowers.

And I think this is the way we live and the way we die. Nothing is wasted in nature, nothing is lost: we come from nature and to nature we will return, and we are part of nature throughout our lives. Our lives will be ended by a wild boar's tusk, but while we wait, we love and we hunt and we run, born from a secret womb, and destined, one day, to make flowers with our blood.

comfort · desire · meaning

Common Ground

ROB COWEN

◆————————◆

⧗ 12 minutes

Rob Cowen teaches us to find nature on our
doorstep, and to seek a different rhythm for our lives.

◆————————◆

Maps transform us. They make birds of us all. They reveal
the patterns of our existence and unlock our cages. If it
wasn't for that map, a second-hand Ordnance Survey
given as a Christmas present, maybe none of this would
have happened. It was New Year's Eve and I lay on the bed
with the town unfolded before me. I felt tired; constrained;
racked with cabin fever. I needed to get out. From a circle
of Biro drawn around my new house I flew up and over the
unfamiliar rooftops and roads, past shops, schools, hair
salons and bookmakers, seeking the nearest open ground.
Below me suburbia slunk down a shallow hill towards
an endless patchwork of delineated farmland. Hemmed
in between the two, I saw it: a tract of white paper, tree
symbols and the varicose vein of a river. It lured me down,
eyes to paper, body to freezing earth.

Somewhere a bell struck five as I cut through the start-stop traffic of the ring road. Exhaust fumes swirled fog-like, landlocked by the plummeting temperature. Underfoot the afternoon rain was hardening into a slippery film; frost feathered lawns. That peculiar post-Christmas malaise, thick with burning coal, pressed down on the houses. As the shrivelled sun disappeared into the mass of pitched roofs, chimney stacks and telegraph wires, I flowed on past a plastic Santa on a roof with no chimney and along a trench of emerging street lights. Either side of me, rows of Victorian terraces morphed into post-war semis before, finally, modern red-brick boxes whirled off the road in car-cluttered cul-de-sacs. Then, after a mile of walking, even their low walls and privet hedges began to thin. Through the gaps the dark, dank countryside of northern England rose like a great black wave.

At the bottom of the hill a rough track bisected the road suddenly and steadfastly, tracing a contour with nineteenth-century arrogance. It was a definitive border. Light and vegetation were in accord. Dimness shrouded the land beyond. Among the bare blackthorn, ash and spider-limbed elder, I spied relics: soot-blackened sand-stone walls, riveted iron plates and the overgrown ditch and mound of a siding. It all uttered a single word: railway. A footstep and I had crossed from the bright lights and right angles of bulbs and bricks into black bushes and trees, whose infinitesimal branches overlapped the track like hair growing over a scar. Unwittingly the railway was fulfilling a different function now – this was the high water mark of the sprawl. Suburbia washed against its southern bank in a mass of rickety fences and scattered bin bags disembowelled by brambles. Down its northern side the town dissolved into something other: a kind of wildness. Winter-beaten meadows stretched into wood before the earth rose again as field and hill that met sky in an unbroken ridge.

I hunkered down by a fence and tried to take it all in. Nothing stirred. There were hints of shapes forming in the distance – stands of larch, pylons, barns – but they were impossible to distinguish. The road I'd followed narrowed and wandered past a squat pub crouching in a hollow, then became lost in the rawness of fields. Tarmac turned to footpath, footpath into soil. Marking the border on opposite sides of the road were two vast oaks thirty metres high. Entwined above me their limbs created an arch, ancient sentinels guarding a forgotten world. I knew it, though. The urban fringe. The no man's land between town and country; this was the edge of things.

*

I can't say what imperceptible force drew me there, only that I needed to reach it. That frontier called me. Maybe a speck of its soil carried in a starling's foot had been drawn down deep into my respiratory system, circulating around my bloodstream and lodging on my temporal lobes, establishing itself as a point of reckoning. Whatever it was, I felt a sense of returning, like a bee to a hive. Weeks had passed since I'd left London with the weightlessness of new horizons in Yorkshire, the place I'd grown up, but far from being the liberating experience I'd imagined, moving house had proved to be an imprisonment. For too long I'd been stuck in an unending cycle of working, painting walls and unpacking boxes, sleeping fitfully in rooms that stank of gloss, acid in my throat, numbed by the cold of open windows. I'd find a whole day had slipped by as I sifted through collections of things that suddenly seemed to belong to a previous life. I'd hardly ventured into the world outside. Soon the shortening days and wintry gloom made familiarising myself with new surroundings even harder. All my routines were jumbled; every light switch was in the wrong place. In truth, the act of handing over the keys to my London flat had signified a greater shift: present to past. All the maps I had once navigated my life by – the routes to work, streets, cafés, flats, parks and pubs – were redundant. They covered a region 220 miles to the south. I was stuck somewhere else, between tenses, between spaces, between lives.

Everything changes continuously, of course, nature is perpetual flux, but we are good at suppressing uncomfortable reminders of the greater cycles. We rope ourselves to imagined, controllable permanence. Clocks are wound to the rhythms of modern anthropocentric existence: the nine-to-five grind, career trajectories, the working week, Saturday nights out, summer holidays, twenty-five-year mortgages, pension plans, retirement. It's how the adverts metronome our lives. Yet staring out over that edge rendered such things irrelevant. Time was a different animal, indifferent, a deer running unseen through the trees. There was nothing by which I might measure the moments passing until the rise and fall of a siren shrieked through town, then silence again. With the cold, clear, descending dark came euphoria; it prickled my neck and released the atom-deep sensation of otherworldliness. It was the blur of joy and terror felt when facing something prior to and greater than the self. My pulse slowed as the adrenalin dispersed and for a second I imagined it was my cells recalibrating to the deeper rhythms of the dark, my body resetting to the land.

Once upon a time the edges were the places we knew best. They were our common ground. Times were hard and spare but the margins around homesteads, villages and towns sustained us. People grazed livestock and collected deadfall for fuel. Access and usage became enshrined as rights and recognised in law. Pigs trotted through trees during 'pannage' – the acorn season from Michaelmas to Martinmas – certain types of game were hunted for the table and heather and fern were cut for bedding. Mushrooms, fruits and berries would be foraged and dried for winter; honey taken from wild beehives; chestnuts hoarded, ground and stored as flour. The fringes provided playgrounds for kids and illicit bedrooms for lovers. Whether consciously or not, these spaces kept us in time and rooted to the rhythms of land and nature. Feet cloyed with clay, we oriented ourselves by rain and sun, day and night, seasons, the slow spinning of stars.

Humans are creatures of habit: we all still go to edges to get perspective, to be sustained and reborn. Recreation is still re-creation after a fashion, only now it occurs in largely virtual worlds. Clouds, hyper-real TV shows, 3D films, multiplayer games, online stores and social media networks – these are today's areas of common ground, the terrains where people meet, work, hunt, play, learn, fall in love even. Ours is a world growing yet shrinking, connected yet isolated, all-knowing but without knowledge. It is one of breadth, shallowness and the endless swimming through cyberspace. All is speed and surface. Digging down deeper into an overlooked patch of ground, one that (in a global sense, at least) few people will ever know about and even fewer visit, felt like the antithesis to all of this. And it felt vitally important. You see, I still believe in the importance of edges. Lying just beyond our doors and fences, the enmeshed borders where human and nature collide are microcosms of our world at large, an extraordinary, exquisite world that is growing closer to the edge every day. These spaces reassert a vital truth: nature isn't just some remote mountain or protected park. It is all around us. It is in us. It is us.

➤

anxiety · comfort · self-knowledge

My First Summer in the Sierra

JOHN MUIR

◆

⧖ 7 minutes

John Muir was a Scottish-American
environmentalist of profoundly mystical bent.
Here he shows us how to find awe in a
storm, and in a single raindrop.

◆

About noon, as usual, big bossy cumuli began to grow
above the forest, and the rainstorm pouring from them
is the most imposing I have yet seen. The silvery zigzag
lightning lances are longer than usual, and the thunder
gloriously impressive, keen, crashing, intensely concentrated, speaking with such tremendous energy it would
seem that an entire mountain is being shattered at every
stroke, but probably only a few trees are being shattered,
many of which I have seen on my walks hereabouts
strewing the ground. At last the clear ringing strokes are
succeeded by deep low tones that grow gradually fainter as
they roll afar into the recesses of the echoing mountains,
where they seem to be welcomed home. Then another and

another peal, or rather crashing, splintering stroke, follows in quick succession, perchance splitting some giant pine or fir from top to bottom into long rails and slivers, and scattering them to all points of the compass. Now comes the rain, with corresponding extravagant grandeur, covering the ground high and low with a sheet of flowing water, a transparent film fitted like a skin upon the rugged anatomy of the landscape, making the rocks glitter and glow, gathering in the ravines, flooding the streams, and making them shout and boom in reply to the thunder.

How interesting to trace the history of a single raindrop! It is not long, geologically speaking, as we have seen, since the first raindrops fell on the newborn leafless Sierra landscapes. How different the lot of these falling now! Happy the showers that fall on so fair a wilderness – scarce a single drop can fail to find a beauty spot – on the tops of the peaks, on the shining glacier pavements, on the great smooth domes, on forests and gardens and brushy moraines, plashing, glinting, pattering, laving. Some go to the high snowy fountains to swell their well-saved stores; some into the lakes, washing the mountain windows, patting their smooth glassy levels, making dimples and bubbles and spray; some into the waterfalls and cascades, as if eager to join in their dance and song and beat their foam yet finer; good luck and good work for the happy mountain raindrops, each one of them a high waterfall in itself, descending from the cliffs and hollows of the clouds to the cliffs and hollows of the rocks, out of the sky-thunder into the thunder of the falling rivers. Some, falling on meadows and bogs, creep silently out of sight to the grass roots, hiding softly as in a nest, slipping, oozing hither, thither, seeking and finding their appointed work. Some, descending through the spires of the woods, sift spray through the shining needles, whispering peace and good cheer to each one of them. Some drops with happy aim glint on the sides of crystals – quartz, hornblende, garnet, zircon, tourmaline, feldspar – patter on grains of gold and heavy way-worn nuggets; some, with blunt plap-plap and low bass drumming, fall on the broad leaves of veratrum, saxifrage, cypripedium. Some happy drops fall straight into the cups of flowers, kissing the lips of lilies. How far they have to go, how many cups to fill, great and small, cells too small to be seen, cups holding half a drop as well as lake basins between the hills, each replenished with equal care, every drop in all the blessed throng a silvery newborn star with lake and river, garden and grow, valley and mountain, all that the landscape holds reflected in its crystal depths, God's messenger, angel of love sent on its way with majesty and pomp and display of power that make man's greatest shows ridiculous.

Now the storm is over, the sky is clear, the last rolling thunder-wave is spent on the peaks, and where are the raindrops now – what has become of all the shining throng? In winged vapour rising some are already has-tening back to the sky, some have gone into the plants, creeping through invisible doors into the round rooms of cells, some are locked in crystals of ice, some in rock crys-tals, some in porous moraines to keep their small springs flowing, some have gone journeying on in the rivers to join the larger raindrop of the ocean. From form to form, beauty to beauty, ever changing, never resting, all are speeding with love's enthusiasm, singing with the stars the eternal song of creation.

beauty · learning · meaning

'Nature'

RALPH WALDO EMERSON

⌛ 7 minutes

How can we learn to reconnect with nature?
To feel the bond we share with plants and rocks
and other animals? We could start with these
words of Ralph Waldo Emerson.

The stars awaken a certain reverence, because though
always present, they are inaccessible; but all natural
objects make a kindred impression, when the mind is open
to their influence. Nature never wears a mean appearance.
Neither does the wisest man extort her secret, and lose his
curiosity by finding out all her perfection. Nature never
became a toy to a wise spirit. The flowers, the animals, the
mountains, reflected the wisdom of his best hour, as much
as they had delighted the simplicity of his childhood. [...]
To speak truly, few adult persons can see nature. Most
persons do not see the sun. At least they have a very superficial seeing. The sun illuminates only the eye of the man,
but shines into the eye and the heart of the child. The
lover of nature is he whose inward and outward senses

are still truly adjusted to each other; who has retained the spirit of infancy even into the era of manhood. His intercourse with heaven and earth becomes part of his daily food. In the presence of nature, a wild delight runs through the man, in spite of real sorrows. Nature says – he is my creature, and maugre all his impertinent griefs, he shall be glad with me. Not the sun or the summer alone, but every hour and season yields its tribute of delight; for every hour and change corresponds to and authorizes a different state of the mind, from breathless noon to grimmest midnight. Nature is a setting that fits equally well a comic or a mourning piece. In good health, the air is a cordial of incredible virtue. Crossing a bare common, in snow puddles, at twilight, under a clouded sky, without having in my thoughts any occurrence of special good fortune, I have enjoyed a perfect exhilaration. I am glad to the brink of fear. In the woods too, a man casts off his years, as the snake his slough, and at what period soever of life, is always a child. In the woods, is perpetual youth. Within these plantations of God, a decorum and sanctity reign, a perennial festival is dressed, and the guest sees not how he should tire of them in a thousand years. In the woods, we return to reason and faith. There I feel that nothing can befall me in life – no disgrace, no calamity (leaving me my eyes), which nature cannot repair. Standing on the bare ground – my head bathed by the blithe air, and uplifted into infinite space – all mean egotism vanishes. I become a transparent eye-ball; I am nothing; I see all; the currents of the Universal Being circulate through me; I am part or particle of God. The name of the nearest friend sounds then foreign and accidental: to be brothers, to be acquaintances – master or servant, is then a trifle and a disturbance. I am the lover of uncontained and immortal beauty. In the wilderness, I find something more dear and connate than in streets or villages. In the tranquil landscape, and especially in the distant line of the horizon, man beholds somewhat as beautiful as his own nature.

The greatest delight which the fields and woods minister is the suggestion of an occult relation between man and the vegetable. I am not alone and unacknowledged. They nod to me, and I to them. The waving of the boughs in the storm, is new to me and old. It takes me by surprise, and yet is not unknown. Its effect is like that of a higher thought or a better emotion coming over me, when I deemed I was thinking justly or doing right.

Yet it is certain that the power to produce this delight does not reside in nature, but in man, or in a harmony of both. It is necessary to use these pleasures with great temperance. For nature is not always tricked in holiday attire, but the same scene which yesterday breathed perfume and glittered as for the frolic of the nymphs, is overspread with melancholy today. Nature always wears the colors of the spirit. To a man laboring under calamity, the heat of his own fire hath sadness in it. Then, there is a kind of contempt of the landscape felt by him who has just lost by death a dear friend. The sky is less grand as it shuts down over less worth in the population.

beauty · learning · meaning

Recollections of a Tour Made in Scotland
A.D. 1803

DOROTHY WORDSWORTH

⧗ 9 minutes

Too often remembered as 'William
Wordsworth's sister', Dorothy Wordsworth was a
great writer in her own right. Here she describes
an encounter with the romantic wildness of the
island of Inchtavannach in Loch Lomond.

Presently after Coleridge joined us, and we determined to
go to the island. [...] We had two rowers and a strong boat;
so I felt myself bold, though there was a great chance of a
high wind. [...] It rained a little when we landed, and I took
my cloak, which afterwards served us to sit down upon in
our road up the hill, when the day grew much finer, with
gleams of sunshine. [...]

We had not climbed far before we were stopped by a
sudden burst of prospect, so singular and beautiful that it
was like a flash of images from another world. We stood
with our backs to the hill of the island, which we were

ascending, and which shut out Ben Lomond entirely, and all the upper part of the lake, and we looked towards the foot of the lake, scattered over with islands without beginning and without end. The sun shone, and the distant hills were visible, some through sunny mists, others in gloom with patches of sunshine; the lake was lost under the low and distant hills, and the islands lost in the lake, which was all in motion with travelling fields of light, or dark shadows under rainy clouds. There are many hills, but no commanding eminence at a distance to confine the prospect, so that the land seemed endless as the water.

What I had heard of Loch Lomond, or any other place in Great Britain, had given me no idea of anything like what we beheld: it was an outlandish scene [...]. The islands were of every possible variety of shape and surface – hilly and level, large and small, bare, rocky, pastoral, or covered with wood. Immediately under my eyes lay one large flat island, bare and green, so flat and low that it scarcely appeared to rise above the water, with straggling peat-stacks and a single hut upon one of its out-shooting promontories for it was of a very irregular shape, though perfectly flat. Another, its next neighbour, and still nearer to us, was covered over with heath and coppice-wood, the surface undulating, with flat or sloping banks towards the water, and hollow places, cradle-like valleys, behind. These two islands, with Inch-ta-vanach, where we were standing, were intermingled with the water, I might say interbedded and interveined with it, in a manner that was exquisitely pleasing. There were bays innumerable, straits or passages like calm rivers, land-locked lakes, and, to the main water, stormy promontories. The solitary hut on the flat green island seemed unsheltered and desolate, and yet not wholly so, for it was but a broad river's breadth from the covert of the wood of the other island. Near to these is a miniature, an islet covered with trees, on which stands a small ruin that looks like the remains of a religious house; it is overgrown with ivy, and were it not that the arch of a window or gateway may be distinctly seen, it would be difficult to believe that it was not a tuft of trees growing in the shape of a ruin, rather than a ruin overshadowed by trees. When we had walked a little further we saw below us, on the nearest large island, where some of the wood had been cut down, a hut, which we conjectured to be a bark hut. It appeared to be on the shore of a little forest lake, enclosed by Inch-ta-vanach, where we were, and the woody island on which the hut stands.

Beyond we had the same intricate view as before, and could discover Dumbarton rock with its double head. There being a mist over it, it had a ghost-like appearance – as I observed to William and Coleridge, something like the Tor of Glastonbury from the Dorsetshire hills. Right before us, on the flat island mentioned before, were several small single trees or shrubs, growing at different distances from each other, close to the shore, but some optical delusion had detached them from the land on which they stood, and they had the appearance of so many little vessels sailing along the coast of it. [...] with the ghostly image of Dumbarton Castle, and the ambiguous ruin on the small island, it was much in the character of the scene, which was throughout magical and enchanting – a new world in its great permanent outline and composition, and changing at every moment in every part of it by the effect of sun and wind, and mist and shower and cloud, and the blending lights and deep shades which took place of each other, traversing the lake in every direction. The whole was indeed a strange mixture of soothing and restless images, of images inviting to rest, and others hurrying the fancy away into an activity still more pleasing than repose. Yet, intricate and homeless, that is, without lasting abiding-place for the mind, as the prospect was, there was no perplexity; we had still a guide to lead us forward.

Wherever we looked, it was a delightful feeling that there was something beyond.

◖▶

anxiety · beauty · meaning

The Old Ways

ROBERT MACFARLANE

◆

⌛ 8 minutes

What is the sound of sailing? Listen to the aural
wonder that Robert Macfarlane recreates.

◆

Mid-morning departure, Stornoway harbour, which is
also known as the Hoil: hints of oil, hints of hooley. Sound
of boatslip, reek of diesel. *Broad Bay*'s wake through the
harbour – a tugged line through the fuel slicks on the
water's surface, our keel slurring petrol-rainbows. Light
quibbling on the swell. We nosed through the chowder
of harbour water: kelp, oranges, plastic milk bottles, sea
gunk. Big seals floating here and there, their nostrils and
eyes just above the water, their blubbery backs looking
like the puffed-up anoraks of murder victims. Nostrils
up, *snort snort*, duck to rinse, and then dive with a final
flip of the flukes. Out we went – by oar, sail and tow –
past the drug-money pleasure-gardens and castle of
James Matheson, who in 1844 used half a million pounds
of the money he made pushing opium to the Chinese to

buy the whole island of Lewis. Out past the lighthouse, out past the headlands, the sea opening like a cone into the Minch. The sun above us, bright and high, but the sky darkening swiftly further out. Black sky-reefs of cloud to the east. The sea: graphite, lightly choppy, white-stippled. The wind: a near-southerly, Force 3 or 4, with just a touch of east in it. A good strength for a little boat like ours, but from the worst of directions. Our sea road led us south-south-east, but it's impossible to sail directly upwind: we would have to make long tacks. Two other boats left the Hoil with us: a full-size *Sgoth Niseach*, called *An Sùlaire* (*The Gannet*), with a crew of five, and a sea-going yacht to keep watch over us in case of trouble. Ian and I were together in little *Broad Bay*.

'Let's get the sail up, show the people that we're leaving well,' said Ian. So I hoofed and hauled the big yard to the spar-top, the mainsheet was tightened and lightly jammed, the terracotta sail luffed then filled, *Broad Bay* surged southwards through the water, and my heart leapt in my chest. Our wake spooling white behind us, our track record. The water going past fast with a hiss like poured sand.

We pursued our long and lonely tacks, like cross-stitches made over the direct line of the sea road, zigzagging south through the Minch towards the Shiants. Inland was the grey-green Lewis coastline, with its sumping sea lochs and high headlands. Eastwards, on the mainland, sun fell full on the Torridon Hills, gilding them such that I could discern peaks I'd known underfoot – Beinn Eighe, Beinn Alligin, Liathach – and whose paths I could remember well. Shifts in light changed the sea's substance. Clouds pulling over and the sea a sheeny steel; sunshine falling and the sea a clean malachite green.

Early afternoon: the Shiants at last starting to show as dark shapes glimpsed. Outline and texture slowly firming up: the islands and their guardian skerries seen as nibs, teeth, tables, gable ends, chapels. Geese coming over in lettersets. When we were perhaps three miles distant, a band of rain swept in from the east, bringing with it a mist that occluded both coastlines and caused the illusion that the Shiants were receding in proportion to our approach. For half an hour or so we passed over the grey water and through that grey mist, and it felt as if we might be sailing towards a mythic archipelago, a scatter of Hy-Brazils: out of the real world and into a realm beyond verification. I recalled the clouds that so often enable the transition in the *immrama* from the known to the imagined. Then we sailed out of the southerly edge of the rain band, and there were the islands, sharp and true to the eye.

'Oh, you can see the shapes standing clear now!' Ian said, gazing ahead. Then, quietly to himself, 'What a life, what a life.' The tide fell slack just as we reached the outstretched arm of Eilean Mhuire, the most easterly of the Shiants, the wind fell light, and *Broad Bay* trembled almost to a halt.

All that paused water, unsure of its obligations, simmering, waiting for command. The lateral drive of the ebb tide canted to the vertical play of the slack tide. Gouts of water bulging up from deep down, polishing areas of ocean. Currents billowing and knotting.

Nature • 247

The light flimsy, filmy. The earth open on its hinges, unsure of its swing. The day fathomable and still.

Suddenly the glossy black fin and back of a minke whale rose a hundred yards astern, two yellow-striped dolphins broke water and plunged cheerily down again, and then the flow of the turned tide could be seen as a chop on the water, small standing waves that indicated the whole Minch was reversing its direction – trillions of tons of brine, a mountain range of water turning in obedience to the invisible force of the moon, starting the long slop back north and carrying our little boat with it.

■

beauty · meaning · potential

The Hawaiian Archipelago

ISABELLA BIRD

◆———

⏳ 14 minutes

Isabella Bird was a Victorian adventurer and
writer, whose life story wouldn't be out of place
in one of the adventure novels of that period.
She once climbed to the top of a volcano in
Hawaii, and faced nature at its darkest, staring
into a crater called Halemaʻumaʻu.

———◆———

Here the last apparent vegetation was left behind, and
the familiar earth. We were in a new Plutonic region of
blackness and awful desolation, the accustomed sights
and sounds of nature all gone. Terraces, cliffs, lakes,
ridges, rivers, mountain sides, whirlpools, chasms of lava
surrounded us, solid, black, and shining, as if vitrified, or
an ashen grey, stained yellow with sulphur here and there,
or white with alum. The lava was fissured and upheaved
everywhere by earthquakes, hot underneath, and emit-
ting a hot breath.

After more than an hour of very difficult climbing we

reached the lowest level of the crater, pretty nearly a mile across, presenting from above the appearance of a sea at rest, but on crossing it we found it to be an expanse of waves and convolutions of ashy-coloured lava, with huge cracks filled up with black iridescent rolls of lava, only a few weeks old. Parts of it are very rough and ridgy, jammed together like field ice, or compacted by rolls of lava which may have swelled up from beneath, but the largest part of the area presents the appearance of huge coiled hawsers, the ropy formation of the lava rendering the illusion almost perfect. These are riven by deep cracks which emit hot sulphurous vapours. Strange to say, in one of these, deep down in that black and awful region, three slender metamorphosed ferns were growing, three exquisite forms, the fragile heralds of the great forest of vegetation, which probably in coming years will clothe this pit with beauty. [...] On our right there was a precipitous ledge, and a recent flow of lava had poured over it, cooling as it fell into columnar shapes as symmetrical as those of Staffa. It took us a full hour to cross this deep depression, and as long to master a steep hot ascent of about four hundred feet, formed by a recent lava-flow from Hale-mau-mau into the basin. This lava hill is an extraordinary sight – a flood of molten stone, solidifying as it ran down the declivity, forming arrested waves, streams, eddies, gigantic convolutions, forms of snakes, stems of trees, gnarled roots, crooked water-pipes, all involved and contorted on a gigantic scale, a wilderness of force and dread. Over one steeper place the lava had run in a fiery cascade about one hundred feet wide. Some had reached the ground, some had been arrested midway, but all had taken the aspect of stems of trees. [...]

As we ascended, the flow became hotter under our feet, as well as more porous and glistening. It was so hot that a shower of rain hissed as it fell upon it. The crust became increasingly insecure, and necessitated our walking in single file with the guide in front, to test the security of the footing. I fell through several times, and always into holes full of sulphurous steam, so malignantly acid that my strong dog-skin gloves were burned through as I raised myself on my hands. [...] Suddenly, just above, and in front of us, gory drops were tossed in air, and springing forwards we stood on the brink of Hale-mau-mau, which was about thirty-five feet below us. I think we all screamed, I know we all wept, but we were speechless, for a new glory and terror had been added to the earth. It is the most unutterable of wonderful things. The words of common speech are quite useless. It is unimaginable, indescribable, a sight to remember for ever, a sight which at once took possession of every faculty of sense and soul, removing one altogether out of the range of ordinary life. Here was the real 'bottomless pit' – the 'fire which is not quenched' – 'the place of hell' – 'the lake which burneth with fire and brimstone' – the 'everlasting burnings' – the fiery sea whose waves are never weary. There were groanings, rumblings, and detonations, rushings, hissings, and splashings, and the crashing sound of breakers on the coast, but it was the surging of fiery waves upon a fiery shore. [...] Such words as jets, fountains, waves, spray, convey some idea of order and regularity, but here there was none. The inner lake, while we stood there, formed a sort of crater within itself, the whole lava sea rose about three feet, a blowing cone about eight feet high was formed, it was never the same two minutes together. And what we saw had no existence a month ago, and probably will be changed in every essential feature a month hence.

What we did see was one irregularly-shaped lake, [...] almost divided into two by a low bank of lava, which extended nearly across it where it was narrowest, and which was raised visibly before our eyes. [...] On one side there was an expanse entirely occupied with blowing cones, and jets of steam or vapour. [...] The prominent object was fire in motion, but the surface of the double lake was continually skinning over for a second or two with a cooled crust of a lustrous grey-white, like frosted silver, broken by jagged cracks of a bright rose-colour. [...] Before each outburst of agitation there was much hissing and a throbbing internal roaring, as of imprisoned gases. Now it seemed furious, demoniacal, as if no power on earth could bind it, then playful and sportive, then for a second languid, but only because it was accumulating fresh force. On our arrival eleven fire fountains were playing joyously round the lakes, and sometimes the six of the nearer lake ran together in the centre to go wallowing down in one vortex, from which they reappeared bulging upwards, till they formed a huge cone thirty feet high, which plunged downwards in a whirlpool only to reappear in exactly the previous number of fountains in different parts of the lake, high leaping, raging, flinging themselves upwards. Sometimes the whole lake [...] took the form of mighty waves, and surging heavily against the partial barrier with a sound like the Pacific surf, lashed, tore, covered it, and threw itself over it in clots of living fire. It was all confusion, commotion, force, terror, glory, majesty, mystery, and even beauty. And the colour! 'Eye hath not seen' it! Molten metal has not that crimson gleam, nor blood that living light! Had I not seen this I should never have known that such a colour was possible.

The crust perpetually wrinkled, folded over, and cracked, and great pieces were drawn downwards to be again thrown up on the crests of waves. The eleven fountains of gory fire played the greater part of the time, dancing round the lake with a strength of joyousness which was absolute beauty. Indeed after the first half hour of terror had gone by, the beauty of these jets made a profound impression upon me, and the sight of them must always remain one of the most fascinating recollections of my life. During three hours, the bank of lava which almost divided the lakes rose considerably, owing to the cooling of the spray as it dashed over it, and a cavern of considerable size was formed within it, the roof of which was hung with fiery stalactites, more than a foot long. Nearly the whole time the surges of the further lake taking a southerly direction, broke with a tremendous noise on the bold craggy cliffs which are its southern boundary, throwing their gory spray to a height of fully forty feet. At times an overhanging crag fell in, creating a vast splash of fire and increased commotion.

Almost close below us there was an intermittent jet of lava, which kept cooling round what was possibly a blowhole forming a cone with an open top, which when we first saw it was about six feet high on its highest side, and about as many in diameter. Up this cone or chimney heavy jets of lava were thrown every second or two, and cooling as they fell over its edge, raised it rapidly before our eyes. Its fiery interior, and the singular sound with which the lava was vomited up, were very awful. There was no smoke rising from the lake, only a faint blue vapour which the wind carried in the opposite direction. The heat was excessive. We were obliged to stand the whole time, and the soles of our boots were burned, and my ear and one side of my face were blistered. Although there was no smoke from the lake itself, there was an awful region to the westward, of smoke and sound, and rolling clouds of steam and vapour whose phenomena it was not safe to investigate, where the blowing cones are, whose fires last night appeared stationary. We were able to stand quite near the margin, and look down into the lake, as you look into the sea from the deck of a ship, the only risk being that the fractured ledge might give way.

Before we came away, a new impulse seized the lava. The fire was thrown to a great height; the fountains and jets all wallowed together; new ones appeared, and danced joyously round the margin, then converging towards the centre they merged into one glowing mass, which upheaved itself pyramidally and disappeared with a vast plunge. Then innumerable billows of fire dashed themselves into the air, crashing and lashing, and the lake dividing itself recoiled on either side, then hurling its fires together and rising as if by upheaval from below, it surged over the temporary rim which it had formed, passing downwards in a slow majestic flow, leaving the central surface swaying and dashing in fruitless agony, as if sent on some errand it failed to accomplish.

adventure · power

Nightwalk

CHRIS YATES

◆

⏳ 8 minutes

When night falls, the door to a different world
opens. Different animals, different scents,
different sounds. Chris Yates explored the night
world of England's West Country, and was
blessed by an encounter with one of the British
Isles' most magical creatures.

◆

The path that runs along the length of the valley inclines
gently to the north and as I headed that way I could feel
a coolness flowing against me. The grass was not exactly
dew-soaked, but my boots swung through it more quietly
and easily than when I was crossing the dry upper pasture.
Tall trees along both slopes accentuated the valley's depth,
increasing the sense of enclosure. Even when the trees
began to thin out it was still easy to imagine I was walking
through a canyon.

Distances do not seem to obey the laws of perspective
after dark. Though the high skyline ahead was clearly
visible, my path disappeared into general darkness after

only about ten yards. Despite my steady pace, the continually limited foreground plus a total lack of any middle distance eventually gave me the impression that I was either walking incredibly slowly or the hill beyond the valley's end, which had seemed so close, was actually a hundred miles away. As long as I kept looking straight ahead the illusion kept working, but then something broke the spell by kicking out of a tussock next to me and sweeping up the slope to my left. I knelt down to get a glimpse of it against the starry sky and saw a rapidly diminishing shape, long and low, yet with long legs – a startled hare that reached its vanishing point in an instant.

Carefully, I went over to where the animal had sprung from, thinking I might have disturbed a female with leverets. Details were obscure, even close to, but I eventually found an opened purse of grass blades that was warm and dry when I pressed my palm into it. There were, however, no infants.

It would have been unusual, though not unheard of, to find a doe with young so close to a footpath.

A few years ago, my son Will discovered a form containing three new-born leverets by the path that crosses the sheep field, and, more recently, I watched a hare making a round-about approach to her nursery just a stone's throw from our house. I was looking out of my window on a late May evening when I saw her appear from under the oaks and lollop slowly round in a wide half-circle across the field. For a minute or two she paused, sitting calmly in the long grass with her ears at half-cock, before trotting forward again and eventually completing the circuit. After another short interval, she began to run slightly faster, her course now describing a gradually tightening spiral, her pace quickening and her ears flat as she wheeled round and round towards the centre, as if she had been caught up in a mysterious vortex. Finally she stopped and slowly sank down out of sight into the grass. I kept my eyes fixed on the spot, but night came on and she did not reappear.

Hares may act eccentrically at times; I have watched them boxing, chasing and somersaulting, yet I have never seen that kind of behaviour before. I presumed it was defensive, an instinctive strategy for preventing a direct approach from a predator that might have picked up her scent. By leading, say, a fox in a circle around her she would have plenty of time to hear or smell it coming and run, drawing it away from the leverets before accelerating and leaving it in a cloud of grass pollen. [...]

A hare is an inquisitive creature; if it hears the squeal-ing of one its kind, which is fairly easy to imitate, I can often persuade it to investigate. As long as I never move once I have the hare's attention it will, hesitantly, begin to approach. Several times I have managed to intrigue an animal to within a few feet of me. During one very close encounter, as I 'called' while sitting back against a fence-post, a hare that seemed almost half the size of a roe deer reared up onto its hind legs and raised its head so that we were looking at each other eye to eye – and what strange high-set eyes they were, staring with a terrible intensity, expressing something much wilder and stranger than I could imagine. I was no threat to it because I remained absolutely motionless, and it looked at me as if I were not really there, or as if I were a conundrum that made no sense. After an electric half minute, it went down onto its forepaws, twitched its whiskers and unhurriedly loped away across a field.

When my daughter Camilla was two years old I drew a picture of a leaping hare and she immediately asked, or rather demanded, that I introduce her to a real one. It was springtime, when the animals are at their most active, and we walked to a field where I had often seen them playing and feeding. As we approached the field's edge I picked Camilla up so that we made just one suspicious shape rather than two. We spotted a hare almost straight away. It was sitting quietly on its own, about seventy yards away, and it turned to face us as soon as I began to squeak at it. After a moment it trotted towards us quite quickly until, just a few paces away, it stopped, sat upright and stared.

'What big ears it has!' I whispered. 'And look at its lovely eyes!'

But then I realized my little girl was not looking. She had been watching as the hare approached, but when it stared at us she covered her face with her hands.

'Eyes!' she said. 'Don't want to see 'em!'

In the valley, not long before midnight, as I set off along the footpath again, I remembered those eyes and felt they were still watching me.

calm · instinct · surprise

'Radical Bears in the Forest Delicious'

AMY LEACH

◆

⏳ 13 minutes

Pandas are the bearers of a strange wisdom.
Here, Amy Leach explores the nature of their
all-consuming obsession with bamboo.

◆

There once was a king of Babylon who was too proud, so he was given the mind of an animal and put out to pasture. For seven years he roamed the fields on all fours and munched on grass, after which period he was allowed to return to his palace and rich robes of purple, his barley beer and skewered locusts and royal hairdresser who gave him back his dignified ringlets. (Along with an animal's mind he had been given the animal's hairstylist.) It is not specified which animal's mind Nebuchadnezzar received, but from his glad return to civilisation and fine cuisine we can infer that it was not the mind of a panda bear. If he had had a panda's mind for seven years, in the end he would have rejected the restitution of his kingdom; he would have somersaulted away, to continue leading a free, elusive, unfollowed life.

Having followers is an honour pandas dream not of. There is no tragopan so trustworthy, no bushpig so dependable, that they would want it tagging along. Pandas even head away from pandas, like the stars in the universe, spreading farther and farther apart (you can never be too far away to say goodbye) – except their territory is neither infinite nor expanding, and in order to deliver more panda bears into existence, they can't just scatter into particles at the end. Pandas come together every two years or so; marriage isn't always marriage of the mind.

Maybe if they had been given a choice they would have picked a less conspicuous coat, one to better correspond with their reclusive spirits. Admirers can be secret admirers and afflictions can be secret afflictions but pandas cannot be secret pandas, since they contrast dramatically with green ferns, grey rocks, pink rhododendrons, and their own bellies and ears and legs. They are showy bears, sensationally visible, which might actually be an advantage for a solitary species: the easier to avoid you, my dear. Camouflaged animals must always be bumping into each other.

What does the animal do all day who is not engaged in society, its duties and pleasures and ferments? There may be some wedging in trees, some gazing into the mist, some fiddle-faddle. Sometimes the panda breaks an icicle off a branch and tosses it into the air over and over till it melts. Sometimes, trotting pigeon-toed across a hillside, he trips, then rolls, because he is round; having enjoyed that, he climbs back up and rolls back down. He might pick wild irises or crocuses and recline among the fern-fronds to eat them, or lounge underneath a weeping willow, munching on the little leaflets that dangle into his mouth.

Mostly what pandas do with their time is eat bamboo. Bamboo, that sturdy wooden grass, makes up to 99 per cent of their diet and they eat it for up to fourteen hours a day. They have to consume it constantly since they are only assimilating about 20 per cent. Their penitential diet is a mystery; pandas are like celery saints – everyone else is convivially dining on stuffed eggs, truffled fingerlings, little pies and oranges, enjoying the tableside crooners, while out behind a bush sits a celery saint with his basket of celery, crunch crunch crunch. Eat enough pies and you can put aside the desire for food and pursue something else, such as a cowhand. Rare is the romance of the celery extremist.

With their carnivorous anatomy and herbivorous behaviour, it is as if pandas are pledged to an ancient covenant – as if they used to be bon vivants like other bears, blood and berry juice staining their muzzles, slugabeds all winter, until one day they fell into a trance and received a deep message: 'You are standing, pandas, on the very borders of the eternal world, but you have become charmed with infatuating food; the subtle poison of sensuality courses through your veins. You must disregard custom and the strong clamouring of appetite and passion. It will take, at times, every particle of willpower which you possess; but give yourselves wholly to a bamboo diet, and guided by firm, unspotted principle your lives will become pure and noble.' Thus was formed that radical sect of bears, the Bambooists. Modern-day Bambooists show a remarkable resistance to temptation: a stream runs by, serving up fresh fish, and what does the panda do? Wades across, to get to a stiff thicket of bamboo on the opposite side.

But willpower might not entirely account for such abstemiousness anymore. Bamboo is not power food, and the bear who eats it is not a power bear, and swiping fish from the river takes energy, as does sleeping all winter. If you're going to sleep for seven months you need to eat your hickory nuts, your ungulates, your honey. Bambooists have to stay awake all winter to eat bamboo – incidentally witnessing the sapphirine sparkles of snow falling from a branch, the cliffs draped with icy fringes, the white snow powdering the green bamboo leaves. (Could any dream compare with winter?)

What does a panda know, who studies just a few cloudy-mountain miles of the world? From her experience she must know about fallibility. Icicles melt, flowers fail, intangibly small babies grow tangible and autonomous, and one day when you come back from foraging to collect yours from the tree fork where you left him, he is gone. Mushrooms, moonlight, everything is ephemeral, with one exception: bamboo. Bamboo never fails, bamboo is eternal, evergreen, green in the orange season, green in the white season, green in the green season, poking up sweet little shoots into the spring rain. Blessed is the bear that trusteth in bamboo.

For lucky pandas it is true, bamboo never fails. Bamboo can be eternal for a hundred years, which is four times as eternal as panda bears; but there is in the character of bamboo a devastating defect. Most grasses stagger their dying, piece by piece, like an orchestra – though a trombonist goes down the collective life carries on. The trouble with bamboo is that it crashes all at once: after a century of continuous availability the entire thicket flowers together, dies together, and like a dead orchestra it can take twenty years to get back on its feet.

At this point an animal might wise up and become a Whateverist. With so many edibles in the world why consume, almost exclusively, a miserably nutritious, erratically fallible one? It's not as if bamboo is pleasant to eat, like horsebeans; bamboo splinters poke and scratch the swallower all the way down. That old covenant was arbitrary and perverse; bamboo is a silly staple; specialism is folly. Consider pragmatists – when the linguini runs out, a pragmatist will eat the centrepiece, and when that is done he will eat the tablecloth. As pragmatists have no principles their numbers are myriad.

But pandas betrayed by bamboo go looking for bamboo. For there is such a thing as specialised hunger, being hungry for one thing – similar to specialised loneliness. Sometimes they don't have to travel far; pandas eat several kinds of bamboo, and even though arrow bamboo collapses, there might be umbrella bamboo growing nearby. Sometimes they have to go farther afield, and sometimes they travel in pitiful directions – would you know which way to go to find a hotbed of celery? – until their coats don't fit very well anymore. Vagrancy used to be easier on the animals, because there used to be more forest. Even if an expedition wasn't efficient, it was foresty all the way, just as the journey from earth to heaven is milky all the way. Now, between patches of forest, there are villages and gravel mines, steep corn fields, dance tents, frightened people waving blankets, mushroomers, other things to avoid.

People have tried to help pandas become pragmatists, to see sense, to switch to alternatives during a bamboo strangulation. And in captivity they comply – they eat the yams and bananas and fish set before them. But compliance is not conversion. When they are set free, pandas return to their ruinous fidelity to bamboo, shuffling past opportunity – for on the far side of that hill might be the Forest Delicious, where they can lie back, in the million-column sanctuary, a bamboo cane in each forefoot, crunching on the one and then the other, munching on happy bundles of leaves. There are fewer than twenty-five hundred free pandas left and they're all in the same boat, made of bamboo. When it goes down they go down with it, into dark water, and they won't switch to another boat, not for all the tea in China. Pandas have their own wisdom, unaccountable and unamendable, whose roots shoot down deeper than we can penetrate, and if they mind anyone at all it is someone more elusive than man.

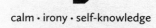

calm · irony · self-knowledge

CHAOS

My house was burgled one night. My wife and I were sleeping. It was the 21st of March – I still remember it because it was the first day of Spring, and I love the first day of Spring. I found it particularly unfair that we had been burgled on one of my favourite days of the year.

We had forgotten to lock our door. There were no signs of a forced entry, but if you don't lock your door, all it takes to open it are a credit card and very basic skills. The burglars just got lucky, the police said. They didn't look like criminal masterminds. They took only two very old mobile phones, my wallet with a few pounds and a debit card they didn't use, plus a battery charger. They hadn't even noticed the iPad lying on the same table with the phones. It had been a quick incursion. The financial damage was negligible.

Even so, it left me sleepless for a couple of months.

Every noise in the house was a step; every whistle of the wind, a voice. Part of me was scared the burglars would try their luck again, part of me wished they would do so, so that my wife and I could have a little southern Italian-style chat with them. I was both sincerely afraid and sincerely willing to engage. But there was a deeper truth beneath these feelings – I felt violated. A home is supposed to be a safe haven. A home is supposed to keep the world outside, well, outside. The burglars had made my home porous, and I hated them for that. The better angels of my nature told me the burglars probably came from a disadvantaged background, and I had to live up to my ideals of empathy and kindness, and try to understand what brought them to risk jail for a battery charger. All the same I wanted them to suffer, I wanted them to fail at everything in life, I wanted them, frankly, to die some horrible, painful death. Because they had invaded my home. Because they had brought Chaos in.

We make doors to keep Chaos at bay, but we know all too well that Chaos is always lurking and might enter at any moment. Any order we build is frail, and it is not a matter of *if* it will fail, but *when*. We just can't go through life without being burgled a few times.

Chaos comes first and never goes away. For the ancient Greeks, Chaos was the first thing that came to be. Nordic creation myth has the primordial void of Ginnungagap. The cosmological theory known as the Big Bang posits the universe exploding and expanding out of a single originating point. Chaos is part of the physical world that surrounds us; it continues to exist, alongside our pathetic attempts to tame it.

While I don't believe you can really tame Chaos, I do believe you can learn to dance with it. We could even say that most stories, with their solid structures and predictable endings, are an attempt to deal with Chaos. The writings in this section are not about taming Chaos, but they are about coping with it. They teach us, among other things, that some forms of Chaos can be enjoyable, if we only allow them to be.

*

The myth of the daughters of Minyas suggests that we should embrace Chaos when it comes knocking at our door. It is one of my favourite Greek myths, because it offers a view of a world very different from our own, where refusing to join in an orgy signals a lack of devotion to the gods.

Rosalind Kerven tells a fairytale about people joining together when Chaos strikes, while Gregory Bateson tells us something about the very nature of order and chaos, through a dialogue between him and his young daughter. Bateson was a hugely influential anthropologist, and his thinking here is as clear as ever.

Alice Hoffman talks to us about magic. Throughout the ages, magic has been one of the weapons people have used to fight back against Chaos. Whether you believe it works or not, there might be a lesson here.

E. M. Forster offers a different strategy: when you are feeling confused by life's complexities, you can just sit down and make something beautiful, in this case by playing a piece of music. (Or by reading aloud, maybe.)

David Mitchell shows that Chaos can be part of the lives of the people around us, without our even noticing it. For some, Chaos is not knocking at the door, it is already inside, leaving no space for enjoyment, or even escape.

Vernon Lee describes a chaotic moment in a place one doesn't normally associate with Chaos: the Sistine Chapel in the Vatican.

Maurice Baring writes about a Russian ritual: the observance of a short period of silence just before the start of a journey. I have adopted this ritual in my own life: I find it helps me cope with anxiety, and with the Chaos that all journeys, even the best ones, inevitably bring.

The Daughters of Minyas

FRANCESCO DIMITRI

———◆———

⏳ 7 minutes

The wine-god Dionysus travels with a procession
of wild, drunken and sexually excited followers.
When he appears, the pious thing to do, the
right thing to do, is join in the revelry and Chaos.
Those who choose not to do so run the risk of
coming to a very bad end.

———◆———

I remember the night Dionysus came to town. We heard
his procession long before we saw it: the drums, the
cymbals, the songs, the roaring of lions and the laughter,
the laughter most of all, cracking open the summer night,
joining at first with the voice of crickets, and then drown-
ing it in a much wilder music. We all rushed out, eager
to celebrate the god's sacred rituals, in drunkenness, and
revelry, and chaos. You know as well as I do that when the
gods call, mortals must answer.

I will never forget the procession appearing at our city's
gates. It was a disorderly line, like a snake made of smoke,
a giant organism whose flesh changed and shifted under

our eyes. A naked young man and a naked young woman were at the helm, as beautiful as you, dancing and leaping on the dusty path without hurting their feet. She had the firmest breasts I have ever seen, and he the biggest cock. Behind them came her fellow Maenads, naked, gorgeous and wild, some of them dancing, some of them drinking, some of them already running their hands all over each other's bodies. I saw the satyrs with their goat hoofs, and, behind them, Dionysus on his carriage, young, ageless, slender, strong, showering his people with his blessing of good red wine. I saw an ass carrying Silenus, the hideous satyr who was Dionysus' teacher, drunk and happy and completely oblivious to his own hideousness.

'To the woods!' Dionysus shouted. 'To the orgy!'

All night long, and longer, maybe, there would be bodies upon bodies: drinking, sweating, fucking, and drinking some more, forgetting the civilised ways of other gods, losing themselves in cock and cunt and wine. The pious, devoted women in town all answered the call, as you should do, always.

But there were three sisters, the daughters of Minyas, who wanted no part of it. When they heard the cymbals, they snorted; when they heard the laughter, they didn't join in; and when they heard Dionysus' call, they shook their heads.

'I'd rather stay home and knit,' said one.

'An orgy? What a ridiculous idea,' said another.

'Ridiculous and shameful,' said the third.

And they all said, 'We're better than that.'

Then someone knocked at the door.

When they opened it, they saw a young man smiling at them, his cheek reddened by wine, a lustful light in his eyes. He was impatient to go. 'Come!' he said. 'Everybody else is already out there, fucking in the woods. Come on, let's go. It's beautiful!'

The sisters sniggered.

'Beautiful? I don't think so.'

'Try stupid.'

'Try pointless.'

'Try vulgar.'

'We're better than that.'

The young man was still smiling. 'Is this your last word?'

'Of course.'

'What else do you expect us to say?'

'We're better than that.'

The young man said, still smiling, 'All right then.'

A cymbal played a note somewhere in the house. Then a flute. Then the drumming began, and then laughter, and roars, and songs, and then there came a moaning, a happy moaning. The three sisters looked around, at a loss, but they couldn't find where the sounds came from: they came from everywhere and nowhere at once.

And the sounds grew, and as they grew, they filled the sisters' heads, filled them completely, leaving no space for other thoughts, no space for sanity. The sisters looked left and right, they ran through the house, scuttling like terrified mice, desperate to find the source of the noise and make it stop. Finally it occurred to them to try to flee the house. But they didn't remember where the door was anymore. The world was sound and chaos and confusion, and they were lost.

The young man was Dionysus in disguise: he had given the three sisters one last chance to amend their ways, and they had refused. He couldn't let such impiety go unpunished. He touched a wall with his nimble fingers, and suddenly all the walls in the house were pouring milk and wine, milk and wine on the floor, milk and wine on the furniture, milk and wine on the sisters.

The three sisters burst in a demented laugh, and began to lick the milk and the wine from the walls and from each other's faces. They gorged themselves on it. And as they licked and lapped their tongues became coarser, and their skin became black and hairy, and their bodies bloated, and their hands transformed into talons.

The three sisters turned into bats.

They found an open window, and they flew out of the house, to disappear in the night, their human nature lost to them for ever.

Dionysus turned his back on the empty house, went back to the woods, and rejoined us in the sacred rites. He told us the story of the three sisters himself, as a warning to always keep pure as we were. I will never forget it; and I will always join in, when Dionysus comes to town.

instinct · rules · temptation · virtue

'The Dead Moon'

ROSALIND KERVEN

———◆———

⌛ 10 minutes

Sometimes a negative form of Chaos encroaches
on our lives, and we feel the presence of
darkness, and unpleasant beings. But never
forget that it is possible to fight back...

———◆———

Keep away from the bog.

It's riddled with unspeakable things. It stinks of death.
There are bogles and rotting corpses; dark, nauseous
shapes that weave in and out of the mud like worms.
There are fleshless, grasping hands out there, and disembodied mouths that gape open and suck everything into
them. There are ghosts and creeping goblins, witches on
cat-back, and treacherous, flickering will-o'-the-wisps.

It's an evil place to pass through, especially at night.
Many have been lost there. That's why the moon herself
came down here once, to try and make things better. She
came in disguise, wrapped in a black, hooded cloak so
that every inch of her was hidden, slipping down from the

sky like a shadow. Through the shifting vapours of the boglands she drifted, gazing this way and that, shuddering at the foul things that surrounded her.

Suddenly, a cry went up: a scream of horror, melting into agony and anguish. Close by the moon was a man: a big, strong, handsome fellow, who was bawling like a baby as the bogles and spooks sank their claws and venomous suckers into him. They tore off his topcoat and shirt, his boots and breeches until he was naked and blue with cold. Cackling and slurping, they began to draw him down into the bottomless, impenetrable dark of the bog.

The moon couldn't bear it. She threw back her hood and let her light shine out. In its beam, the dark things shrivelled and shrank away, and the man found the strength to flail and struggle. He hauled himself from the heaving mud and kicked out at the monsters that had snared him. Thanks to the good moon, he could now see the path clearly, which only moments before had been lost to him. He ran down it with a cry of joy, heading towards dry land and the village.

But there was no escape for the moon: now the evil ones had seen her, they would not let her escape. They came crowing round, fingering her cloak with their bare-boned hands, snorting poison out through their gaping nostrils and covering her with reeking slime. Twisted limbs shot out to trip her. When she was down, they dragged her into a deep hole and pushed a heavy stone on top.

So the moon was lost.

After that, every night was completely dark in the boglands. Even the stars shunned the sky that hung over those parts. It was terrible for the folk who lived there. Their lives dwindled. No one dared go out after nightfall. They sealed their windows tightly and laid salt, straw and buttons on the sills for protection.

As for the bogles and ghosts and witches, they grew even bolder. They came creeping out of the bog, slithering over mud and grass and right into the village. No one even dared to slip out to the privy at night, for the beasties hung around the houses, waiting for a door to open. It was human flesh they craved, and also human souls. Where else could they sate their hunger, since folk didn't travel through the bog anymore?

At first, no one could guess why the moon had stopped shining. But then the traveller she had rescued on that fateful night found the courage to look back on what had happened. He recalled how, just as he was about to die, a dazzling light had saved him. He brooded on the memory. Supposing, he thought, the moon herself had sacrificed her life for him? Guilt overwhelmed him.

He set off to see the wise old woman who lived in the ruined old mill. She listened carefully to the outpourings of this troubled soul, then took her Bible from the high shelf, glanced quickly into her mirror, and gazed long and deep into her brew pot. Finally, she told him what to do.

The traveller went back to the village and knocked on his neighbours' doors. He assembled a band of nine strong men. When dusk fell, each man put a stone in his mouth, broke a twig from a hazel tree and grasped it in his hand.

The twilight thickened into darkness. The nine men did what none had done for the past three months: they walked out into the night. Shoulder to shoulder they went, but none spoke or even sighed, for the wise woman had warned them to keep absolutely silent.

They stepped on to the bog. The wind screamed at them. They were surrounded by hisses and whispers. In single file now, they pressed on. This is what they were seeking: a candle, a cross and a coffin.

The man who was leading the way halted suddenly. He nudged the man behind him and pointed. The signal passed quickly back along the line. The nine men all stared...

For a will-o'-the-wisp was flickering before them: that was surely meant as the candle. It lit up a stump of dry, crumbling wood with two gnarled branches jutting from each side: that was the cross. From its base there stretched an expanse of long, cold stone.

That was the moon's coffin.

The nine men gathered around it. In the ghostly light they looked at each other and nodded, then in unison their lips began to move. No sound came from them, for they must not break their silence. But in their minds, in their hearts, they recited the Lord's Prayer.

They recited it forwards, to honour the Cross. They recited it backwards, to drive away the beasties and bogles. Then they leaned forward together, and heaved up the stone.

It came free with a terrible wrenching and creaking sound, spraying them all – near blinding them – with bog water and mud. For an instant, they caught a glimpse of a pale, luminescent face beneath the stone, filled with unearthly beauty. Then light rushed past them, over-whelming them with such exquisite sadness and joy that each man felt the ground beneath him falling away...

When they came to, there was the moon, back in her rightful place in the sky! The nine bold men who had rescued her were all lying on high ground. Below them, in the moonlight, the bog lay strangely still.

From then on, the folk who lived around the bogs had nothing more to fear. For the gentle moon was ever mindful of how they had rescued her, and vowed to cast her light most strongly over their own bleak lands for ever more.

companionship · hope · magic

'Why Do Things Get in a Muddle?'

from *Steps to an Ecology of Mind*

GREGORY BATESON

◆

⏳ **12 minutes**

For all our striving to keep our desks tidy and our
houses clean, the order we impose never seems
to last very long. Dirty socks soon start piling
up on the floor, pencils get lost. But how is this
possible, when we try so hard to prevent Chaos?
Anthropologist Gregory Bateson provides us
with an answer, in a dialogue with his daughter.

◆

Daughter: Daddy, why do things get in a muddle?

Father: What do you mean? Things? Muddle?

D: Well, people spend a lot of time tidying things, but they
never seem to spend time muddling them. Things just
seem to get in a muddle by themselves. And then people
have to tidy them up again.

F: But do your things get in a muddle if you don't touch them?

D: No – not if *nobody* touches them. But if you touch them – or if anybody touches them – they get in a muddle and it's a worse muddle if it isn't me.

F: Yes – that's why I try to keep you from touching the things on my desk. Because my things get in a worse muddle if they are touched by somebody who isn't me.

D: But do people *always* muddle other people's things? Why do they, Daddy?

F: Now, wait a minute. It's not so simple. First of all, what do you mean by a muddle?

D: I mean – so I can't find things, and so it *looks* all muddled up. The way it is when nothing is straight.

F: Well, but are you sure you mean the same thing by muddle that anybody else would mean?

D: But, Daddy, I'm sure I do – because I'm not a very tidy person and if I say things are in a muddle, then I'm sure everybody else would agree with me.

F: All right – but do you think you mean the same thing by 'tidy' that other people would? If your mummy makes your things tidy, do you know where to find them?

D: Hmm... *sometimes*. [...] Daddy, do you and I mean the same thing by 'tidy'?

F: I doubt it, my dear – I doubt it.

D: But, Daddy, isn't that a funny thing – that everybody means the same when they say 'muddled' but everybody means something different by 'tidy'. But 'tidy' is the opposite of 'muddled', isn't it?

F: Now we begin to get into more difficult questions. Let's start again from the beginning. You said *'Why do things always get in a muddle?'* Now we have made a step or two – and let's change the question to 'Why do things get in a state which Cathy calls 'not tidy'? Do you see why I want to make that change?

D: ...Yes, I think so – because if I have a special meaning for 'tidy' then some of other people's 'tidies' will look like muddles to me – even if we do agree about most of what we call muddles.

F: That's right. Now – let's look at what *you* call tidy. When your paint box is put in a tidy place, where is it?

D: Here on the end of this shelf.

F: Okay – now if it were anywhere else?

D: No, that would not be tidy.

F: What about the other end of the shelf, here? Like this?

D: No, that's not where it belongs, and anyhow it would have to be *straight*, not all crooked the way you put it.

F: Oh – in the right place *and* straight.

D: Yes.

F: Well, that means that there are only very few places which are 'tidy' for your paint box.

D: Only *one* place—

F: No – very *few* places, because if I move it a little bit, like this, it is still tidy.

D: All right – but very, very few places.

F: All right, very, very few places. Now what about the teddy bear and your doll, and the Wizard of Oz and your sweater, and your shoes? It's the same for all the things, isn't it, that each thing has only a very, very few places which are 'tidy' for that thing?

D: Yes, Daddy – but the Wizard of Oz could be anywhere on that shelf. And Daddy – do you know what? I hate, hate it when my books get all mixed up with your books and Mummy's books.

F : Yes, I know. (Pause)

D: Daddy, you didn't finish. Why do my things get the way I say isn't tidy?

F: But I *have* finished – it's just because there are more ways which you call 'untidy' than there are ways which you call 'tidy.'

D: But that isn't a reason why.

F: But, yes, it is. And it is the real and only and very important reason.

D: Oh, Daddy! Stop it.

F: No, I'm not fooling. That is the reason, *and all of science is hooked up with that reason*. Let's take another example. If I put some sand in the bottom of this cup and put some sugar on the top of it, and now stir it with a teaspoon, the sand and the sugar will get mixed up, won't they?

D: Yes, but, Daddy, is it fair to shift over to talking about 'mixed up' when we started with 'muddled up?'

F: Hmm... I wonder... but I think so – Yes – because let's say we can find somebody who thinks it is more tidy to have all the sand underneath all the sugar. [...] take another example. Sometimes in the movies you will see a lot of letters of the alphabet all scattered over the screen, all higgledy-piggledy and some even upside down. And then something shakes the table so that the letters start to move, and then as the shaking goes on, the letters all come together to spell the title of the film.

D: Yes, I've seen that – they spelled DONALD.

F: It doesn't matter what they spelled. The point is that you saw something being shaken and stirred up and instead of getting more mixed up than before, the letters came together into an order, all right way up, and spelled a word – they made up something which a lot of people would agree is *sense*.

D: Yes, Daddy, but you know...

F: No, I don't know; what I am trying to say is that in the real world things never happen that way. It's only in the movies.

D: But, Daddy...

F: I tell you it's only in the movies that you can shake things and they seem to take on more order and sense than they had before...

D: But, Daddy...

F: Wait till I've finished this time... And they make it look like that in the movies by doing the whole thing backwards. They put the letters all in order to spell DONALD and then they start the camera and then they start shaking the table. [...] There's only one way of spelling DONALD. Agreed?

D: Yes.

F: All right. And there are millions and millions and millions of ways of scattering six letters on the table. Agreed?

D: Yes. I suppose so. Can some of these be upside down?

F: Yes – just in the sort of higgledy-piggledy muddle they were in in the film. But there could be millions and millions and millions of muddles like that, couldn't there? And only one DONALD? [...]

D: Daddy? Are you still talking about the same question we started with? 'Why do things get in a muddle?'

F: Yes.

[...]

D: Oh – I was just wondering, that's all.

F: Now, let's see if I can get it said this time. Let's go back to the sand and the sugar, and let's suppose that somebody says that having the sand at the bottom is 'tidy' or 'orderly'.

D: Daddy, does somebody have to *say* something like that before you can go on to talk about how things are going to get mixed up when you stir them?

F: Yes – that's just the point. They say what they hope will happen and then I tell them it won't happen because there are so *many* other things that might happen. And I know that it is more likely that one of the many things will happen and not one of the few.

D: Daddy, you're just an old bookmaker, backing all the other horses against the *one* horse that I want to bet on.

F: That's right, my dear. I get them to bet on what they call the 'tidy' way – I know that there are infinitely many muddled ways – so things will always go toward muddle and mixedness.

D: But why didn't you say that at the beginning, Daddy? I could have understood *that* all right.

F: Yes, I suppose so. Anyhow, it's now bedtime.

D: Daddy, why do grownups have wars, instead of just fighting the way children do?

F: No – bedtime. Be off with you. We'll talk about wars another time.

◗

anxiety · learning · meaning

Practical Magic

ALICE HOFFMAN

◆

⌛ 13 minutes

Perhaps what we really need – to make sense
of the world, to understand life, and to
keep Chaos at bay – is some magic.

◆

Two hundred years ago, people believed that a hot and
steamy July meant a cold and miserable winter. The
shadow of a groundhog was carefully studied as an indi-
cator for bad weather. The skin of an eel was commonly
used to prevent rheumatism. Cats were never allowed
inside a house, since it was well known that they could
suck the breath right out of an infant, killing the poor
baby in his cradle. People believed that there were reasons
for everything, and that they could divine these reasons
easily. If they could not, then something wicked must
be at work. Not only was it possible to converse with the
devil, but some in their midst actually made bargains with
him. Anyone who did was always found out in the end,
exposed by his or her own bad fortune or the dreadful
luck of those close by.

When a husband and wife were unable to have a child, the husband placed a pearl beneath his wife's pillow, and if she still failed to conceive, there'd be talk about her, and concern about the true nature of her character. If all the strawberries in every patch were eaten by earwigs, suddenly and overnight, then the old woman down the road, who was cross-eyed and drank until she was as unmovable as a stone, was brought into the town hall for questioning. Even after a woman proved herself innocent of any wrongdoing – if she managed to walk through water and not dissolve into smoke and ashes or if it was discovered that the strawberries in the entire Commonwealth had been affected – that still didn't mean she'd be welcome in town or that anyone believed she wasn't guilty of something.

These were the prevailing attitudes when Maria Owens first came to Massachusetts with only a small satchel of belongings, her baby daughter, and a packet of diamonds sewn into the hem of her dress. Maria was young and pretty, but she dressed all in black and didn't have a husband. In spite of this, she possessed enough money to hire the twelve carpenters who built the house on Magnolia Street, and she was so sure of herself and what she wanted that she went on to advise these men in such matters as what wood to use for the mantel in the dining room and how many windows were needed to present the best view of the back garden. People became suspicious, and why shouldn't they be? Maria Owens' baby girl never cried, not even when she was bitten by a spider or stung by a bee. Maria's garden was never infested with earwigs or mice. When a hurricane struck, every house on Magnolia

Street was damaged, except for the one built by the twelve carpenters; not one of the shutters was blown away, and even the laundry forgotten out on the line stayed in place, not a single stocking was lost.

If Maria Owens chose to speak to you, she looked you straight in the eye, even if you were her elder or better. She was known to do as she pleased, without stopping to deliberate what the consequences might be. Men who shouldn't have fell in love with her and were convinced that she came to them in the middle of the night, igniting their carnal appetites. Women found themselves drawn to her and wanted to confess their own secrets in the shadows of her porch, where the wisteria had begun to grow and was already winding itself around the black-painted railings.

Maria Owens paid attention to no one but herself and her daughter and a man over in Newburyport who none of her neighbours even knew existed, although he was well known and quite well respected in his own town. Three times every month, Maria bundled up her sleeping baby, then she put on her long wool coat and walked across the fields, past the orchards and the ponds filled with geese. Drawn by desire, she traveled quickly, no matter what the weather might be. On some nights, people thought they saw her, her coat billowing out behind her, running so fast it seemed she was no longer touching the ground. There might be ice and snow, there might be white flowers on every apple tree; it was impossible to tell when Maria might walk through the fields. Some people never even knew she was passing right by their houses; they would simply hear something out beyond where they lived, out where the raspberries grew, where the horses were sleeping, and a wash of desire would filter over their own skins, the women in their nightgowns, the men exhausted from the hard work and boredom of their lives. Whenever they did see Maria in daylight, on the road or in a shop, they looked at her carefully, and they didn't trust what was before them – the pretty face, the cool gray eyes, the black coat, the scent of some flower no one in their town could name.

And then one day, a farmer winged a crow in his cornfield, a creature that had been stealing from him shamelessly for months. When Maria Owens appeared the very next morning with her arm in a sling and her right hand wound up in a white bandage, people felt certain they knew the reason why. They were polite enough when she came into their stores, to buy coffee or molasses or tea, but as soon as her back was turned they made the sign of the fox, raising pinky and forefinger in the air, since this motion was known to unravel a spell. They watched the night sky for anything strange; they hung horseshoes over their doors, hammered in with three strong nails, and some people kept bunches of mistletoe in their kitchens and parlors, to protect their loved ones from evil.

Every Owens woman since Maria has inherited those clear gray eyes and the knowledge that there is no real defense against evil. Maria was no crow interested in harassing farmers and their fields. It was love that had wounded her. The man who was the father of her child, whom Maria had followed to Massachusetts in the first place, had decided he'd had enough. His ardor had cooled, at least for Maria, and he'd sent her a large sum of money to keep her quiet and out of the way. Maria refused to believe he would treat her this way; still he had failed to meet her three times, and she just couldn't wait any longer. She went to his house in Newburyport, something he'd absolutely forbidden, and she'd bruised her own arm and broken a bone in her right hand by pounding on his door. The man she loved would not answer her cries; instead he shouted at her to go away, with a voice so distant anyone would have guessed they were little more than strangers. But Maria would not go away, she knocked and she knocked, and she didn't even notice that her knuckles were bloody; welts had already begun to appear on her skin.

Finally, the man Maria loved sent his wife to the door, and when Maria saw this plain woman in her flannel nightgown, she turned and ran all the way home, across the fields in the moonlight, fast as a deer, faster even, entering into people's dreams. The next morning most people in town awoke out of breath, with their legs shaking from exertion, so tired it seemed as though they hadn't slept a wink. Maria didn't even realize what she'd done to herself until she tried to move her right hand and couldn't, and she thought it only fitting that she'd been marked this way. From then on, she kept her hands to herself.

Of course, bad fortune should be avoided whenever possible, and Maria was always prudent when it came to matters of luck. She planted fruit trees in the dark of the moon, and some of the hardier perennials she tended continue to sprout among the rows in the aunts' garden; the onions are still so fiery and strong it's easy to understand why they were thought to be the best cure for dog bites and toothaches. Maria always made certain to wear something blue, even when she was an old lady and couldn't get out of bed. The shawl across her shoulders was blue as paradise, and when she sat on the porch in her rocking chair it was difficult to tell where she ended and where the sky began.

Until the day she died, Maria wore a sapphire the man she'd loved had given her, just to remind herself of what was important and what was not. For a very long time after she was gone, some people insisted they saw an icy blue figure in the fields, late at night, when the air was cold and still. They swore that she walked past the orchards, traveling north, and that if you were very quiet, if you didn't move at all, but stayed down on one knee beside the old apple trees, her dress would brush against you, and from that day forward you'd be lucky in all matters, as would your children after you, and their children as well.

▶

anxiety · desire · learning · magic

A Room with a View

E. M. FORSTER

◆————————◆

⧖ 3 minutes

Lucy Honeychurch discovers that one of
the best ways to remain calm in the face
of Chaos is to lose oneself in music.

◆————————◆

It so happened that Lucy, who found daily life rather
chaotic, entered a more solid world when she opened the
piano. She was then no longer either deferential or patron-
izing; no longer either a rebel or a slave. The kingdom
of music is not the kingdom of this world; it will accept
those whom breeding and intellect and culture have alike
rejected. The commonplace person begins to play, and
shoots into the empyrean without effort, whilst we look
up, marvelling how he has escaped us, and thinking how
we could worship him and love him, would he but trans-
late his visions into human words, and his experiences
into human actions. Perhaps he cannot; certainly he does
not, or does so very seldom. Lucy had done so never.

She was no dazzling executante; her runs were not

at all like strings of pearls, and she struck no more right notes than was suitable for one of her age and situation. Nor was she the passionate young lady, who performs so tragically on a summer's evening with the window open. Passion was there, but it could not be easily labelled; it slipped between love and hatred and jealousy, and all the furniture of the pictorial style. And she was tragical only in the sense that she was great, for she loved to play on the side of Victory. Victory of what and over what – that is more than the words of daily life can tell us. But that some sonatas of Beethoven are written tragic no one can gainsay; yet they can triumph or despair as the player decides, and Lucy had decided that they should triumph.

A very wet afternoon at the Bertolini permitted her to do the thing she really liked, and after lunch she opened the little draped piano. A few people lingered round and praised her playing, but finding that she made no reply, dispersed to their rooms to write up their diaries or to sleep. She took no notice of Mr Emerson looking for his son, nor of Miss Bartlett looking for Miss Lavish, nor of Miss Lavish looking for her cigarette-case. Like every true performer, she was intoxicated by the mere feel of the notes: they were fingers caressing her own; and by touch, not by sound alone, did she come to her desire.

◖▮

anxiety · calm · music · power · self-knowledge

Black Swan Green

DAVID MITCHELL

◆

⏳ **6 minutes**

It is 1982, and a thirteen-year-old boy is about
to learn how difficult life can be – and that
Chaos lurks in unexpected places.

◆

Run across a field of daisies at warp speed but keep your
eyes on the ground. It's ace. Petalled stars and dandelion comets streak the green universe. Moran and I got to
the barn at the far side, dizzy with intergalactic travel. I
was laughing more than Moran 'cause Moran's dry trainer
wasn't dry any more, it was glistening in cow shit. Bales of
straw made a ramp up to the griddly barn roof, so up we
climbed. The cockerel tree you can see from my bedroom
wasn't running left to right now, it was running right to
left. 'Skill place for a machine-gun nest, this barn,' I said,
displaying my military expertise.

Moran squidged off the shitty trainer and lay back.

I lay back too. The rusty iron was warm as a hotty.

'This is the life,' sighed Moran, after a bit.

'You can say that again,' I said, after a bit.

'This is the life,' said Moran, straight off.

I *knew* he would. 'That's *so* original.'

Sheep and lambs were bleating, fields behind us.

A tractor was chuntering, fields ahead.

'Does *your* old man ever get pissed?' Moran asked.

If I said yes I'd be lying, but if I said no it'd look gay. 'He has a drink or two, when my uncle Brian visits.'

'Not a drink or two. I mean does he get so *fucking plastered* he... he can hardly speak?

'No.'

That *No* turned the three feet between into three miles.

'No.' Moran'd shut his eyes. 'Don't look the type, your dad.'

'But yours doesn't, either. He's really friendly and funny...'

An aeroplane glinted, mercury bright in the dark high blue.

'Maxine calls it like this, she calls it "Daddy's going dark". She's right. He goes dark. He starts... y'know, on a few cans, and gets loud and makes shite jokes we have to laugh at. Shouts and stuff. The neighbours bang on the wall to complain. Dad bangs back, calls 'em all the names under the sun... then he locks himself in his room but he's got bottles in there. We hear them smash. One by one. Then he sleeps it off. Then afterwards, when he's all so sorry, it's all, "Oh, I'm never touchin' the stuff again..." That's almost worse... Tell you what it's like, it's like this whiny shitty nasty weepy man who isn't my dad takes my dad over for however long the bender lasts, but only I – and Mum and Kelly and Sally and Max – know it *isn't him*. The rest of the world doesn't know that, see. They just say, *Frank Moran showing his true colours, that is*. But it ain't.' Moran twisted his head at me. 'But it is. But it *ain't*. But it is. But it *ain't*. Oh, how am *I* s'posed to know?'

A painful minute went by.

Green is made of yellow and blue, nothing else, but when you *look* at green, where've the yellow and blue gone? Somehow this is to do with Moran's dad. Somehow this is to do with everyone and everything. But too many things'd've gone wrong if I'd tried to say this to Moran.

Moran sniffed. 'Fancy a nice, cool bottle of Woodpecker?'

'Cider? You've brought cider?'

'No. My dad drunk 'em all. *But*,' Moran fumbled in his bag, 'I've got a can of Irn Bru.'

Irn Bru's fizzy liquid bubblegum, but I said, 'Sure,' 'cause I hadn't brought any drink myself and Irn Bru's better than nothing. I'd imagined I could drink from fresh springs but the only water I'd seen so far was that farty ditch.

The Irn Bro exploded in Moran's hand like a grenade. 'Shit!'

'Watch out with that Irn Bru. It'll be all shaken up.'

'You don't flamin' say so!' Moran gave me first swig, as he licked his hand clean. In return, I gave him some Cadbury's Caramel. It'd oozed out of its wrapper, but we picked off the bits of pocket fluff and it tasted okay. I got a hayfever attack and sneezed ten or twenty times into a nuggety hanky.

A vapour tail gashed the sky.
But the sky healed itself. Without fuss.

companionship · resilience

'A Pontifical Mass at the Sixtine Chapel'

VERNON LEE

◆

⧗ 6 minutes

Vernon Lee, aka Violet Paget, describes a joyous Chaos:
a colourful papal mass in Rome. Lee was visiting the
Sistine Chapel with a friend she refers to as 'M.P.' –
but she might as well be alone, immersed as she is
in an intense and overheated spirituality.

◆

I never knew so many hours pass so pleasantly as in this
tribune, surrounded by those whispering, elbowing,
plunging, veiled women in black, under the wall painted
with Perugino's Charge of St Peter, and dadoed with imi-
tation Spanish leather, superb gold and blue scrolls of
Rhodian pomegranate pattern and Della Rovere shields
with the oak-tree.

My first impression is of the magnificence of all these
costumes, the Swiss with their halberts, the Knights of
Malta, the Chamberlains like so many Rubenses or Frans
Halses, the Prelates and cardinals, each with his little
train of purple priestlets; particularly of the perfection

in wearing these clothes, something analogous to the brownish depth of the purple, the carnation vividness of the scarlet, due to all these centuries of tradition. At the same time, an impression of the utter disconnectedness of it all, the absence of all spirit or meaning; this magnificence being as the turning out of a great rag bag of purple and crimson and gold, of superb artistic things all out of place, useless, patternless, and almost odious: pageantry, ritual, complicated Palestrina music, crowded Renaissance frescoes, that huge Last Judgment, that mass of carefully grouped hideous nudities, brutal, butcher-like, on its harsh blue ground; that ceiling packed with superb pictures and figures, symmetrical yet at random, portentous arm and thighs and shoulders hitting one as it were in the eye. The papal procession, white robes, gold candlesticks, a wizen old priest swaying, all pale with sea-sickness, above the crowd, above the halberts and plumes, between the white ostrich fans, and dabbing about benedictions to the right and left. The shuffle of the people down onto their knees, and scuffle again onto their feet, the shrill reading of the Mass, and endless unfinished cadences, overtopped by unearthly slightly sickening quaverings of the choir; the ceaseless moving about of all this mass of black backs, veils, cloaks, outlines of cheek and ear presenting every now and then among the various kinds of rusty black; no devotion, no gravity, no quiet anywhere, among these creatures munching chocolates and adjusting opera-glasses. M.P.'s voice at my ear, now about Longus and Bonghi's paganism, now about the odiousness of her neighbour who won't let her climb on her seat, the dreadful grief of not seeing the Cardinal's tails, the wonderfulness of Christianity having come out of people like the Apostles (I having turned out Gethsemane in St Matthew in the Gospel which she brought, together with a large supply of chocolate and the Fioretti di S. Francesco), the ugliness of the women, &c. &c. And meanwhile the fat pink profile perdu, the *toupé* of grey hair like powder of a colossal soprano sways to and fro fatuously over the gold grating above us.

All this vaguely on for a space of time seeming quite indeterminate. Little by little, however, a change came over things, or my impression of them. Is it that one's body being well broken, one's mind becomes more susceptible of homogeneous impressions? I know not. But the higher light, the incense, fills the space above all those black women's heads, over the tapers burning yellow on the carved marble balustrades with the Rovere arms, with a luminous grey vagueness; the blue background of the *Last Judgment* grows into a kind of deep hyacinthine evening sky, on which twist and writhe like fleshy snakes the group of demons and damned, the naked Christ thundering with His empty hand among them; the voices moving up and down, round and round in endless unended cadences, become strange instruments (all sense of register and vocal cords departing), unearthly harps and bugles and double basses, rasping often and groaning like a broken-down organ, above which warbles the hautboy quaver of the sopranos. And the huge things on the ceiling, with their prodigious thighs and toes and arms and jowls crouch and cower and scowl, and hang uneasily on arches, and strain themselves wearily on brackets, dreary, magnificent, full of inexplicable feelings all about nothing: the colossal prophetic creature in green and white over the altar, on the keystone of the vault, striking out his arms – to pull it all down or prop it all up? The very creation of the world becoming the creation of chaos, the Creator scudding away before Himself as He separates the light from the darkness. Chaos, chaos, and all these things moving, writhing, making fearful efforts, in a way living, all about nothing and in nothing, much like those voices grating and quavering endlessly long.

◖▮

beauty · power

'Half a Minute's Silence'

MAURICE BARING

———◆———

⧖ 8 minutes

Maurice Baring, a dramatist, novelist and
translator who travelled widely in Russia in the
early years of the twentieth century, describes
a simple ritual which might help you to prepare
yourself to face Chaos in any form. The wisdom
of silence can teach us important things, useful
things, about ourselves and about the world.

———◆———

It is the custom in Russia for people when they are starting
on a journey and leaving a house, to sit down and spend
half a minute in silence. Not only the departing guest or
members of the family, but those who are remaining, take
part in this little silent ceremony. Everybody concerned
sits down in silence for about half a minute. They have
their little armistice after the bustle of packing is over and
before the bustle of the journey (for those who are going)
and the routine of everyday life (for those who are remaining behind) begins once more.

And some say that the meaning of this custom was religious; that the half-minute's silence was originally given to silent prayer; but others say not. Certainly in the home I am about to describe, although the family to which it belonged was deeply religious and scrupulously orthodox, and although their daily life was interwoven with minute observances of religious ritual, the half-minute's silence here was not specially religious.

There were nineteen people sitting in the – well, not a hall, and not a drawing-room, but in the large open living-room of Prince A.'s country home, an untidy, one-storeyed, shabby Grand Trianon, full of stiff divans and card-tables scored with chalk; it looked out on a dishevelled garden on one side; on the other side on to the drive. During the half-minute's silence on that particular September morning this is what those nineteen people were thinking of.

Princess A., the hostess, caught sight of a tree at the bottom of the garden, a stunted willow. She thought, 'For the last twenty years I have told the gardener to cut that tree down almost every day – certainly every time I have seen him; and each time he has agreed with alacrity, but it has never been done. Tomorrow I will do it myself.' Then she added to herself, 'How often I have said to myself, "tomorrow I will do it", and yet the tree is there.' Then she looked at the church and thought of something else.

B., who was a journalist and dabbled in belles-lettres, was wondering whether two roubles was too little to give the butler. He had only stayed a night. He had packed his own clothes. He had given no trouble. He had a ten-rouble note. That was too much – he reflected that the butler's wages were proportionally greater than his precarious salary, and far more secure; on the other hand, he remembered a servant once telling him that needy professional people were as a rule far more generous than the rich; and he further reflected that a boy who had rich parents at a school needed a tip just as badly as a boy who had poor parents, and then he thought, 'What, after all, is ten roubles?'

V. was a foreigner. He was glad to be going; he had looked forward to the visit; but no sooner had he arrived than he had said to himself, 'Only an insane man can leave his own house to mingle with eighteen unknown people of different habits, with not one of whom he feels in complete sympathy.' And yet now during this half-minute he felt as sad at going away as if he were going to school for the first time [...].

E. (who was a neighbour, middle-aged, and rather fat) suddenly became aware that all the carefully constructed stopping had come out of his wisdom tooth, leaving, as it seemed, an unfathomable abyss. Would he have to go back to the dentist so soon? So very soon? [...]

G. (seven years old and a boy) looked at an old man with a white beard who had promised him some Persian stamps, and was calculating by what post they could arrive after the old gentleman's departure. He hoped he wouldn't die. [...]

Miss J. [...] Five people wanted to marry her, and one man had shot himself because she had told him he had no will. In that half-minute she made a decision: she decided (*a*) that she would be a woman doctor; (*b*) that she would eventually, somewhere and somehow, marry a kind man.

K., the old man with a beard who had promised the Persian stamps, was thinking – he was a diplomatist – of last night's game of cards and wondering if he would have won if he had doubled hearts. Not that he cared. [...]

Q. was thirty-five. He was engaged to be married to a nice girl. He had had rather a tumultuous past; debts were its main feature – debts which still remained to be paid. The wedding was to be next week. That morning he had had a letter from Isaaks, the moneylender, demanding to be paid – capital and interest – 500,000 roubles [...]. It was impossible. What was to be done? He made up his mind he would shoot Isaaks, shoot him dead.

A man came in and said the horses were there.

The little boy was the first to rise. He had been told ever since he could remember to get up first from his chair on these occasions. Prince A., the host, started from his reverie. He had been looking at the church through the window, and thinking of what he always thought of. He always thought of one thing: his son who was buried in that church.

The little armistice was at an end.

■●

calm · potential · self-knowledge

LIGHTNESS

WE DON'T PLAY REMOTELY enough. When you say, 'I'm not playing here,' what you mean is, I'm up to serious business here. Important business. Not play, no, that's for children.

But there is a strong argument to be made for the importance of play, for doing something not because it is useful or intensely pleasurable, but just because it is *fun*. The Dutch cultural historian Johan Huizinga, in his *Homo Ludens*, argued that play is so fundamental that it is, in fact, one of the activities that make us human. We are wise and smart apes *because* we are playful apes. Other animals play too, but none does so at the level of *Homo sapiens*. Our societies, our religion, our culture, are built – among many other things – on play.

Sometimes we don't need to find the love of our life, just a half-decent one-night stand. Sometimes we are not looking for deeper meaning, but mindless fun. Sometimes we don't want Beethoven's late quartets or John Coltrane, but a sweaty bop to Beyoncé. Sometimes we just need to lighten up.

This is no easy task for a grown-up. We are besieged by reasons to worry. Have you checked your bank account recently? You might find it's not quite as healthy as you thought. And as for the state of politics... has the world gone mad? And what about your children? – or indeed your lack of them. You have a thousand things to worry about, important things, serious things. I get that. I have them too.

The secret is, if you lighten up a bit, you will not be *less* effective, but *more* so. Alex Soojung-Kim Pang, a Silicon Valley consultant, argues (in his book *Rest: Why You Get More Done When You Work Less*) for the importance of taking time off. The idea that in order to get things done we should be doing things all the time is just wrong: we get *more* done when we take time to unwind.

*

This chapter is a celebration of lightness, and contains pieces that you could read aloud to a friend just to cheer her up. They have no specific target or goal; they are just fun, and could be read to anybody, at any time. They are toys to pick up and play with.

The myth of the birth of Hermes is a celebration of playfulness: Hermes has always been a thief and a liar, but he is such fun, and so charming, that the other gods let him get away with it.

Katherine Mansfield describes a perfect bank holiday. This is one of my favourite pieces for a rainy winter's day: even if you can't actually go out to play, you can still do so in your mind and your imagination. One of the great things stories do is allow us to live vicariously. So this is one for your dullest days.

Mark Twain's speech is about how to age his way, or

about how *not* to. P. G. Wodehouse graces us with a brilliant piece and a brilliant idea: the exquisite pleasure of *not doing things*.

Aleister Crowley, once billed 'the wickedest man in the world' (though it was the tabloids who described him thus, which says something), wrote an 'autohagiography'. In this extract he praises – lavishly – the work of his favourite author: himself.

G. K. Chesterton celebrates a simple pleasure: running after your hat. Most people would consider this an annoyance, but Chesterton shows us another point of view.

The Birth of Hermes

FRANCESCO DIMITRI

⏳ 8 minutes

The *Homeric Hymn to Hermes* tells the story of
Hermes' birth. Hermes demonstrated certain...
inclinations from the outset.

Hermes was just born and already bored. His mum and
dad (Maia, the nymph, and Zeus) had wrapped him in
silky bands and left him in a luxurious cradle in a cave in
Arcadia. It was all right, sort of, if you like it safe and dull.
Hermes didn't.

Zeus was on Mount Olympus, and Maia was busy
doing what nymphs do in the shade of the woods, so
Hermes had the day to himself, and he had no intention
of spending it *in a cradle*, thank you very much. He twisted
and turned and wriggled free of his bands, and jumped
out, impatient to get to know the Arcadian sun.

On the threshold of the cave he found a turtle.

'Hello sister,' he said. 'What a charming little thing
you are.'

He picked the turtle up. The wind was whistling

through a clump of swaying reeds, which gave him an idea. 'We could do with some music,' he said to the turtle. 'Come on, my friend, help me out.'

There and then he killed the turtle, and used its shell, some reeds, and some cowhide to make a lyre. The day – sunny and flower-scented – was just perfect for hanging out and strumming lazily.

But after a while Hermes grew bored again. Even worse, he got *hungry*. And it wasn't the sort of hunger you can satisfy with milk. A nice steak was what he craved.

Hermes had heard his father Zeus speak of the quality of Apollo's cattle. Only the best would do for him. He wouldn't ask, of course. There's no point in asking when you know the answer will be *no*. So he just walked to the place where the gods kept their cattle, found Apollo's (which, to be honest, were indeed the best), and took them. He made them walk with their feet turned the other way round, so as to hide their hoofprints – Apollo wasn't exactly renowned for his forgiveness, and Hermes didn't want any messy business. He sacrificed two cows to the gods, and kept the others for himself. By now night had fallen; Hermes yawned and went back to his cradle, satisfied with a job well done.

The next day Apollo found he had been robbed. An old man had spotted Hermes stealing the cattle, and sent Apollo his way. Apollo burst into the cave, shouting, 'Where's my cattle?'

'Your what?' Maia said. She was sitting next to the cradle, in contemplation of the simple, innocent, face of her baby.

'My cattle! Your son stole them!'

'He did not.'

'Oh yes he did!'

Hermes chose that moment to wake up and rub his huge chestnut eyes with his tiny, chubby hands. 'What's going on?' he asked.

'I want my cattle back!'

Hermes said, 'Did someone take them? I'm so sorry.'

'*You* took them!'

'I'm a baby,' Hermes said. 'I'm not strong enough to steal. Oh, and also, I'm not clever enough, not yet, you know.'

Apollo crossed the cave, closing in on the cradle.

Hermes cried, 'You're a big bully. Mummy, he's a big bully.'

'Apollo, don't be a bully,' said Maia.

'I'm not a bully!' Apollo shouted.

Hermes burst in tears.

'Look what you've done!' said Maia.

Apollo, frustrated, punched the wall of the cave. 'I want to talk to Zeus.'

'Yes,' Hermes sobbed out. 'Yes, let's ask Dad.'

So Apollo and Hermes went to Zeus, who had them tell the story all over again. When Hermes came to the point at which he said what a big bully Apollo was, Zeus couldn't help himself, and burst out laughing. 'Son,' he said to Hermes, 'I know you.'

'I'm just a baby.'

'Yeah, yeah. You stole the cattle, Hermes. You can't lie to *me*.'

'So it's true then! He's a thief,' said Apollo, with self-righteous satisfaction.

'He is,' Zeus conceded. 'But he's an entertaining thief. Boys, sort it out between you: I have better things to do with my day. Hermes, show Apollo where the cattle are.'

Hermes shrugged, and turned to Apollo. 'Come on, let's go,' he said, with a smile. When a strategy fails, you don't insist, you change the strategy.

Hermes took Apollo to the little glade where the cattle were grazing, and chatted amiably on the way. Now that everything had been solved, Apollo shared Zeus's amusement.

'I sacrificed two cows to you and the other Olympian gods,' said Hermes, when they got to the glade.

'That's fine,' said Apollo. He started counting the surviving cows.

While Apollo counted, Hermes took out his lyre, as if the idea had only just crossed his mind, and began to play, and to sing stories. To the accompaniment of simple tunes on his lyre, he told stories of gods and mortals, stories of love and loss and magic, and everything that makes life so beautiful and tragic.

Apollo stopped counting, engrossed. 'That toy of yours,' he said. 'It's magnificent.'

Hermes held out the lyre to Apollo. 'It's called a lyre. There, it's yours.'

'Really?'

'Really. I can teach you a few tunes too. And a couple of those songs I was singing.'

'Thank you. Thank you!' Apollo took the lyre. He

looked at the cattle. He didn't want to look like a miser. 'You can keep the cattle then. It's a fair bargain.'

Hermes shrugged. 'If it makes you happy.'

They spent the day singing and playing, and they became close friends.

Hermes is the god of commerce, thieves, and communication.

Make of it what you will.

➡

creativity · irony · music

'Bank Holiday'

KATHERINE MANSFIELD

◆———————◆

⏳ 9 minutes

We long for bank holidays and, sometimes, when
they arrive, we are disappointed. The weather
is awful; we have work to do. But other times
they turn out to be every bit as blissful as
they are supposed to be...

◆———————◆

A stout man with a pink face wears dingy white flannel
trousers, a blue coat with a pink handkerchief showing,
and a straw hat much too small for him, perched at the
back of his head. He plays the guitar. A little chap in
white canvas shoes, his face hidden under a felt hat like a
broken wing, breathes into a flute; and a tall thin fellow,
with bursting over-ripe button boots, draws ribbons –
long, twisted, streaming ribbons – of tune out of a fiddle.
They stand, unsmiling, but not serious, in the broad sunlight opposite the fruit-shop; the pink spider of a hand
beats the guitar, the little squat hand, with a brass-and-
turquoise ring, forces the reluctant flute, and the fiddler's
arm tries to saw the fiddle in two.

A crowd collects, eating oranges and bananas, tearing off the skins, dividing, sharing. One young girl has even a basket of strawberries, but she does not eat them. 'Aren't they dear!' She stares at the tiny pointed fruits as if she were afraid of them. The Australian soldier laughs. 'Here, go on, there's not more than a mouthful.' But he doesn't want her to eat them, either. He likes to watch her little frightened face, and her puzzled eyes lifted to his: 'Aren't they a price!' He pushes out his chest and grins. Old fat women in velvet bodices – old dusty pin-cushions – lean old hags like worn umbrellas with a quivering bonnet on top; young women, in muslins, with hats that might have grown on hedges, and high pointed shoes; men in khaki, sailors, shabby clerks, young Jews in fine cloth suits with padded shoulders and wide trousers, 'hospital boys' in blue – the sun discovers them – the loud, bold music holds them together in one big knot for a moment. The young ones are larking, pushing each other on and off the pavement, dodging, nudging; the old ones are talking: 'So I said to 'im, if you wants the doctor to yourself, fetch 'im, says I.'

'An' by the time they was cooked there wasn't so much as you could put in the palm of me 'and!'

The only ones who are quiet are the ragged children. They stand, as close up to the musicians as they can get, their hands behind their backs, their eyes big. Occasionally a leg hops, an arm wags. A tiny staggerer, overcome, turns round twice, sits down solemn, and then gets up again.

'Ain't it lovely?' whispers a small girl behind her hand.

And the music breaks into bright pieces, and joins together again, and again breaks, and is dissolved, and the crowd scatters, moving slowly up the hill.

At the corner of the road the stalls begin.

'Ticklers! Tuppence a tickler! 'Ool 'ave a tickler? Tickle 'em up, boys.' Little soft brooms on wire handles. They are eagerly bought by the soldiers.

'Buy a golliwog! Tuppence a golliwog!'

'Buy a jumping donkey! All alive-oh!'

'Su-perior chewing gum. Buy something to do, boys.'

'Buy a rose. Give 'er a rose, boy. Roses, lady?'

'Fevvers! Fevvers!' They are hard to resist. Lovely, streaming feathers, emerald green, scarlet, bright blue, canary yellow. Even the babies wear feathers threaded through their bonnets.

And an old woman in a three-cornered paper hat cries as if it were her final parting advice, the only way of saving yourself or of bringing him to his senses: 'Buy a three-cornered 'at, my dear, an' put it on!'

It is a flying day, half sun, half wind. When the sun goes in a shadow flies over; when it comes out again it is fiery. The men and women feel it burning their backs, their breasts and their arms; they feel their bodies expanding, coming alive... so that they make large embracing gestures, lift up their arms, for nothing, swoop down on a girl, blurt into laughter.

Lemonade! A whole tank of it stands on a table covered with a cloth; and lemons like blunted fishes blob in the yellow water. It looks solid, like a jelly, in the thick glasses. Why can't they drink it without spilling it? Everybody spills it, and before the glass is handed back the last drops are thrown in a ring.

Round the ice-cream cart, with its striped awning and bright brass cover, the children cluster. Little tongues lick, lick round the cream trumpets, round the squares. The cover is lifted, the wooden spoon plunges in; one shuts one's eyes to feel it, silently scrunching.

'Let these little birds tell you your future!' She stands beside the cage, a shrivelled ageless Italian, clasping and unclasping her dark claws. Her face, a treasure of delicate carving, is tied in a green-and-gold scarf. And inside their prison the love-birds flutter towards the papers in the seed-tray.

'You have great strength of character. You will marry a red-haired man and have three children. Beware of a blonde woman.' Look out! Look out! A motor-car driven by a fat chauffeur comes rushing down the hill. Inside there a blonde woman, pouting, leaning forward – rushing through your life – beware! beware!

'Ladies and gentlemen, I am an auctioneer by profession, and if what I tell you is not the truth I am liable to have my licence taken away from me and a heavy imprisonment.' He holds the licence across his chest; the sweat pours down his face into his paper collar; his eyes look glazed. When he takes off his hat there is a deep pucker of angry flesh on his forehead. Nobody buys a watch.

Look out again! A huge barouche comes swinging down the hill with two old, old babies inside. She holds up a lace parasol; he sucks the knob of his cane, and the fat old bodies roll together as the cradle rocks, and the steaming horse leaves a trail of manure as it ambles down the hill.

Under a tree, Professor Leonard, in cap and gown, stands beside his banner. He is here 'for one day,' from the London, Paris and Brussels Exhibition, to tell your fortune from your face. And he stands, smiling encouragement, like a clumsy dentist. When the big men, romping and swearing a moment before, hand across their sixpence, and stand before him, they are suddenly serious, dumb, timid, almost blushing as the Professor's quick hand notches the printed card. They are like little children caught playing in a forbidden garden by the owner, stepping from behind a tree.

The top of the hill is reached. How hot it is! How fine it is! The public-house is open, and the crowd presses in. The mother sits on the pavement edge with her baby, and the father brings her out a glass of dark, brownish stuff, and then savagely elbows his way in again. A reek of beer floats from the public-house, and a loud clatter and rattle of voices.

The wind has dropped, and the sun burns more fiercely than ever. Outside the two swing-doors there is a thick mass of children like flies at the mouth of a sweet-jar.

And up, up the hill come the people, with ticklers and golliwogs, and roses and feathers. Up, up they thrust into the light and heat, shouting, laughing, squealing, as though they were being pushed by something, far below, and by the sun, far ahead of them – drawn up into the full, bright, dazzling radiance to... what?

calm · comfort

Speech made on his seventieth birthday

MARK TWAIN

——————◆——————

⏳ 6 minutes

If you want to reach a ripe old age, you should
follow a healthy lifestyle. Or possibly not.

——————◆——————

I have achieved my seventy years in the usual way: by sticking strictly to a scheme of life which would kill anybody else. It sounds like an exaggeration, but that is really the common rule for attaining old age. [...] I will offer here, as a sound maxim, this: that we can't reach old age by another man's road.

I will now teach, offering my way of life to whomsoever desires to commit suicide by the scheme which has enabled me to beat the doctor and the hangman for seventy years. Some of the details may sound untrue, but they are not. I am not here to deceive: I am here to teach.

We have no permanent habits until we are forty. Then they begin to harden, presently they petrify, then business begins. Since forty I have been regular about going to bed and getting up – and that is one of the main things. I have made it a rule to go to bed when there wasn't anybody left to sit up with; and I have made it a rule to get up when I had to. This has resulted in an unswerving regularity of irregularity. It has saved me sound, but it would injure another person.

In the matter of diet – which is another main thing – I have been persistently strict in sticking to the things which didn't agree with me until one or the other of us got the best of it. Until lately I got the best of it myself. But last spring I stopped frolicking with mince-pie after midnight; up to then I had always believed it wasn't loaded. For thirty years I have taken coffee and bread at eight in the morning, and no bite nor sup until seven-thirty in the evening. Eleven hours. That is alright for me, and is wholesome, because I have never had a headache in my life, but headachy people would not reach seventy comfortably by that road, and they would be foolish to try it. And I wish to urge upon you this – which I think is wisdom – that if you find you can't make seventy by any but an uncomfortable road, don't you go. [...]

I have made it a rule never to smoke more than one cigar at a time. I have no other restriction as regards smoking. [...] As an example to others, and not that I care for moderation myself, it has always been my rule never to smoke when asleep, and never to refrain when awake. It is a good rule. I mean, for me; but some of you know quite well that it wouldn't answer for everybody that's trying to get to be seventy.

I smoke in bed until I have to go to sleep; I wake up in

the night, sometimes once, sometimes twice, sometimes three times, and I never waste any of these opportunities to smoke. This habit is so old and dear and precious to me that I would feel as you, sir, would feel if you should lose the only moral you've got [...] if you've got one: I am making no charges. [...]

As for drinking, I have no rule about that. When the others drink I like to help; otherwise I remain dry, by habit and preference. This dryness does not hurt me, but it could easily hurt you, because you are different. Let it alone.

Since I was seven years old I have seldom taken a dose of medicine, and have still seldom needed one. But up to seven I lived exclusively on allopathic medicines. Not that I needed them, for I don't think I did; it was for economy; my father took a drug-store for a debt, and it made cod-liver oil cheaper than the other breakfast foods. We had nine barrels of it, and it lasted me seven years. Then I was weaned. [...] By the time the drugstore was exhausted my health was established, and there has never been much the matter with me since. But you know very well it would be foolish for the average child to start for seventy on that basis. It happened to be just the thing for me, but that was merely an accident; it couldn't happen again in a century.

I have never taken any exercise, except sleeping and resting, and I never intended to take any. Exercise is loathsome. And it cannot be any benefit when you are tired: and I was always tired. But let another person try my way, and see where he will come out.

To Read Aloud · 328

I desire now to repeat and emphasise that maxim: we can't reach old age by another man's road. My habits protect my life, but they would assassinate you.

◖▶

irony · resilience · self-knowledge · temptation

The Confessions of Aleister Crowley: an Autohagiography

ALEISTER CROWLEY

———◆———

⏳ 3 minutes

Aleister Crowley believed he was the prophet
of a new age. Not many agreed, so he wrote an
'autohagiography' to further his cause. Here he
praises the *oeuvre* of his favourite poet – himself.
When he mentions something called 'Nephesch'
he refers to what, in occult theory, is the
lowest part of the human soul.

———◆———

The years 1907 and 1908 may be described as years of fulfilment. No new current came to stir my life; but the seeds
which had been sown in the past came many of them to
harvest. I had come to my full stature as a poet. My technique was perfect; it had shaken off from its sandals the
last dust which they had acquired by walking in the ways
of earlier masters. I produced lyric and dramatic poetry
which shows an astounding mastery of rhythm and rime,
a varied power of expression which has no equal in the

history of the language, and an intensity of idea which eats into the soul of the reader like vitriol.

I should have been assigned publicly my proper place among my peers of the past without difficulty had it not been for one fatal fact. My point of view is so original, my thoughts so profound, and my allusions so recondite, that superficial readers, carried away by the sheer music of the words, found themselves, so to speak, intoxicated and unable to penetrate to the pith. People did not realize that my sonorous similes possessed a subtle sense intelligible only to those whose minds were familiar with the subject. It is, in fact, necessary to study almost any poem of mine like a palimpsest. The slightest phrase is essential; each one must be interpreted individually, and the poem read again until its personality presents itself. People who like my poetry, bar those who are simply tickled by the sound or what they imagine to be the sense, agree that it spoils them for any other poetry.

For instance, if I mention a beetle I expect the reader to understand an allusion to the sun at midnight in its moral sense of Light-in-Darkness; if a pelican, to the legend that she pierces her own breast to feed her young on her heart's bleed; if a goat, to the entire symbolism of Capricornus, the god Pan, Satan or Jesus (Jesus being born at the winter solstice, when the sun enters Capricorn); if a pearl, to the correspondences of that stone as a precious and glittering secretion of the oyster, by which I mean that invertebrate animal life of man, the Nephesch.

It must not be supposed that I am obscure on purpose. I have thought in the language of correspondences continuously, and it never occurs to me that other people have not at their fingers' ends the whole rosary of symbols.

▶

irony · self-knowledge

'The Secret Pleasures of Reginald'

P. G. WODEHOUSE

⧗ 7 minutes

There is a very specific form of pleasure
we could all benefit from. Wodehouse's
friend turns it into an art form.

I found Reggie in the club one Saturday afternoon. He
was reclining in a long chair, motionless, his eyes fixed
glassily on the ceiling. He frowned a little when I spoke.
'You don't seem to be doing anything,' I said.

'It's not what I'm doing, it's what I am not doing that
matters.'

It sounded like an epigram, but epigrams are so little
associated with Reggie that I ventured to ask what he
meant.

He sighed. 'Ah well,' he said. 'I suppose the sooner I tell
you, the sooner you'll go. Do you know Bodfish?'

I shuddered. 'Wilkinson Bodfish? I do.'

'Have you ever spent a weekend at Bodfish's place in
the country?'

I shuddered again. 'I have.'

'Well, I'm not spending the weekend at Bodfish's place in the country.'

'I see you're not. But—'

'You don't understand. I do not mean that I am simply absent from Bodfish's place in the country. I mean that I am deliberately not spending the weekend there. When you interrupted me just now, I was not strolling down to Bodfish's garage, listening to his prattle about his new car.'

I glanced around uneasily.

'Reggie, old man, you're – you're not – This hot weather—'

'I am perfectly well, and in possession of all my faculties. Now tell me. Can you imagine anything more awful than to spend a weekend with Bodfish?'

On the spur of the moment I could not.

'Can you imagine anything more delightful, then, than not spending a weekend with Bodfish? Well, that's what I'm doing now. Soon, when you have gone – if you have any other engagements, please don't let me keep you – I shall not go into the house and not listen to Mrs Bodfish on the subject of young Willie Bodfish's premature intelligence.'

I got his true meaning. 'I see. You mean that you will be thanking your stars that you aren't with Bodfish.'

'That is it, put crudely. But I go further. I don't indulge in a mere momentary self-congratulation, I do the thing thoroughly. If I were weekending at Bodfish's, I should have arrived there just half an hour ago. I therefore selected that moment for beginning not to weekend with Bodfish. I settled myself in this chair and I did not have my back slapped at the station. A few minutes later I was not whirling along the country roads, trying to balance the car with my legs and an elbow. Time passed, and I was not shaking hands with Mrs Bodfish. I have just had the most corking half-hour, and shortly – when you have remembered an appointment – I shall go on having it. What I am really looking forward to is the happy time after dinner. I shall pass it in not playing bridge with Bodfish, Mrs Bodfish, and a neighbor. Sunday morning is the best part of the whole weekend, though. That is when I shall most enjoy myself. Do you know a man named Pringle? Next Saturday I am not going to stay with Pringle. I forget who is not to be my host the Saturday after that. I have so many engagements of this kind that I lose track of them.'

'But, Reggie, this is genius. You have hit on the greatest idea of the age. You might extend this system of yours.'

'I do. Some of the jolliest evenings I have spent have been not at the theatre.'

'I have often wondered what it was that made you look so fit and happy.'

'Yes. These little non-visits of mine pick me up and put life into me for the coming week. I get up on Monday morning feeling like a lion. The reason I selected Bodfish this week, though I was practically engaged to a man named Stevenson who lives out in Connecticut, was that I felt rundown and needed a real rest. I shall be all right on Monday.'

'And so shall I,' I said, sinking into the chair beside him.

'You're not going to the country?' he asked regretfully.

'I am not. I, too, need a tonic. I shall join you at Bodfish's. I really feel a lot better already.'

I closed my eyes, and relaxed, and a great peace settled upon me.

happiness · self-knowledge · shift of perspective

'On Running After One's Hat'

G. K. CHESTERTON

◆———

⏳ **10 minutes**

Packed trains, tight deadlines, noisy neighbours:
life can be bothersome. And yet, we might change
the way we look at the things which annoy us,
and that might transform them completely.

———◆———

I feel an almost savage envy on hearing that London has been flooded in my absence, while I am in the mere country. My own Battersea has been, I understand, particularly favoured as a meeting of the waters. Battersea was already, as I need hardly say, the most beautiful of human localities. Now that it has the additional splendour of great sheets of water, there must be something quite incomparable in the landscape (or waterscape) of my own romantic town. Battersea must be a vision of Venice. The boat that brought the meat from the butcher's must have shot along those lanes of rippling silver with the strange smoothness of the gondola. The greengrocer who brought cabbages to the corner of the Latchmere Road must have leant upon the oar with the unearthly grace of the gondolier. There is nothing so perfectly poetical as an island; and when a district is flooded it becomes an archipelago.

Some consider such romantic views of flood or fire slightly lacking in reality. But really this romantic view of such inconveniences is quite as practical as the other. The true optimist who sees in such things an opportunity for enjoyment is quite as logical and much more sensible than the ordinary 'Indignant Ratepayer' who sees in them an opportunity for grumbling. Real pain, as in the case of being burnt at Smithfield or having a toothache, is a positive thing; it can be supported, but scarcely enjoyed. But, after all, our toothaches are the exception, and as for being burnt at Smithfield, it only happens to us at the very longest intervals. And most of the inconveniences that make men swear or women cry are really sentimental or imaginative inconveniences – things altogether of the mind. For instance, we often hear grown-up people complaining of having to hang about a railway station and wait for a train. Did you ever hear a small boy complain of having to hang about a railway station and wait for a train? No; for to him to be inside a railway station is to be inside a cavern of wonder and a palace of poetical pleasures. Because to him the red light and the green light on the signal are like a new sun and a new moon. Because to him when the wooden arm of the signal falls down suddenly, it is as if a great king had thrown down his staff as a signal and started a shrieking tournament of trains. I myself am of little boys' habit in this matter. They also serve who only stand and wait for the two-fifteen. Their meditations may be full of rich and fruitful things. Many of the most purple hours of my life have been passed at Clapham Junction, which is now, I suppose, under water. I have been there in many moods so fixed and mystical that the water might well have come up to my waist before I noticed it particularly. But in the case of all such annoyances, as I have said, everything depends upon the emotional point of view. You can safely apply the test to almost every one of the things that are currently talked of as the typical nuisance of daily life.

For instance, there is a current impression that it is unpleasant to have to run after one's hat. Why should it be unpleasant to the well-ordered and pious mind? Not merely because it is running, and running exhausts one. The same people run much faster in games and sports. The same people run much more eagerly after an uninteresting little leather ball than they will after a nice silk hat. There is an idea that it is humiliating to run after one's hat; and when people say it is humiliating they mean that it is comic. It certainly is comic; but man is a very comic creature, and most of the things he does are comic – eating, for instance. And the most comic things of all are exactly the things that are most worth doing – such as making love. A man running after a hat is not half so ridiculous as a man running after a wife.

Now a man could, if he felt rightly in the matter, run after his hat with the manliest ardour and the most sacred joy. He might regard himself as a jolly huntsman pursuing a wild animal, for certainly no animal could be wilder. In fact, I am inclined to believe that hat-hunting on windy days will be the sport of the upper classes in the future.

There will be a meet of ladies and gentlemen on some high ground on a gusty morning. They will be told that the professional attendants have started a hat in such-and-such a thicket, or whatever be the technical term. Notice that this employment will in the fullest degree combine sport with humanitarianism. The hunters would feel that they were not inflicting pain. Nay, they would feel that they were inflicting pleasure, rich, almost riotous pleasure, upon the people who were looking on. When last I saw an old gentleman running after his hat in Hyde Park, I told him that a heart so benevolent as his ought to be filled with peace and thanks at the thought of how much unaffected pleasure his every gesture and bodily attitude were at that moment giving to the crowd.

The same principle can be applied to every other typical domestic worry. A gentleman trying to get a fly out of the milk or a piece of cork out of his glass of wine often imagines himself to be irritated. Let him think for a moment of the patience of anglers sitting by dark pools, and let his soul be immediately irradiated with gratification and repose. Again, I have known some people of very modern views driven by their distress to the use of theological terms to which they attached no doctrinal significance, merely because a drawer was jammed tight and they could not pull it out. A friend of mine was particularly afflicted in this way. Every day his drawer was jammed, and every day in consequence it was something else that rhymes to it. But I pointed out to him that this sense of wrong was really subjective and relative; it rested entirely upon the assumption that the drawer could, should, and would come out easily. 'But if,' I said, 'you picture to yourself that you are pulling against some powerful and oppressive enemy, the struggle will become merely exciting and not exasperating. Imagine that you are tugging up a lifeboat out of the sea. Imagine that you are roping up a fellow-creature out of an Alpine crevass. Imagine even that you are a boy again and engaged in a tug-of-war between French and English.' Shortly after saying this I left him; but I have no doubt at all that my words bore the best possible fruit. I have no doubt that every day of his life he hangs on to the handle of that drawer with a flushed face and eyes bright with battle, uttering encouraging shouts to himself, and seeming to hear all round him the roar of an applauding ring.

So I do not think that it is altogether fanciful or incredible to suppose that even the floods in London may be accepted and enjoyed poetically. Nothing beyond inconvenience seems really to have been caused by them; and inconvenience, as I have said, is only one aspect, and that the most unimaginative and accidental aspect of a really romantic situation. An adventure is only an inconvenience rightly considered. An inconvenience is only an adventure wrongly considered. The water that girdled the houses and shops of London must, if anything, have only increased their previous witchery and wonder. For as the Roman Catholic priest in the story said: 'Wine is good with everything except water,' and on a similar principle, water is good with everything except wine.

◖

irony · shift of perspective

WONDER

THERE IS A SECRET source inside us, which takes different shapes and leads us to take different paths in life – that of the scientist, the actor, the artist, the teacher, the priest. That source is our sixth sense, the sense of wonder.

Sense of wonder is that ineffable mixture of reverence and disquiet we all feel at some point in life: when you look at the ocean from a windswept cliff, when you see a star-prickled sky on a rare clear night in the Highlands of Scotland, when you understand how fully your partner loves you, when you allow a work of art to cast its spell upon you. Sense of wonder makes you feel there is something bigger than you, something more important and fundamental than your daily worries. It is a spiritual feeling, though not necessarily a religious one.

Sense of wonder comes naturally to children, who believe in magic and all sorts of odd things, but as we grow older, it slips away. We know that there is an answer – a mundane one – to every mystery, even when we don't know what the answer is. The dizziness we felt on the top of that windswept cliff? A physiological reaction. The perfection of that work of art? That's what you can achieve when you've got the skills. As grown-ups we have to navigate a complicated world of jobs, domestic responsibilities, taxes and slippery politics, and we just don't have time to wonder anymore. You can't stay up all night to watch the sky, because you have a performance review tomorrow.

We pay a terrible price for our loss of wonder. When I said just now that sense of wonder is a source, I meant it quite literally: only things (or people) that make you wonder will make you curious, and only things (or people) that make you curious will make you passionate. And we are at our most creative, and most fulfilled, when we are giving ourselves to projects and people we are passionate about. Scientific revolutions, art, religious insights, they all happen by the workings of wonder. Without wonder there's no passion, and without passion, it is a dull, dull life. Albert Einstein famously said that those who have lost the ability to wonder are 'as good as dead'.

*

The pieces in this section are intended to arouse your sense of wonder and to help rekindle an awestruck appreciation of all that is strange and beautiful in the world. They are perfect for friends who are going through a life crisis, or who are creatively stuck, or who are looking for something deeper, more fundamental, than just another cosy weekend.

The myth offers a personal riff on the tale of the death of Pan, originally told by Plutarch. The story seems to imply that the age of wonders is over, that gods no longer walk the land. But then again, maybe that is not the case...

Olaf Stapledon helps us understand how small we are next to the immensity of the Universe.

Dion Fortune offers intense and eccentric reflections on Glastonbury Tor, which I hope will re-enchant the landscape for you.

W. B. Yeats re-enchants the woods, by telling of the fairies you will encounter there.

The piece by Algernon Blackwood is another that dwells on the natural world, but in this case, the supernatural turns out to be a very natural phenomenon, and yet no less enchanting for that.

Jo Walton has a simple, straightforward story of magic to tell, in which the magic might be real or not, but strange things happen anyway, just as they sometimes do in our lives.

From Kenneth Graham comes a famous description of a meeting with a god of nature; from Tana French her take on the wonder of youth and friendship.

And finally, Kelly Link provides instructions on how to go to hell: a bracing, if occasionally rather scary, kind of holiday.

The Death of Pan

FRANCESCO DIMITRI

◆

⧖ 7 minutes

They say the great Pan is dead, and the other
gods died with him. I beg to differ.

◆

'The great Pan is dead!'

The sailors heard this cry (so the legend goes) over
the sea. They heard a sorrowful howl, and then a voice
without a body cried, 'The great Pan is dead!'

The voice told them to bring the message to shore, to
Emperor Tiberius. A new light of reason was dawning: the
world was no place for strange gods anymore. Wildness
would be tamed, horrors would be conquered, and life
would be safer than ever before.

Why then, I wonder, did the sailors mourn?

Let me tell you about Pan. He would sit in the cool
shade of trees at midday and play his pipes: you might
think his was a peaceful way to while away the time, until
you realise that those pipes were made of a living being.

There was a nymph in Arcadia called Syrinx, who kept

herself chaste in honour of Artemis. Every day she would walk to a river bank, sit in the waters, and sing, and all those who passed by, humans, gods, and spirits alike, would be overjoyed at hearing her voice.

Pan, too.

Pan enjoyed Syrinx's voice very much. He also enjoyed Syrinx's face, the curve of her breasts, the curly hair drawing a soft triangle on the delicious space between her legs. For some time he contented himself with looking at her from a hiding place: he would keep his eyes on her, and masturbate happily. But that couldn't last for long.

One day, when the sun was at its hottest, and was scorching the land, Pan came out of the shadow of the pine trees, his gigantic cock erect, his hands on his hips, his face monstrous. He ogled Syrinx, and he nodded.

After a moment in which she was frozen in shock, Syrinx fled. Pan ran behind her – this is how he liked it. His goat legs were fast, his hoofs were strong. He always caught his prey.

Syrinx ran and ran, under the Arcadian sun, until she reached the river, and there she had to stop, exhausted. She could hear Pan closing in. 'Artemis,' she prayed, 'my goddess, please help me.'

When Pan arrived, the nymph had disappeared; all he could see were the slender stems of water reeds. Pan roared in frustration. The reeds answered with a melodious voice. He recognised it: it was *her* voice. So Pan strode to the reeds, and cut them, and fashioned his pipes out of them.

Think of this, when you remember him playing in the shade of trees. Every time Pan touched his pipes, he was kissing Syrinx, he was putting his lips on her most private parts. I am not sure Artemis thought it through that time. Or maybe she had her own plans, who knows.

There are many other stories about Pan. His sexual appetites were so vigorous and so catholic that he would happily have his way with a goat. He slept with Selene, goddess of the moon. He had sex with all the Maenads. The size of his cock was matched only by the scope of his desires and his fantasies. He would often be jolly, but his favours could turn to violence in the blink of an eye. You might stumble upon him taking an afternoon nap in the woods of Arcadia, and his face would look content. But if you – by mistake or stupidity – awoke him, he would instantly put a mortal fear in your heart, a panic which would drive you, literally, crazy. You should never, ever, wake up Pan from his slumber.

So this was Pan, before he died. More than a spirit of the woods, less than an Olympian god, something other than a human being – mysterious, dangerous, and above all unpredictable. But he was one of the immortals, and if he died, there was only one possible reason for that: the age of immortals was over. Pan was not as mighty as Zeus, or Mars, or Hermes, so he was the first to go. The other gods would follow suit.

That is what, I think, the sailors were mourning that day: the passing of the gods.

In time the gods fell, and they were forgotten, and died. Aphrodite lost her beauty (what a blasphemous thought!), Athena stopped cracking the secrets of the universe, and nymphs and satyrs faded like mirages in the

Mediterranean sun. Gone, all gone. Arcadia was no more: the great Pan was dead.

Only, I don't think so.

I think the voice was wrong.

Pan is napping, but didn't die. Arcadia cannot be lost, Arcadia is never lost. Arcadia didn't exist *before* our time, it exists *above* our time, *around* our time. We built walls and cities and theories to keep Arcadia out, to protect ourselves from Pan's lust, from Mars' rage, Aphrodite's pride, and Hermes' tricks, and we didn't think that when you get rid of terror, you must give up wonder too. But they are all here still. You only need to walk in the woods at the right time, in the right frame of mind, and you will meet them. You only need to walk out of the walls of the city you built.

So be careful, in the woods. Pan is still there, napping.

Someone will wake him up, sooner or later.

Someone will wake him up.

◗

desire · meaning · regret · hope

Star Maker

OLAF STAPLEDON

⧗ 10 minutes

The sheer *immensity* of the universe is almost
impossible to conceive. But let's try, with
a little help from Olaf Stapledon.

Overhead obscurity was gone. From horizon to horizon
the sky was an unbroken spread of stars. Two planets
stared, unwinking. The more obtrusive of the constellations asserted their individuality. Orion's four-square
shoulders and feet, his belt and sword, the Plough, the
zigzag of Cassiopeia, the intimate Pleiades, all were duly
patterned on the dark. The Milky Way, a vague hoop of
light, spanned the sky.

Imagination completed what mere sight could not
achieve. Looking down, I seemed to see through a transparent planet, through heather and solid rock, through
the buried graveyards of vanished species, down through
the molten flow of basalt, and on into the Earth's core of
iron; then on again, still seemingly downwards, through

the southern strata to the southern ocean and lands, past the roots of gum trees and the feet of the inverted antipodeans, through their blue, sun-pierced awning of day, and out into the eternal night, where sun and stars are together. For there, dizzyingly far below me, like fishes in the depth of a lake, lay the nether constellations. The two domes of the sky were fused into one hollow sphere, star-peopled, black, even beside the blinding sun. The young moon was a curve of incandescent wire. The completed hoop of the Milky Way encircled the universe. In a strange vertigo, I looked for reassurance at the little glowing windows of our home. There they still were; and the whole suburb, and the hills. But stars shone through all.

It was as though all terrestrial things were made of glass, or of some more limpid, more ethereal vitreosity. Faintly the church clock chimed for midnight. Dimly, receding, it tolled the first stroke.

Imagination was now stimulated to a new, strange mode of perception.

Looking from star to star, I saw the heaven no longer as a jewelled ceiling and floor, but as depth beyond flashing depth of suns. And though for the most part the great and familiar lights of the sky stood forth as our near neighbours, some brilliant stars were seen to be in fact remote and mighty, while some dim lamps were visible only because they were so near. On every side the middle distance was crowded with swarms and streams of stars. But even these now seemed near; for the Milky Way had receded into an incomparably greater distance. And through gaps in its nearer parts appeared vista beyond vista of luminous mists, and deep perspectives of stellar populations.

The universe in which fate had set me was no spangled chamber, but a perceived vortex of star-streams. No! It was more. Peering between the stars into the outer darkness, I saw also, as mere flecks and points of light, other such vortices, such galaxies, sparsely scattered in the void, depth beyond depth, so far afield that even the eye of imagination could find no limits to the cosmical, the all-embracing galaxy of galaxies. The universe now appeared to me as a void wherein floated rare flakes of snow, each flake a universe. [...]

But now, once more shunning these immensities, I looked again for the curtained windows of our home, which, though star-pierced, was still more real to me than all the galaxies. But our home had vanished, with the whole suburb, and the hills too, and the sea. The very ground on which I had been sitting was gone. Instead there lay far below me an insubstantial gloom. And I myself was seemingly disembodied, for I could neither see nor touch my own flesh. And when I willed to move my limbs, nothing happened. I had no limbs. The familiar inner perceptions of my body, and the headache which had oppressed me since morning, had given way to a vague lightness and exhilaration. [...]

I noticed that the obscurity which had taken the place of the ground was shrinking and condensing. The nether stars were no longer visible through it. Soon the earth below me was like a huge circular table-top, a broad disc of darkness surrounded by stars. I was apparently soaring away from my native planet at incredible speed. The sun, formerly visible to imagination in the nether heaven, was once more physically eclipsed by the Earth. Though by now I must have been hundreds of miles above the ground, I was not troubled by the absence of oxygen and atmospheric pressure. I experienced only an increasing exhilaration and a delightful effervescence of thought. The extraordinary brilliance of the stars excited me. For, whether through the absence of obscuring air, or through my own increased sensitivity, or both, the sky had taken on an unfamiliar aspect. Every star had seemingly flared up into higher magnitude. The heavens blazed. The major stars were like the headlights of a distant car. The Milky Way, no longer watered down with darkness, was an encircling, granular river of light.

[...] The Earth appeared now as a great bright orb hundreds of times larger than the full moon. In its centre a dazzling patch of light was the sun's image reflected in the ocean. The planet's circumference was an indefinite breadth of luminous haze, fading into the surrounding blackness of space. Much of the northern hemisphere, tilted somewhat toward me, was an expanse of snow and cloud-tops. I could trace parts of the outlines of Japan and China, their vague browns and greens indenting the vague blues and greys of the ocean. Toward the equator, where the air was clearer, the ocean was dark. A little whirl of brilliant cloud was perhaps the upper surface of a hurricane. The Philippines and New Guinea were precisely mapped. Australia faded into the hazy southern limb.

Wonder · 355

The spectacle before me was strangely moving. Personal anxiety was blotted out by wonder and admiration; for the sheer beauty of our planet surprised me. It was a huge pearl, set in spangled ebony. It was nacreous, it was an opal. No, it was far more lovely than any jewel. Its patterned colouring was more subtle, more ethereal. It displayed the delicacy and brilliance, the intricacy and harmony of a live thing.

Strange that in my remoteness I seemed to feel, as never before, the vital presence of Earth as of a creature alive but tranced and obscurely yearning to wake.

adventure · anxiety · shift of perspective

Glastonbury: Avalon of the Heart

DION FORTUNE

◆

⏳ **14 minutes**

Dion Fortune was an occultist and a mystic,
with a background in psychotherapy. Here
she captures the wonder, strangeness and
magic of Glastonbury Tor.

◆

In the northern part of Somerset, where it borders upon
Gloucester, there is a triangular plain, bounded upon two
of its sides by the Mendips and the Poldens, and upon the
third by the sea. In the centre of this plain rises a strange
pyramidal hill crowned with a tower. So strange is this
hill, so symmetrical in form and rising so abruptly from
the wide-stretching levels, that no-one looking upon it for
the first time but is impelled to ask what it may be, for
it has that subtle thing which, strange as the word may
seem when applied to a hill, we cannot call other than
personality.

Seen from a distance, the Tor is a perfect pyramid;
but as we draw nearer, a central hill detaches itself from

the crowding foot-hills, and we see that it is shaped like a couch lion bearing a tower upon its crest, and round the central portion, in three great spirals, sweeps a broad, graded track, known as the Pilgrim Way.

The whole hill seems to radiate a strange and potent influence, whether seen afar off from the top of Mendip or glimpsed unexpectedly from a bedroom window as the curtain is drawn back in the dark. Whether the full moon is sailing serenely in the night sky behind the tower or whether a dark mass blots out the stars, whether the sun is blazing in a sky of Italian blue or shreds of cloud are driving past in storm, the Tor dominates Glastonbury. The busy little market town at its foot is occupied with the daily life of men, but on the Tor:

> The Old Gods guard their ground,
> And in her secret heart,
> The heathen kingdom Wilfred found,
> Dreams, as she dwells apart.

In the centre of this, 'the holiest erthe in Englande' rises the most pagan of hills. [...]

Round about the sacred Blood Well, so the story runs, certain hermits made their cells. But these holy men were so troubled by the principalities and powers that the ancient ritual had summoned to the Tor that in self-defence they built a church upon its summit and dedicated it to St Michael, the mighty archangel whose function it is to hold down the powers of the underworld.

But even St Michael was helpless against the Powers of Darkness, concentrated by ritual, and in the earthquake of A.D. 1000 the body of the church fell down, leaving only the tower standing. Thus was the Christian symbol of a cruciform church changed into the pagan symbol of an upstanding tower, and the Old Gods held their own. [...]

The Tor is indeed the Hill of Vision for any one whose eyes have the least inclination to open upon another world. Innumerable stories are told about it. There are some who, visiting Glastonbury for the first time, are amazed to see before them a Hill of Dreams which they have already known in sleep. More than one has told of this experience. Many times the tower is reported to have been seen rimmed in light; a warm glow, as of a furnace, beats up from the ground on wild winter nights, and the sound of chanting is heard from the depths of the hill. Towering forms of shadow and light are seen moving among the ancient thorn-trees that clothes the lower slopes, and something which no eye can see drives the grazing cattle down from the heights; and they do not fly from it in panic, but go quietly and orderly at the bidding of the invisible shepherd, who leads them away in order that the Sun-temple on the heights, not made with hands, eternal in the heavens, may be made ready for those who come to worship there. On more than one occasion we who live upon its flank have been called upon to minister comfort and consolation to those who have actually seen what they went to look for.

Wonderful as is the view from the Tor by day when half Somerset lies spread at one's feet, with the far hills of Devon to the south across Bridgwater Bay, and, in clear air after rain, even the hills of Wales to the west, far more wonderful is the sight by night for those who dare to climb in the dark. Most wonderful of all, perhaps, is to climb the Tor at sunset and watch the sun go down over the far Atlantic. From the Tor we see two sunsets – the sun himself in his glory in the west, and the reflection upon the clouds in the eastern sky. To see the moon rising through the rose-pink glow of the low clouds over the darkening marshes is a thing never to be forgotten. [...]

There is one time above all others when it is well to ascend the Tor at nightfall, and that is at the full moon of the autumnal equinox, round about the Mass of St Michael. The nights are coming cold then, but the days are still warm with the afterglow of summer, and the cold of the darkness, chilling the warm breath of the meadows, causes a thick but shallow mist to form over the levels. Through this the cattle wade knee-deep as in water, and trees cast shadows in the moonlight, black upon silver. As night closes in the mist deepens, like the rising tide in an estuary it fills the hollows. Trees and barns slowly drown. Only the few scattered knolls like St Bride's Bakery remain as islands in the mist. Lights on the far roads flit like fire-flies in the white gloom. Gradually they too fade as the mist thickens, and Avalon is an island again.

Local folk call this shallow mist that lies upon the levels the Lake of Wonder. Through it comes slowly the black barge, rowed by the dumb man, bearing the three weeping queens who bring Arthur, wounded unto death at Lyonesse, that he may heal him of his grievous wound in our green coombes among the apple-trees. Into the Lake of Wonder Sir Bedivere flings the magic sword Excalibur, graven with strange runes in an unknown tongue. And the white arm of the Lady of the Lake, rising from the rushes, seizes it and draws it under. To this day its jewels, gemming the rusting blade, lie among the marshes, waiting to be found.

All these, and many more, come back to Avalon when the Lake of Wonder rises from its faery springs under the Hunter's Moon.

But I have seen a stranger thing even than the Lake of Wonder by moonlight. There are times when there falls upon the Glastonbury levels what is known locally as the Blight. A strange heaviness that will not turn to thunder is in the summer air. The sun glows dully like a copper disk through the low-lying clouds, and in the oppressive dimness and heat, nerves are on edge with restlessness and uneasiness.

On one such occasion, driven desperate by the oppressiveness of the Levels, we set out to climb the Tor. Up and up through densest mist, moving in a circle some ten feet in diameter, shut in by a white wall impenetrable as stone – we climbed to the very summit, and there in a white blindness, came out of the mist as suddenly as a train runs out of a tunnel. The crest of the Tor was above the cloud-line.

The sky was of that deep indigo-blue often seen at Avalon – a blue that should be seen through the boughs of an apple-tree in blossom. From marge to marge no cloud flecked its depths, but below our feet there stretched to the very horizon a rolling, billowing sea of purest white with purple in the hollows. Above our heads was the tower, its shadow flung far out over the cloudy floor. It was as if the world had sunk in the sea and we were the last of mankind. No sound rose through the mist, no bird circled above us. There was nothing but blue sky, grey tower, billowing mist and blazing sun.

There was no air moving. All was still and silent as the moon. Time went by unaccounted, till presently a slight air began to stir; soon it strengthened to a breeze. Then the clouds began to move. They rolled and banked into great billows and flowed towards the sea. Faster and faster as the wind freshened they went shouldering past below our feet. Soon long rifts began to open their mass, and we saw the dark Butleigh woods for a moment, wrapped in deepest shadow. Rifts closed and opened again, giving us glimpses of the peat cuttings over to Ashcott and the red roofs of Street. Then the water-cuts began to show as silver wires through the mist; sounds began to rise up faintly through the thinning cloud – a cock crowing, a dog barking, distant bells. Then the last of the mist rolled back bodily and went in a flying wall towards the coast, and the levels lay spread in golden sunshine. Twice have I seen that from the Tor, and the sight is never to be forgotten.

▄▄▶

beauty · magic · memory · time

'Enchanted Woods'

from *The Celtic Twilight*

W. B. YEATS

⧖ 13 minutes

There are a few lucky people who can still
see spirits in nature. I don't know whether those
spirits exist, but I would love to see them too.

Last summer, whenever I had finished my day's work, I
used to go wandering in certain roomy woods, and there
I would often meet an old countryman, and talk to him
about his work and about the woods, and once or twice a
friend came with me to whom he would open his heart
more readily than to me. He had spent all his life lopping
away the witch elm and the hazel and the privet and the
hornbeam from the paths, and had thought much about
the natural and supernatural creatures of the wood. He
has heard the hedgehog – 'grainne oge,' he calls him –
'grunting like a Christian,' and is certain that he steals
apples by rolling about under an apple tree until there is

an apple sticking to every quill. He is certain too that the cats, of whom there are many in the woods, have a language of their own – some kind of old Irish. He says, 'Cats were serpents, and they were made into cats at the time of some great change in the world. That is why they are hard to kill, and why it is dangerous to meddle with them. If you annoy a cat it might claw or bite you in a way that would put poison in you, and that would be the serpent's tooth.' Sometimes he thinks they change into wild cats, and then a nail grows on the end of their tails; but these wild cats are not the same as the marten cats, who have been always in the woods. The foxes were once tame, as the cats are now, but they ran away and became wild. He talks of all wild creatures except squirrels – whom he hates – with what seems an affectionate interest, though at times his eyes will twinkle with pleasure as he remembers how he made hedgehogs unroll themselves when he was a boy, by putting a wisp of burning straw under them.

*

I am not certain that he distinguishes between the natural and supernatural very clearly. He told me the other day that foxes and cats like, above all, to be in the 'forths' and lisses after nightfall; and he will certainly pass from some story about a fox to a story about a spirit with less change of voice than when he is going to speak about a marten cat – a rare beast now-a-days. Many years ago he used to work in the garden, and once they put him to sleep in a garden-house where there was a loft full of apples, and all night he could hear people rattling plates and knives and forks over his head in the loft. Once, at any rate, he has seen an unearthly sight in the woods. He says, 'One time I was out cutting timber over in Inchy, and about eight o'clock one morning when I got there I saw a girl picking nuts, with her hair hanging down over her shoulders, brown hair, and she had a good, clean face, and she was tall and nothing on her head, and her dress no way gaudy but simple, and when she felt me coming she gathered herself up and was gone as if the earth had swallowed her up. And I followed her and looked for her, but I never could see her again from that day to this, never again.' He used the word clean as we would use words like fresh or comely.

*

Others too have seen spirits in the Enchanted Woods. A labourer told us of what a friend of his had seen in a part of the woods that is called Shanwalla, from some old village that was before the weed. He said, 'One evening I parted from Lawrence Mangan in the yard, and he went away through the path in Shanwalla, an' bid me good-night. And two hours after, there he was back again in the yard, an' bid me light a candle that was in the stable. An' he told me that when he got into Shanwalla, a little fellow about as high as his knee, but having a head as big as a man's body, came beside him and led him out of the path an' round about, and at last it brought him to the lime-kiln, and then it vanished and left him.'

*

A woman told me of a sight that she and others had seen by a certain deep pool in the river. She said, 'I came over the stile from the chapel, and others along with me; and a great blast of wind came and two trees were bent and broken and fell into the river, and the splash of water out of it went up to the skies. And those that were with me saw many figures, but myself I only saw one, sitting there by the bank where the trees fell. Dark clothes he had on, and he was headless.'

*

A man told me that one day, when he was a boy, he and another boy went to catch a horse in a certain field, full of boulders and bushes of hazel and creeping juniper and rock-roses, that is where the lake side is for a little clear of the woods. He said to the boy that was with him, 'I bet a button that if I fling a pebble on to that bush it will stay on it,' meaning that the bush was so matted the pebble would not be able to go through it. So he took up 'a pebble of cow-dung, and as soon as it hit the bush there came out of it the most beautiful music that ever was heard.' They ran away, and when they had gone about two hundred yards they looked back and saw a woman dressed in white, walking round and round the bush. 'First it had the form of a woman, and then of a man, and it was going round the bush.'

*

I often entangle myself in argument more complicat- ed than even those paths of Inchy as to what is the true nature of apparitions, but at other times I say as Socrates said when they told him a learned opinion about a nymph of the Illissus, 'The common opinion is enough for me.' I believe when I am in the mood that all nature is full of people whom we cannot see, and that some of these are ugly or grotesque, and some wicked or foolish, but very many beautiful beyond any one we have ever seen, and that these are not far away when we are walking in pleasant and quiet places. Even when I was a boy I could never walk in a wood without feeling that at any moment I might find before me somebody or something I had long looked for without knowing what I looked for. And now I will at times explore every little nook of some poor coppice with almost anxious footsteps, so deep a hold has this imagination upon me. You too meet with a like imagination, doubtless, somewhere, wherever your ruling stars will have it, Saturn driving you to the woods, or the Moon, it may be, to the edges of the sea. I will not of a certainty believe that there is nothing in the sunset, where our forefathers imagined the dead following their shepherd the sun, or nothing but some vague presence as little moving as nothing. If beauty is not a gateway out of the net we were taken in at our birth, it will not long be beauty, and we will find it better to sit at home by the fire and fatten a lazy body or to run hither and thither in some foolish sport than to look at the finest show that light and shadow ever made among green leaves. I say to myself, when I am well out of that thicket of argument, that they are surely there, the divine people, for only we who have neither simplicity nor wisdom have denied them, and the simple of all times and the wise men of ancient times have seen them and even spoken to them. They live out their passionate lives not far off, as I think, and we shall be among them when we die if we but keep our natures simple and passionate. May it not even be that death shall unite us to all romance, and that some day we shall fight dragons among blue hills, or come to that whereof all romance is but

'Foreshadowings mingled with the images
Of man's misdeeds in greater days than these,'

as the old men thought in *The Earthly Paradise* when they were in good spirits.

◗

beauty · magic · hope

'The Messenger'

ALGERNON BLACKWOOD

◆

⏳ 10 minutes

Sometimes a sense of wonder hits us
unexpectedly. It might come from the most
mundane of sources – revealing to us that those
sources were never mundane in the first place.

◆

I have never been afraid of ghostly things, attracted
rather with a curious live interest, though it is always out
of doors that strange Presences get nearest to me, and in
Nature I have encountered warnings, messages, presenti-
ments, and the like, that, by way of help or guidance, have
later justified themselves. I have, therefore, welcomed
them. But in the little rooms of houses things of much
value rarely come, for the thick air chokes the wires, as it
were, and distorts or mutilates the clear delivery.

But the other night, here in the carpenter's house,
where my attic windows beckon to the mountains and the
woods, I woke with the uncomfortably strong suggestion
that something was on the way, and that I was not ready.

It came along the by-ways of deep sleep. I woke abruptly, alarmed before I was even properly awake. Something was approaching with great swiftness – and I was unprepared.

Across the lake there were faint signs of colour behind the distant Alps, but terraces of mist still lay grey above the vineyards, and the slim poplar, whose tip was level with my face, no more than rustled in the wind of dawn. A shiver, not brought to me by any wind, ran through my nerves, for I knew with a certainty no arguing could lessen nor dispel that something from immensely far away was deliberately now approaching me. The touch of wonder in advance of it was truly awful; its splendour, size, and grandeur belonged to conditions I had surely never known. It came through empty spaces – from another world. While I lay asleep it had been already on the way.

I stood there a moment, seeking for some outward sign that might betray its nature. The last stars were fading in the northern sky, and blue and dim lay the whole long line of the Jura, cloaked beneath still slumbering forests. There was a rumbling of a distant train. Now and then a dog barked in some outlying farm. The Night was up and walking, though as yet she moved but slowly from the sky. Shadows still draped the world. And the warning that had reached me first in sleep rushed through my tingling nerves once more with a certainty not far removed from shock. Something from another world was drawing every minute nearer, with a speed that made me tremble and half-breathless. It would presently arrive. It would stand close beside me and look straight into my face. Into these very eyes that searched the mist and shadow for an outward sign it would gaze intimately with a Message brought for me alone. But into these narrow walls it could only come with difficulty. The message would be maimed. There still was time for preparation. And I hurried into clothes and made my way downstairs and out into the open air.

Thus, at first, by climbing fast, I kept ahead of it, and soon the village lay beneath me in its nest of shadow, and the limestone ridges far above dropped nearer. But the awe and terrible deep wonder did not go. Along these mountain paths, whose every inch was so intimate that I could follow them even in the dark, this sense of breaking grandeur clung to my footsteps, keeping close. Nothing upon the earth – familiar, friendly, well-known, little earth – could have brought this sense that pressed upon the edges of true reverence. It was the awareness that some speeding messenger from spaces far, far beyond the world would presently stand close and touch me, would gaze into my little human eyes, would leave its message as of life or death, and then depart upon its fearful way again – it was this that conveyed the feeling of apprehension that went with me.

And instinctively, while rising higher and higher, I chose the darkest and most sheltered way. I sought the protection of the trees, and ran into the deepest vaults of the forest. The moss was soaking wet beneath my feet, and the thousand tapering spires of the pines dipped upwards into a sky already brightening with palest gold and crimson. There was a whispering and a rustling overhead as the trees, who know everything before it comes, announced to one another that the thing I sought to hide from was already very, very near. Plunging deeper into the woods to hide, this detail of sure knowledge followed me and laughed: that the speed of this august arrival was one which made the greatest speed I ever dreamed of a mere standing still...

I hid myself where possible in the darkness that was growing every minute more rare. The air was sharp and exquisitely fresh. I heard birds calling. The low, wet branches kissed my face and hair. A sense of glad relief came over me that I had left the closeness of the little attic chamber, and that I should eventually meet this huge Newcomer in the wide, free spaces of the mountains. There must be room where I could hold myself unmanacled to meet it... The village lay far beneath me, a patch of smoke and mist and soft red-brown roofs among the vineyards. And then my gaze turned upwards, and through a rift in the close-wrought ceiling of the trees I saw the clearness of the open sky. A strip of cloud ran through it, carrying off the Night's last little dream... and down into my heart dropped instantly that cold breath of awe I have known but once in life, when staring through the stupendous mouth within the Milky Way – that opening into the outer spaces of eternal darkness, unlit by any single star, men call the Coal Hole.

The futility of escape then took me bodily, and I renounced all further flight. From this speeding Messenger there was no hiding possible. His splendid shoulders already brushed the sky. I heard the rushing of his awful wings... yet in that deep, significant silence with which light steps upon the clouds of morning.

And simultaneously I left the woods behind me and stood upon a naked ridge of rock that all night long had watched the stars.

Then terror passed away like magic. Cool winds from the valleys bore me up. I heard the tinkling of a thousand cowbells from pastures far below in a score of hidden valleys. The cold departed, and with it every trace of little fears. My eyes seemed for an instant blinded, and I knew that deep sense of joy which seems so 'unearthly' that it almost stains the sight with the veil of tears. The soul sank to her knees in prayer and worship.

For the messenger from another world had come. He stood beside me on that dizzy ledge. Warmth clothed me, and I knew myself akin to deity. He stood there, gazing straight into my little human eyes. He touched me everywhere. Above the distant Alps the sun came up. His eye looked close into my own.

◗

anxiety · instinct · power

Among Others

JO WALTON

───────◆───────

⏳ 9 minutes

Children play with make-believe creatures.
Sometimes those creatures play with children, too.

───────◆───────

The Phurnacite factory in Abercwmboi killed all the trees
for two miles around. We'd measured it on the mile-
ometer. It looked like something from the depths of hell,
black and looming with chimneys of flame, reflected in a
dark pool that killed any bird or animal that drank from
it. The smell was beyond description. We always wound
up the car windows as tight as tight when we had to pass
it, and tried to hold our breath, but Grampar said nobody
could hold their breath that long, and he was right. There
was sulphur in that smell, which was a hell chemical as
everyone knew, and other, worse things, hot unnameable
metals and rotten eggs.

My sister and I called it Mordor, and we'd never been
there on our own before. We were ten years old. Even so,
big as we were, as soon as we got off the bus and started

looking at it we started holding hands.

It was dusk, and as we approached the factory loomed blacker and more terrible than ever. Six of the chimneys were alight; four belched out noxious smokes.

'Surely it is a device of the Enemy,' I murmured.

Mor didn't want to play. 'Do you really think this will work?'

'The fairies were sure of it,' I said, as reassuringly as possible.

'I know, but sometimes I don't know how much they understand about the real world.'

'Their world is real,' I protested. 'Just in a different way. At a different angle.'

'Yes.' She was still staring at the Phurnacite, which was getting bigger and scarier as we approached. 'But I don't know how much they understand about the angle of the everyday world. And this is definitely in that world. The trees are dead. There isn't a fairy for miles.'

'That's why we're here,' I said.

We came to the wire, three straggly strands, only the top one barbed. A sign on it read 'No Unauthorised Admittance. Beware Guard Dogs.' The gate was far around the other side, out of sight.

'Are there dogs?' she asked. Mor was afraid of dogs, and dogs knew it. Perfectly nice dogs who would play with me would rouse their hackles at her. My mother said it was a method people could use to tell us apart. It would have worked, too, but typically of her, it was both terrifyingly evil and just a little crazily impractical.

'No,' I said.

'How do you know?'

'It would ruin everything if we go back now, after having gone to all this trouble and come this far. Besides, it's a quest, and you can't give up on a quest because you're afraid of dogs. I don't know what fairies would say. Think of all the things people on quests have to put up with.' I knew this wasn't working. I squinted forward into the deepening dusk as I spoke. Her grip on my hand had tightened. 'Besides, dogs are animals. Even trained guard dogs would try to drink the water, and then they'd die. If there really were dogs, there would be at least a few dog bodies at the side of the pool, and I don't see any. They're bluffing.'

We crept below the wire, taking turns holding it up. The still pool was like old unpolished pewter, reflecting the chimney flames as unfaithful wavering streaks. There were lights below them, lights the evening shift worked by.

There was no vegetation here, not even dead trees. Cinders crunched underfoot, and clinker and slag threatened to turn our ankles. There seemed to be nothing alive but us. The star-points of windows on the hill opposite seemed ridiculously out of reach. We had a school friend who lived there, we had been to a party once, and noticed the smell, even inside the house. Her father worked at the plant. I wondered if he was inside now.

At the edge of the pool we stopped. It was completely still, without even the faintest movement of natural water. I dug in my pocket for the magic flower. 'Have you got yours?'

'It's a bit crushed,' she said, fishing it out. I looked at them. Mine was a bit crushed too. Never had what we were doing seemed more childish and stupid than standing in the centre of that desolation by that dead pool holding a pair of crushed pimpernels the fairies had told us would kill the factory.

I couldn't think of anything appropriate to say. 'Well, un, dai, tri!' I said, and on 'Three' as always we cast the flowers forward into the leaden pool, where they vanished without even a ripple. Nothing whatsoever happened. Then a dog barked far away, and Mor turned and ran and I turned and pelted after her.

'Nothing happened,' she said, when we were back on the road, having covered the distance back in less than a quarter of the time it had taken us as distance out.

'What did you expect?' I asked.

'The Phurnacite to fall and become a hallowed place,' she said, in the most matter-of-fact tone imaginable. 'Well, either that or huorns.'

I hadn't thought of huorns, and I regretted them extremely. 'I though the flowers would dissolve and ripples would spread out and then it would crumble to ruin and the trees and ivy come swarming over it while we watched and the pool would become real water and a bird would come and drink from it and then the fairies would be there and thank us and take it for their palace.'

'But nothing at all happened,' she said, and sighed. 'We'll have to tell them it didn't work tomorrow. Come one, are we going to walk home or wait for a bus?'

It had worked, though. The next day, the headline in the Aberdare *Leader* was 'Phurnacite Plant Closing: Thousands of Jobs Lost.'

companionship · magic · shift of perspective

The Wind in the Willows

KENNETH GRAHAME

◆

⌛ 11 minutes

We can find Wonder in the hearth of nature; if we
are lucky, we might even meet the gods there.

◆

Then a change began slowly to declare itself. The horizon
became clearer, field and tree came more into sight, and
somehow with a different look; the mystery began to
drop away from them. A bird piped suddenly, and was
still; and a light breeze sprang up and set the reeds and
bulrushes rustling. Rat, who was in the stern of the boat,
while Mole sculled, sat up suddenly and listened with a
passionate intentness. Mole, who with gentle strokes was
just keeping the boat moving while he scanned the banks
with care, looked at him with curiosity.

'It's gone!' sighed the Rat, sinking back in his seat again.
'So beautiful and strange and new! Since it was to end so
soon, I almost wish I had never heard it. For it has roused a
longing in me that is pain, and nothing seems worth while
but just to hear that sound once more and go on listening

to it for ever. No! There it is again!' he cried, alert once more. Entranced, he was silent for a long space, spellbound.

'Now it passes on and I begin to lose it,' he said presently. 'O Mole! The beauty of it! The merry bubble and joy, the thin, clear, happy call of the distant piping! Such music I never dreamed of, and the call in it is stronger even than the music is sweet! Row on, Mole, row! For the music and the call must be for us.'

The Mole, greatly wondering, obeyed. 'I hear nothing myself,' he said, 'but the wind playing in the reeds and rushes and osiers.'

The Rat never answered, if indeed he heard. Rapt, transported, trembling, he was possessed in all his senses by this new divine thing that caught up his helpless soul and swung and dandled it, a powerless but happy infant in a strong sustaining grasp.

In silence Mole rowed steadily, and soon they came to a point where the river divided, a long backwater branching off to one side. With a slight movement of his head Rat, who had long dropped the rudder-lines, directed the rower to take the backwater. The creeping tide of light gained and gained, and now they could see the colour of the flowers that gemmed the water's edge.

'Clearer and nearer still,' cried the Rat joyously. 'Now you must surely hear it! Ah – at last – I see you do!'

Breathless and transfixed the Mole stopped rowing as the liquid run of that glad piping broke on him like a wave, caught him up, and possessed him utterly. He saw the tears on his comrade's cheeks, and bowed his head and understood. For a space they hung there, brushed by the purple loose-strife that fringed the bank; then the clear imperious summons that marched hand-in-hand with the intoxicating melody imposed its will on Mole, and mechanically he bent to his oars again. And the light grew steadily stronger, but no birds sang as they were wont to do at the approach of dawn; and but for the heavenly music all was marvellously still.

On either side of them, as they glided onwards, the rich meadow-grass seemed that morning of a freshness and a greenness unsurpassable. Never had they noticed the roses so vivid, the willow-herb so riotous, the meadow-sweet so odorous and pervading. Then the murmur of the approaching weir began to hold the air, and they felt a consciousness that they were nearing the end, whatever it might be, that surely awaited their expedition.

A wide half-circle of foam and glinting lights and shining shoulders of green water, the great weir closed the backwater from bank to bank, troubled all the quiet surface with twirling eddies and floating foam-streaks, and deadened all other sounds with its solemn and soothing rumble. In midmost of the stream, embraced in the weir's shimmering arm-spread, a small island lay anchored, fringed close with willow and silver birch and alder. Reserved, shy, but full of significance, it hid whatever it might hold behind a veil, keeping it till the hour should come, and, with the hour, those who were called and chosen.

Slowly, but with no doubt or hesitation whatever, and in something of a solemn expectancy, the two animals passed through the broken, tumultuous water and moored their boat at the flowery margin of the island. In silence they landed, and pushed through the blossom and scented herbage and undergrowth that led up to the level ground, till they stood on a little lawn of a marvellous green, set round with Nature's own orchard-trees – crab-apple, wild cherry and sloe.

'This is the place of my song-dream, the place the music played to me,' whispered the Rat, as if in a trance. 'Here, in this holy place, here if anywhere, surely we shall find Him!'

Then suddenly the Mole felt a great Awe fall upon him, an awe that turned his muscles to water, bowed his head, and rooted his feet to the ground. It was no panic terror – indeed he felt wonderfully at peace and happy – but it was an awe that smote and held him and, without seeing, he knew it could only mean that some august Presence was very, very near. With difficulty he turned to look for his friend, and saw him at his side cowed, stricken, and trembling violently. And still there was utter silence in the populous bird-haunted branches around them; and still the light grew and grew.

Perhaps he would never have dared to raise his eyes, but that, though the piping was now hushed, the call and the summons seemed still dominant and imperious. He might not refuse, were Death himself waiting to strike him instantly, once he had looked with mortal eye on things rightly kept hidden. Trembling he obeyed, and raised his humble head; and then, in that utter clearness of the imminent dawn, while Nature, flushed with fulness of incredible colour, seemed to hold her breath for the event, he looked in the very eyes of the Friend and Helper;

saw the backward sweep of the curved horns, gleaming in the growing daylight; saw the stern, hooked nose between the kindly eyes that were looking down on them humourously, while the bearded mouth broke into a half-smile at the corners; saw the rippling muscles on the arm that lay across the broad chest, the long supple hand still holding the pan-pipes only just fallen away from the parted lips; saw the splendid curves of the shaggy limbs disposed in majestic ease on the sward; saw, last of all, nestling between his very hooves, sleeping soundly in entire peace and contentment, the little, round, podgy, childish form of the baby otter. All this he saw, for one moment breathless and intense, vivid on the morning sky; and still, as he looked, he lived; and still, as he lived, he wondered.

'Rat!' he found breath to whisper, shaking. 'Are you afraid?'

'Afraid?' murmured the Rat, his eyes shining with unutterable love. 'Afraid! Of *Him*? O, never, never! And yet – and yet – O, Mole, I am afraid!'

Then the two animals, crouching to the earth, bowed their heads and did worship.

Sudden and magnificent, the sun's broad golden disc showed itself over the horizon facing them; and the first rays, shooting across the level water-meadows, took the animals full in the eyes and dazzled them. When they were able to look once more, the Vision had vanished, and the air was full of the carol of birds that hailed the dawn.

beauty · magic · power

The Secret Place

TANA FRENCH

◆

⧖ 6 minutes

Wonder is not always a solitary experience.
Sometimes you can sense it in the company of
your friends; and indeed, it is sometimes *through*
your friends that you get to feel it.

◆

They've never listened to the sounds of the school falling
asleep before, not this way, ears stretched like animals'. At
first the flickers are constant: a burst of giggles through
the wall, a faraway squeal, a patter of slippers as someone
runs to the toilet. Then they drift farther apart. Then
there's silence.

When the clock at the back of the main building strikes
on, Selena sits up.

They don't talk. They don't flick on torches, or bedside
lights: anyone going down the corridor would see the
flicker through the glass above the transom. In the window
the moon is enormous, more than enough. They strip off
their pyjamas and stuff their pillows under their sheets,

pull on final jumpers and coats, deft and synchronised as if they'd been practising. When they're ready they stand by their beds, boots dangling from their hands. They look at each other like explorers in the doorway of a long journey, all of them caught motionless in the moment before one of them takes the first step.

'If you weirdos are serious about this,' Julia says, 'let's do it.'

No one leaps out at them from a doorway, no stair creaks. On the ground floor Matron is snoring. When Becca fits the key into the door to the main building, it turns like the lock's been oiled. By the time they reach the maths classroom and Julia reaches up to the fastening of the sash window, they already know the watchman is asleep or on the phone and will never look their way. Boots on and out of the window, one two three four quick and slick and silent, and they're standing on the grass and it's not a game any more.

The grounds are still as a set for a ballet, waiting for the first shivering run of notes from a flute; for the light girls to run in and stop, poised perfect and impossible, barely touching the grass. The white light comes from everywhere. The frost sings high in their ears.

They run. The great spread of grass rolls out to greet them and they skim down it, the crackle-cold air flowing like spring water into their mouths and running their hair straight out behind them when their hoods fall back and none of them can stop to pull them up again. They're invisible, they could stream laughing past the night watchman and tweak off his cap as they went, leave him grabbing at air and gibbering at the wild unknown that's suddenly everywhere, and they can't stop running.

Into the shadows and down the narrow paths enclosed by dark spiky weaves of branches, past leaning trunks wrapped with years of ivy, through smells of cold earth and wet layers of leaves. When they burst out of that tunnel it's into the white waiting glade.

They've never been here before. The tops of the cypresses blaze with frozen fire like great torches. There are things moving in the shadows, things that when they manage to catch a hair-thin glimpse are shaped like deer and wolves but they could be anything, circling. High in the shining column of air above the clearing, birds whirl arc-winged, long threads of savage cries trailing behind them

The four of them open their arms and whirl too. The breath is spun out of them and the world rocks around them and they keep going. They're spun out of themselves, spun to silver dust flying, they're nothing but a rising arm or a curve of cheek in and out of ragged white bars of light. They dance till they collapse.

When they open their eyes they're in the glade they know again. Darkness, and a million stars, and silence.

The silence is too big for any of them to burst, so they don't talk. They lie on the grass and feel their own moving breath and blood. Something white and luminous is arrowing through their bones, the cold or the moonlight maybe, they can't tell for sure; it tingles but doesn't hurt. They lie back and let it do its work.

Selena was right: this is nothing like the thrill of necking vodka or taking the piss out of Sister Ignatius, nothing like a snog in the Field or forging your mum's signature for ear-piercing. This has nothing to do with what anyone else in all the world would approve or forbid. This is all their own.

After a long time they straggle back to the school, dazzled and rumple-haired, heads buzzing. *Forever*, they say, at the threshold of the window, with their boots in their hands and the moonlight turning in their eyes. *I'll remember this forever. Yes forever. Oh forever.*

beauty · companionship · happiness · magic · potential

'Going to hell. Instructions and advice'

KELLY LINK

◆ — ◆

⧖ 5 minutes

Go to hell. No, really.

◆ — ◆

Listen, because I'm only going to do this once. You'll have to get there by way of London. Take the overnight train from Waverly. Sit in the last car. Speak to no one. Don't fall asleep.

When you arrive at Kings Cross, go down into the Underground. Get on the Northern line. Sit in the last car. Speak to no one. Don't fall asleep.

The Northern line stops at Angel, at London Bridge, at Elephant and Castle, Tooting Broadway. The last marked station is Morden: stay in your seat. Other passengers will remain with you in the car. Speak to no one.

These are some of the unlisted stations you will pass: Howling Green. Duke's Pit. Sparrowkill. Stay in your seat. Don't fall asleep. If you look around the car, you may notice that the other passengers have started to glow. The bulbs on the car dim as the passengers give off more and more light. If you look down you may find that you your-self are casting light into the dark car.

The final stop is Bonehouse.

[...] It is late morning when you arrive at Bonehouse, but the sky is dark. As you walk, you must push aside the air, like heavy cloth. Your foot stumbles on the mute ground.

You are in a flat place where the sky presses down, and the buildings creep close along the streets, and all the doors stand open. Grass grows on the roofs of the houses; the roofs are packed sod, and the grass raises up tall like hair on a scalp. Follow the others. They are dead and know the way better than you. Speak to no one.

At last you will arrive at a door in an alley, with a dog asleep on the threshold. He has many heads and each head has many teeth, and his teeth are sharp and eager as knives.

[...] As the others step over the dog he doesn't wake. If you step over him, he will smell live flesh and he will tear you to pieces.

Take this perfume with you and when you come to Bonehouse, dab it behind your ears, at your wrists and elbows, at the back of your knees. Stroke it into the vee of your sex, as you would for a lover. The scent is heavy and rich, like the first cold handful of dirt tossed into the dug grave. It will trick the dog's nose.

Inside the door, there is no light but the foxfire glow of your own body. The dead flicker like candles around you. They are burning their memories for warmth. They may brush up against you, drawn to what is stronger and hotter and brighter in you. Don't speak to them.

Wonder · 389

There are no walls, no roof above you except darkness. There are no doors, only the luminous windows that the dead have become. Unravel the left arm of his sweater and let it fall to the ground.

[...] 'If you don't let the sweater fall from your hands, if you follow the sleeve until it is only yarn, it will lead you to him. He won't be as you remember him, he's been eating his memories to keep warm. He is not asleep, but if you kiss him he'll wake up. Just like the fairy tales. His lips will be cold at first.'

'Say to him, *Follow* me, and unravel the right arm of the sweater. It will take you to a better place, little thief. If you do it right and don't look back, then you can steal him out of the Bonehouse.'

irony · magic · adventure

CODA:
DELICACIES FOR
DISCUSSION

TABOO TOPICS

W E ARE TOO POLITE, too pleasant, to touch upon certain topics. For all but the most skilful of conversationalists, politics, spirituality and sex are taboo subjects – reefs on which existing friendships can founder or budding ones expire before they have had a chance to take wing. And yet, is there anything that matters more than sex, politics and spirituality? These are taboo topics *because* they are so important. They make us hot under the collar, they make us passionate, they make us say things we don't mean (but actually we *do* mean). There is something adolescent about them – a fire, a spark, a potential for explosiveness that is absent from the polite pleasantries of much adult conversation. So yes, of course, they can often lead to disagreements, but isn't it good and healthy to disagree, sometimes? Isn't it a thousand times better than the soul-crushing safety of small talk?

These three pieces, therefore, have been chosen as conversation starters, possibly incendiary conversation starters. Read them to a friend, or a group of friends, and enjoy the verbal sparring that will ensue. There's nothing like literature for helping to break taboos.

*

The great American writer Henry David Thoreau asks whether obeying the law is always the right thing to do. Perhaps there are higher moral principles that have a greater claim to our adherence than the laws devised by governments? And maybe the best and most responsible citizens are those who accept the need sometimes to disobey, when this higher morality dictates it?

Arthur Conan Doyle, the creator of Sherlock Holmes, was far less rational than his fictional detective. He was fascinated by the paranormal and believed in spirits and fairies. Here he makes a case for their existence, as he argues for the authenticity of a series of photographs of fairies taken by two young girls. The photographs themselves have been since proved to be fakes, but what about the general point Conan Doyle makes? Does it still stand?

Catherine Millet reveals to us the pleasures and worries of group sex. Should sex only happen between a couple in love, or can it also be a beautiful and enriching experience to be savoured by a group of friends, and not just *à deux*? And where does a conversation such this lead, if all those who take part happen to agree?

———◆———

Civil Disobedience

H. D. THOREAU

⏳ 13 minutes

———◆———

I heartily accept the motto, 'That government is best which governs least'; and I should like to see it acted up to more rapidly and systematically. Carried out, it finally amounts to this, which also I believe – 'That government is best which governs not at all'; and when men are prepared for it, that will be the kind of government which they will have. Government is at best but an expedient; but most governments are usually, and all governments are sometimes, inexpedient. The objections which have been brought against a standing army, and they are many and weighty, and deserve to prevail, may also at last be brought against a standing government. The standing army is only an arm of the standing government. The government itself, which is only the mode which the people have chosen to execute their will, is equally liable to be abused and perverted before the people can act through it. Witness the present Mexican war, the work of comparatively a few individuals using the standing government as their tool; for, in the outset, the people would not have consented to this measure.

This American government – what is it but a tradition, though a recent one, endeavoring to transmit itself unimpaired to posterity, but each instant losing some of its integrity? It has not the vitality and force of a single living man; for a single man can bend it to his will. It is a sort of wooden gun to the people themselves. But it is not the less necessary for this; for the people must have some complicated machinery or other, and hear its din, to satisfy that idea of government which they have. Governments show thus how successfully men can be imposed on, even impose on themselves, for their own advantage. It is excellent, we must all allow. Yet this government never of itself furthered any enterprise, but by the alacrity with which it got out of its way. *It* does not keep the country free. *It* does not settle the West. *It* does not educate. The character inherent in the American people has done all that has been accomplished; and it would have done somewhat more, if the government had not sometimes got in its way. For government is an expedient by which men would fain succeed in letting one another alone; and, as has been said, when it is most expedient, the governed are most let alone by it. Trade and commerce, if they were not made of india-rubber, would never manage to bounce over the obstacles which legislators are continually putting in their way; and, if one were to judge these men wholly by the effects of their actions and not partly by their intentions, they would deserve to be classed and punished with those mischievous persons who put obstructions on the railroads.

But, to speak practically and as a citizen, unlike those who call themselves no-government men, I ask for, not *at once* no government, but at once a better government. Let every man make known what kind of government would command his respect, and that will be one step toward obtaining it.

After all, the practical reason why, when the power is once in the hands of the people, a majority are permitted, and for a long period continue, to rule is not because they are most likely to be in the right, nor because this seems fairest to the minority, but because they are physically the strongest. But a government in which the majority rule in all cases cannot be based on justice, even as far as men understand it. Can there not be a government in which majorities do not virtually decide right and wrong, but conscience? – in which majorities decide only those questions to which the rule of expediency is applicable? Must the citizen ever for a moment, or in the least degree, resign his conscience to the legislation? Why has every man a conscience, then? I think that we should be men first, and subjects afterward. It is not desirable to cultivate a respect for the law, so much as for the right. The only obligation which I have a right to assume is to do at any time what I think right. It is truly enough said that a corporation has no conscience; but a corporation of conscientious men is a corporation *with* a conscience.

Law never made men a whit more just; and, by means of their respect for it, even the well-disposed are daily made the agents of injustice. A common and natural result of an undue respect for law is, that you may see a file of soldiers, colonel, captain, corporal, privates, powder-monkeys, and all, marching in admirable order over hill and dale to the wars, against their wills, ay, against their common sense and consciences, which makes it very steep marching indeed, and produces a palpitation of the heart. They have no doubt that it is a damnable business in which they are concerned; they are all peaceably inclined. Now, what are they? Men at all? or small movable forts and magazines, at the service of some unscrupulous man in power? Visit the Navy-Yard, and behold a marine, such a man as an American government can make, or such as it can make a man with its black arts – a mere shadow and reminiscence of humanity, a man laid out alive and standing, and already, as one may say, buried under arms with funeral accompaniments, though it may be,

> Not a drum was heard, not a funeral note,
> As his corse to the rampart we hurried;
> Not a soldier discharged his farewell shot
> O'er the grave where our hero we buried.

The mass of men serve the state thus, not as men mainly, but as machines, with their bodies. They are the standing army, and the militia, jailers, constables, posse comitatus, etc. In most cases there is no free exercise whatever of the judgment or of the moral sense; but they put themselves on a level with wood and earth and stones;

and wooden men can perhaps be manufactured that will serve the purpose as well. Such command no more respect than men of straw or a lump of dirt. They have the same sort of worth only as horses and dogs. Yet such as these even are commonly esteemed good citizens. Others – as most legislators, politicians, lawyers, ministers, and office-holders – serve the state chiefly with their heads; and, as they rarely make any moral distinctions, they are as likely to serve the devil, without *intending* it, as God. A very few – as heroes, patriots, martyrs, reformers in the great sense, and *men* – serve the state with their consciences also, and so necessarily resist it for the most part; and they are commonly treated as enemies by it. A wise man will only be useful as a man, and will not submit to be 'clay,' and 'stop a hole to keep the wind away,' but leave that office to his dust at least:

> I am too high-born to be propertied,
> To be a secondary at control,
> Or useful serving-man and instrument
> To any sovereign state throughout the world.

He who gives himself entirely to his fellow-men appears to them useless and selfish; but he who gives himself partially to them is pronounced a benefactor and philanthropist.

How does it become a man to behave toward this American government today? I answer, that he cannot without disgrace be associated with it. I cannot for an instant recognize that political organization as *my* government which is the *slave's* government also.

All men recognize the right of revolution; that is, the right to refuse allegiance to, and to resist, the government, when its tyranny or its inefficiency are great and unendurable. But almost all say that such is not the case now. But such was the case, they think, in the Revolution of '75. If one were to tell me that this was a bad government because it taxed certain foreign commodities brought to its ports, it is most probable that I should not make an ado about it, for I can do without them. All machines have their friction; and possibly this does enough good to counterbalance the evil. At any rate, it is a great evil to make a stir about it. But when the friction comes to have its machine, and oppression and robbery are organized, I say, let us not have such a machine any longer. In other words, when a sixth of the population of a nation which has undertaken to be the refuge of liberty are slaves, and a whole country is unjustly overrun and conquered by a foreign army, and subjected to military law, I think that it is not too soon for honest men to rebel and revolutionize. What makes this duty the more urgent is the fact that the country so overrun is not our own, but ours is the invading army.

self-knowledge

The Coming of the Fairies

ARTHUR CONAN DOYLE

⌛ 10 minutes

We are accustomed to the idea of amphibious creatures who may dwell unseen and unknown in the depths of the waters, and then some day be spied sunning themselves upon a sandbank, whence they slip into the unseen once more. If such appearances were rare, and if it should so happen that some saw them more clearly than others, then a very pretty controversy would arise, for the sceptics would say, with every show of reason, 'Our experience is that only land creatures live on the land, and we utterly refuse to believe in things which slip in and out of the water; if you will demonstrate them to us we will begin to consider the question.' Faced by so reasonable an opposition, the others could only mutter that they had seen them with their own eyes, but that they could not command their movements. The sceptics would hold the field.

Something of the sort may exist in our psychic arrangements. One can well imagine that there is a dividing line, like the water edge, this line depending upon what we vaguely call a higher rate of vibrations. Taking the vibration theory as a working hypothesis, one could conceive that by raising or lowering the rate the creatures could move from one side to the other of this line of material visibility, as the tortoise moves from the water to the land, returning for refuge to invisibility as the reptile scuttles back to the surf. This, of course, is supposition, but intelligent supposition based on the available evidence is the pioneer of science, and it may be that the actual solution will be found in this direction. I am alluding now, not to spirit return, where seventy years of close observation has given us some sort of certain and definite laws, but rather to those fairy and phantom phenomena which have been endorsed by so many ages, and still even in these material days seem to break into some lives in the most unexpected fashion.

Victorian science would have left the world hard and clean and bare, like a landscape in the moon; but this science is in truth but a little light in the darkness, and outside that limited circle of definite knowledge we see the loom and shadow of gigantic and fantastic possibilities around us, throwing themselves continually across our consciousness in such ways that it is difficult to ignore them.

There is much curious evidence of varying value concerning these borderland forms, which come or go either in fact or imagination – the latter most frequently, no doubt.

And yet there remains a residue which, by all human standards, should point to occasional fact. Lest I should be too diffuse, I limit myself in this essay to the fairies, and passing all the age-long tradition, which is so universal and consistent, come down to some modern instances which make one feel that this world is very much more complex than we had imagined, and that there may be upon its surface some very strange neighbours who will open up inconceivable lines of science for our posterity, especially if it should be made easier for them, by sympathy or other help, to emerge from the deep and manifest upon the margin.

Taking a large number of cases which lie before me, there are two points which are common to nearly all of them. One is that children claim to see these creatures far more frequently than adults. This may possibly come from greater sensitiveness of apprehension, or it may depend upon these little entities having less fear of molestation from the children. The other is, that more cases are recorded in which they have been seen in the still, shimmering hours of a very hot day than at any other time. 'The action of the sun upon the brain,' says the sceptic. Possibly – and also possibly not. If it were a question of raising the slower vibrations of our surroundings one could imagine that still, silent heat would be the very condition which might favour such a change. What is the mirage of the desert? What is that scene of hills and lakes which a whole caravan can see while it faces in a direction where for a thousand miles of desert there is neither hill nor lake, nor any cloud or moisture to produce refraction? I can ask the question, but I do not venture to give an answer. It is clearly a phenomenon which is not to be confused with the erect or often inverted image which is seen in a land of clouds and of moisture.

If the confidence of children can be gained and they are led to speak freely, it is surprising how many claim to have seen fairies. My younger family consists of two little boys and one small girl, very truthful children, each of whom tells with detail the exact circumstances and appearance of the creature. To each it happened only once, and in each case it was a single little figure, twice in the garden, once in the nursery. Inquiry among friends shows that many children have had the same experience, but they close up at once when met by ridicule and incredulity. Sometimes the shapes are unlike those which they would have gathered from picture-books. 'Fairies are like nuts and moss,' says one child in Lady Glenconner's charming study of family life. My own children differ in the height of the creatures, which may well vary, but in their dress they are certainly not unlike the conventional idea, which, after all, may also be the true one.

There are many people who have a recollection of these experiences of their youth, and try afterwards to explain them away on material grounds which do not seem adequate or reasonable.

magic

◆

The Sexual Life of Catherine M.

CATHERINE MILLET

⏳ 6 minutes

◆

It was in June or July, it was hot and somebody suggested that we should all take our clothes off and jump into the big pond. I heard André's voice saying his girlfriend wouldn't be bashful in coming forward, and his words sounded a little muffled because I did indeed already have my T-shirt over my head. I forget when and why I stopped wearing underwear (even though as soon as I was thirteen or fourteen my mother had me wear an underwired bra and a panty girdle on the pretext that a woman 'should be held in place'). In any event, I was naked almost immediately. The other girl started getting undressed too, but in the end no one went in the water. The garden was exposed; and that is probably why the next set of images that come back to me are in a bedroom, me nestled in a tall, cast iron bed, all I can see through the metal bars are the brightly lit walls, aware of the other girl lying on a divan in one corner of the room. André fucked me first, quite slowly and calmly as was his manner. Then he stopped abruptly. I was overcome with an ineffable feeling of anxiety, just long enough to see him moving away, walking slowly, his back arched, towards the other girl. Ringo came and took his place on top of me, while the third boy, who was more reserved and spoke less than the other two, rested on one elbow beside us and ran his hand over my upper body. Ringo's body was very different from André's and I liked it better. He was taller, more wiry, and Ringo was one of those men who isolate the action of the pelvis from the rest of the body, who hammer without smothering, supporting their torso on their arms. But André seemed more mature to me (he was in fact older and had served in Algeria), his flesh was not so spare, he already had less hair, and I liked going to sleep cuddled up next to him with my buttocks against his belly, telling him we were a perfect fit. Ringo withdrew and the one who had been watching and stroking me took his turn even though I had been resisting a terrible urge to urinate for some time. I had to go. The shy boy was piqued. When I came back he was with the other girl. I no longer remember whether it was André or Ringo who took the precaution of telling me that the shy boy had only gone to 'finish off' with her.

I stayed in Lyon for about two weeks. My friends worked during the day and I spent the afternoons with the student I had met in London. [...]

*

The little gang would come and wait for me late in the afternoon at the end of the road. They were happy and playful, and, spotting them one day, the student's father said with a cordial note in his voice that I must be a hell of a girl to have all these boys at my disposal. In fact, I had given up counting. I had completely forgotten my childhood investigation into the permitted number of husbands. I was not a 'collector', and I thought that the boys and the girls that I saw at parties mauling and being mauled, and mouth-to-mouth kissing until their breath gave out with as many people as possible so that they could boast about it the next day, were somehow offensive. I was happy simply to discover that the delicious giddiness I felt at the ineffably soft touch of a stranger's lips, or when a hand fitted itself over my pubis, could be experienced an indefinite number of times because the world was full of men predisposed to do just that. Nothing else really mattered.

▶

companionship · desire

THE 'READ ALOUD' TOOLKIT

1. Reading Prescriptions

LOVE

Myth: Baucis and Philemon

This is a piece for the person you have always loved, or for the one you might love for ever. Alternatively, read it to your parents, to celebrate them; or to a good friend, and wonder together if such a love is, indeed, possible.

Alain de Botton, 'What Nice Men Never Tell Nice Women'

Read this to a friend who complains about being too nice, or one who seems never to find a man who is nice enough. Or read it just for fun to anyone, anywhere.

Kate Chopin, 'A Respectable Woman'

Read this to explore one of the most thorny, and dangerous, issues in a relationship – cheating.

Cicero, *De Amicitia*

Read this to your best friends, or to those who could do with a little more understanding of the values of camaraderie.

Jane Austen, *Pride and Prejudice*
Charles Dickens, *Great Expectations*

Read each of these pieces, or both of them together, to friends, lovers, someone you are dating.

J. R. R. Tolkien, *The Return of the King*

Read this to friends or partners, and let Tolkien's words express the strength of your commitment.

Julie de L'Espinasse, letter to Hippolyte de Guibert

Read this to show your love for the first or hundredth time – or to show the kind of love you might be capable of.

LOSS

Myth: **Alcestis**

Read this to a friend who is facing a difficult choice, entailing a renunciation. Should I go freelance or keep a regular pay cheque?

Neil Gaiman, 'The Sweeper of Dreams'

Read this to a friend who has recently experienced a disappointment, or who gets too caught up in his own world.

Simone de Beauvoir, *A Very Easy Death*

Read this to a grieving friend, or to someone who is interested in exploring their grief.

Oscar Wilde, *De Profundis*

Read this to a friend who is undergoing a life crisis.

E. Nesbit, 'Uncle Abraham's Romance'

Read this to friends who are having regrets, to those who like to dwell in the past, or to those who need to come to terms with some mistake they made or think they made.

Joe Hill, 'Scheherazade's Typewriter'

Read this to a friend who is grieving, or mourning a loss of any kind. It is a gentle piece, which might help us understand the importance of moving on.

Daphne du Maurier, *Rebecca*

Read this to a friend who is moving house, moving to a new city, or just moving on in life.

Graham Joyce, *The Limits of Enchantment*

Read this to a friend looking for closure.

CHANGE

Myth: Persephone and Demeter

Read this to a friend who needs to be reassured about a difficult situation she is going through.

Ray Bradbury, *Dandelion Wine*

Read this to your most nostalgic friends, those who like to indulge in memories of things past.

Joyce Carol Oates, 'The Scarf'

Read this to your parents, or to friends who find themselves negotiating a new relationship with theirs.

Lewis Carroll, *The Life and Letters of Lewis Carroll*

Read this to a friend who is going through a transformation: it is a hymn to change itself, and a guide to how to make the most of it.

Francesco Dimitri, 'The Oak in my Garden'

Read this to inspire a friend to quietly appreciate the mystery of change.

Olive Schreiner, 'The Woman's Rose'

Read this to a friend who is going through a rough time with her friends, co-workers, or family.

Zora Neale Hurston, *Dust Tracks on a Road*

Read this to a friend who finds himself slightly lost, a bit stuck, and is impatient for change to happen.

Rebecca Solnit, *A Field Guide to Getting Lost*

Read this to a friend who is afraid of change; or to one who seeks it always.

PLEASURE

Myth: **Psyche and Eros**

Read this to a friend who needs to learn mindless abandon.

Jim Dodge, *Stone Junction*

Read this to a friend on a warm rainy day – and see what happens.

Joanne Harris, *Chocolat*

Read this to a foodie, or to someone you think might benefit from appreciating food a little more.

Anaïs Nin, 'Manuel'

Read it for fun, to a friend you want to share a laugh with.

Jorge Amado, *Gabriela, Clove and Cinnamon*

Read this to a friend who wants to think about how to make a relationship work.

Lillian Beckwith, *The Hills is Lonely*

Read it for the joy of it.

Epicurus, Letter to Menoeceus

Read it to the philosophically inclined among your friends.

D. H. Lawrence, *Lady Chatterley's Lover*
John Cleland, *Fanny Hill: or, Memoirs of a Woman of Pleasure*

I'm sure you don't need any suggestions about who to read these two pieces to.

Giacomo Leopardi, 'Dialogue of Torquato Tasso and his Familiar Genius'

Read it to a friend who is obsessed with the past, or worried about the future.

WORK

Myth: Pygmalion

Read it to a friend who is passionate about what she does, or one who is starting something new.

Joe R. Lansdale, *Captains Outrageous*
George Orwell, *Down and Out in Paris and London*

Read these to friends stuck in jobs they don't like, or who often complain about their jobs.

Virginia Woolf, 'Professions for Women'

Read this to a girlfriend in need of support, or to any friend – female or male – who is trying to articulate a new identity for herself or himself.

Anthony Trollope, *Autobiography*

Read this to a friend who is thinking of embarking on a creative profession, or one who complains he doesn't have one.

H. G. Wells, *Kipps*

Read this to a friend who has had a bad induction to a new job, or to a friend who is going to go through an induction soon.

Elizabeth Gaskell, *Cranford*

Read this to a friend who is anxious about her finances.

John Fante, *The Brotherhood of the Grape*

Read this to a friend who always seems to pick the wrong job; or maybe to one who seems to have just found her way.

NATURE

Myth: **Adonis**

Read this to a friend who believes there is nothing interesting beyond the city walls.

Rob Cowen, *Common Ground*

Read this to a friend who thinks that nature is distant and dangerous, and has given up looking for it.

John Muir, *My First Summer in the Sierra*

Read this to a friend who could do with some beauty in her life.

Ralph Waldo Emerson, 'Nature'

Read this to those who are a little too focused on city life, and never look out of their window.

Dorothy Wordsworth, *Recollections of a Tour Made in Scotland*

Read this for the sheer joy of taking a friend on a journey of the mind.

Robert Macfarlane, *The Old Ways*

Read this to a friend who enjoys being on the water, or just to rejoice in the soundscape Macfarlane creates.

Isabella Bird, *The Hawaiian Archipelago*

Read this to friends who believe Nature is always benevolent, to gently tease them for their views.

Chris Yates, *Nightwalk*

Read this to a friend, to share with her Yates's joy and wonder.

Amy Leach, 'Radical Bears in the Forest Delicious'

Read this to give a friend a glimpse of the strangeness that the natural world hides in plain sight, and of the lessons we could take from it.

CHAOS

Myth: **The Daughters of Minyas**
Read this to help a friend navigate troublesome times:
it might inspire her to enjoy Chaos, rather than fear it.

Rosalind Kerven, 'The Dead Moon'
Read this to a friend who needs to understand that going it
alone is not always the wisest thing to do; or to a friend who
needs some hope to see him through a dark time.

Gregory Bateson, 'Why Do Things Get in a Muddle?'
Read this to someone who is trying to make sense of the
Chaos in her life.

Alice Hoffman, *Practical Magic*
Read this to the dreamers among your friends.

E. M. Forster, *A Room with a View*
Read this to friends who are looking for a balance of sorts.

David Mitchell, *Black Swan Green*
Read this to a friend who just needs to feel understood.

Vernon Lee, 'A Pontifical Mass at the Sixtine Chapel'
Read this to embrace the more positive sides of Chaos.

Maurice Baring, 'Half a Minute's Silence'
Read this to a friend who is anxious about a journey, be it
a physical journey or any new venture in his life; or to any
friend who travels a lot.

LIGHTNESS

Myth: **The Birth of Hermes**

Read this to a friend who might need to learn how effective you can be when you keep it light.

Katherine Mansfield, 'Bank Holiday'

One of the great things stories do is to allow us to live vicariously. So this is one for your dullest days.

Mark Twain, Speech made on his seventieth birthday

Read this to a friend who is a bit *too* obsessed with cardio, calorie counting, dietary fads, and so on.

Aleister Crowley, *The Confessions of Aleister Crowley: an Autohagiography*

Read this to a friend who is a bit too proud, or not proud enough, of her achievements.

P. G. Wodehouse, 'The Secret Pleasures of Reginald'

Read this to a friend who relishes the pleasure of *not doing things*.

G. K. Chesterton, 'On Running After One's Hat'

Read this to a friend who feels frustrated by the daily grind, or who has simply been a bit tired recently. Life can be much more playful than we make it, if only we look at it from a lighter perspective.

WONDER

Myth: **The Death of Pan**
Read this to a friend who feels dejected, her energy spent.

Olaf Stapledon, *Star Maker*
Read this to a friend who needs some perspective on their problems, or just for pleasure, to share a moment of awe together.

Dion Fortune, *Glastonbury: Avalon of the Heart*
W. B. Yeats, 'Enchanted Woods'
Read these pieces to friends who are searching for a different relationship with the world around them, even if they live in a city and never walk the woods and the hills.

Algernon Blackwood, 'The Messenger'
Read this to a friend who believes that science kills wonder, or the other way round.

Jo Walton, *Among Others*
Read this to a friend who enjoys oddities, or who could do with a few more of them.

Kenneth Graham, *The Wind in the Willows*
Read it to a friend who has been feeling exhausted, and might be looking for a deeper inner life.

Tana French, *The Secret Place*
Read this to friends who might find wonder in human connections.

Kelly Link, 'Going to hell. Instructions and advice'

Read this to a friend who might benefit from visiting other worlds.

CODA

H. D. Thoreau, *Civil Disobedience*

Read this piece to one or more friends, to have a fight about politics.

Arthur Conan Doyle, *The Coming of the Fairies*

Read this piece to one or more friends, to have a fight about spirituality.

Catherine Millet, *The Sexual Life of Catherine M.*

Read this piece to one or more friends, to make war or make love.

2. List of reading times

3 MINUTES

Aleister Crowley, *The Confessions of Aleister Crowley: an Autohagiography*

E. M. Forster, *A Room with a View*

Neil Gaiman, *The Sweeper of Dreams*

Giacomo Leopardi, 'Dialogue of Torquato Tasso and his Familiar Genius'

Julie de L'Espinasse, letter to Hippolyte de Guibert

Rebecca Solnit, *A Field Guide to Getting Lost*

4 MINUTES

Lewis Carroll, *The Life and Letters of Lewis Carroll*

Zora Neale Hurston, *Dust Tracks on a Road*

Graham Joyce, *The Limits of Enchantment*

Daphne du Maurier, *Rebecca*

5 MINUTES

Jim Dodge, *Stone Junction*

Epicurus, Letter to Menoeceus

Elizabeth Gaskell, *Cranford*

Kelly Link, 'Going to hell. Instructions and advice'

J. R. R. Tolkien, *The Return of the King*

Anthony Trollope, *Autobiography*

6 MINUTES

Cicero, *De Amicitia*

Lillian Beckwith, *The Hills is Lonely*

Tana French, *The Secret Place*

Vernon Lee, 'A Pontifical Mass at the Sixtine Chapel'

Catherine Millet, *The Sexual Life of Catherine M.*

David Mitchell, *Black Swan Green*

George Orwell, *Down and Out in Paris and London*

Mark Twain, Speech made on his seventieth birthday

7 MINUTES

Alain de Botton, 'What Nice Men Never Tell Nice Women'

Myth: The Daughters of Minyas

Myth: The Death of Pan

Ralph Waldo Emerson, 'Nature'

John Muir, *My First Summer in the Sierra*

Myth: Persephone and Demeter

Myth: Pygmalion

P. G. Wodehouse, 'The Secret Pleasures of Reginald'

8 MINUTES

Myth: Adonis

Maurice Baring, 'Half a Minute's Silence'

Simone de Beauvoir, *A Very Easy Death*

Myth: The Birth of Hermes

Joanne Harris, *Chocolat*

Joe R. Lansdale, *Captains Outrageous*

Robert Macfarlane, *The Old Ways*

Chris Yates, *Nightwalk*

9 MINUTES

Myth: Alcestis

Katherine Mansfield, 'Bank Holiday'

Jo Walton, *Among Others*

Oscar Wilde, *De Profundis*

Dorothy Wordsworth, *Recollections of a Tour Made in Scotland*

10 MINUTES

Myth: Baucis and Philemon

Algernon Blackwood, 'The Messenger'

G. K. Chesterton, 'On Running After One's Hat'

Arthur Conan Doyle, *The Coming of the Fairies*

Joe Hill, 'Scheherazade's Typewriter'

Rosalind Kerven, 'The Dead Moon'

E. Nesbit, 'Uncle Abraham's Romance'

Anaïs Nin, 'Manuel'

Olaf Stapledon, *Star Maker*

H. G. Wells, *Kipps*

11 MINUTES

Kenneth Grahame, *The Wind in the Willows*

Myth: Psyche and Eros

12 MINUTES

Gregory Bateson, 'Why Do Things Get in a Muddle?', from *Steps to an Ecology of Mind*

Rob Cowen, *Common Ground*

Francesco Dimitri, 'The Oak in my Garden'

John Fante, *The Brotherhood of the Grape*

D. H. Lawrence, *Lady Chatterley's Lover*

Olive Schreiner, 'The Woman's Rose'

13 MINUTES

Ray Bradbury, *Dandelion Wine*

Amy Leach, 'Radical Bears in the Forest Delicious'

Alice Hoffman, *Practical Magic*

H. D. Thoreau, *Civil Disobedience*

W. B. Yeats, 'Enchanted Woods', from *The Celtic Twilight*

14 MINUTES

Jorge Amado, *Gabriela, Clove and Cinnamon*

Isabella Bird, *The Hawaiian Archipelago*

Kate Chopin, 'A Respectable Woman'

Dion Fortune, *Glastonbury: Avalon of the Heart*

Virginia Woolf, 'Professions for Women'

15 MINUTES

Jane Austen, *Pride and Prejudice*

John Cleland, *Fanny Hill: or, Memoirs of a Woman of Pleasure*

Charles Dickens, *Great Expectations*

Joyce Carol Oates, 'The Scarf'

3. Index of tags

Adventure 22, 94, 143, 172, 249, 352, 388

Anxiety 19, 47, 63, 67, 114, 125, 128, 197, 211, 214, 228, 241, 282, 290, 296

Beauty 85, 105, 234, 238, 241, 245, 302, 357, 363, 379, 384

Calm 112, 256, 260, 296, 306, 321

Comfort 14, 77, 161, 224, 228, 321

Companionship 14, 28, 44, 55, 85, 119, 137, 143, 167, 190, 277, 298, 374, 384, 405

Consolation 85

Creativity 77, 146, 203, 316

Desire 38, 47, 94, 167, 186, 224, 290, 348, 405

Generosity 55

Happiness 14, 38, 94, 112, 137, 155, 179, 186, 333, 384

Honesty 19, 28

Hope 28, 38, 44, 55, 67, 114, 119, 125, 277, 348, 363

Instinct 22, 137, 143, 146, 150, 155, 164, 167, 256, 273, 369

Irony 19, 22, 31, 150, 161, 172, 190, 194, 206, 211, 214, 260, 316, 326, 330, 337, 388

Learning 119, 128, 172, 186, 197, 206, 234, 238, 282, 290

Luck 150

Magic 14, 60, 71, 77, 85, 146, 277, 290, 363, 374, 379, 384, 388, 401

Married life 14, 22, 114, 137, 155

Meaning 67, 98, 105, 143, 224, 234, 238, 241, 245, 245, 282, 348

Memory 82, 85, 98, 105, 357

Music 31, 296, 316

Potential 114, 125, 128, 146, 179, 186, 214, 245, 306, 384

Power 249, 296, 302, 369, 379

Regret 63, 67, 71, 179, 348

Resilience 38, 44, 60, 112, 125, 190, 194, 197, 214, 298, 326

Rules 22, 31, 137, 155, 167, 203, 273

Self-knowledge 19, 22, 63, 164, 228, 260, 296, 306, 326, 330, 333, 395

Shift of perspective 19, 333, 337, 352, 374

Surprise 256

Temptation 22, 273, 326

Time 71, 77, 82, 98, 105, 125, 146, 357

Virtue 273

4. Notes on the authors

JORGE AMADO (1912–2001) was a Brazilian writer. He was a member of the Brazilian Academy of Letters, and his works are well known around the world. *Gabriela, Clove and Cinnamon* was first published in English in 1962.

JANE AUSTEN (1775–1817) laid bare the manners of the landed gentry of her era. She published her novels anonymously, but is today one of the most admired and best-loved of English writers.

MAURICE BARING (1874–1945) was an English author with a wide social circle. He travelled extensively, spending time in Russia in the first years of the twentieth century.

GREGORY BATESON (1904–80) was an academic with a wide range of interests. His book *Steps to an Ecology of Mind* has been immensely influential. His 'Metalogue: Why Do Things Get in a Muddle?' was written in 1948.

SIMONE DE BEAUVOIR (1908–86) was a French intellectual. Her book *The Second Sex* is considered a feminist master-work and a landmark text.

The semi-autobiographical books of the English-born LILLIAN BECKWITH (1916–2004) are mostly set in Scotland, where she moved in the 1940s.

Unjustly forgotten today, the Victorian adventurer ISABELLA BIRD (1831–1904) was the first woman fellow of the Royal Geographical Society and a fine writer.

ALGERNON BLACKWOOD (1869–1951) was one of the foremost English writers of the fantastic, fond of practical magic and the outdoor life.

ALAIN DE BOTTON (b. 1969) is a writer, philosopher, and essayist, and the founder of the international organisation The School of Life.

RAY BRADBURY (1920–2012) was an American writer of science fiction, fantasy, horror, and other genres. *Fahrenheit 451* is perhaps his most famous novel.

MARCUS TULLIUS CICERO (106 BC–43 BC) was a Roman politician and orator. His works span philosophy, politics and history, and his influence on Western culture has been vast.

G. K. CHESTERTON (1874–1936) invented the seminal character of Father Brown, paving the way for the figure of the priest-sleuth. An acute and humorous writer, he was also a celebrated essayist.

KATE CHOPIN (1850–1904) was a Louisiana author who started writing following a period of depression. Her novel *The Awakening* was considered scandalous for its depiction of women's sexuality.

JOHN CLELAND (1709–89) finished his *Memoirs of a Woman of Pleasure*, better known as *Fanny Hill*, while doing time for debt in London's Fleet Prison. He wrote other novels, and plays, but with little success.

ARTHUR CONAN DOYLE (1859–1930) was quite different from his fictional detective Sherlock Holmes. Where Sherlock is utterly rational, Doyle was fascinated by spirits, fairies and other strange beings.

ROB COWEN is an award-winning nature writer, speaker, broadcaster and journalist.

ALEISTER CROWLEY (1875–1945), at one time dubbed 'the wickedest man in the world', was an occultist and a poet, and was also known for his feats of mountaineering. After his death he became a counter-culture icon.

CHARLES DICKENS (1812–70) was the most celebrated English novelist of the nineteenth century. Extraordinarily success-ful in his lifetime, he gave public readings of his works on both sides of the Atlantic.

FRANCESCO DIMITRI (b. 1981) is an Italian author living in London.

JIM DODGE (b. 1945) is an American writer. His book *Stone Junction* was appreciated by Thomas Pynchon, who wrote an introduction for it. He teaches Creative Writing at Humboldt State University, California.

RALPH WALDO EMERSON (1803–82) was the father of the brand of American romanticism known as transcendental-ism. He was a friend of H. D. Thoreau, and a remarkable writer in his own right.

EPICURUS (341–270 BC) was a Greek philosopher. At the core of his thinking was the notion that pleasure is the most important thing in life, but that finding real pleasure is not easy, and requires restraint and philosophical reflection.

JULIE DE L'ESPINASSE (1732–76), a French salonnière, left behind a corpus of witty, charming and revealing letters.

JOHN FANTE (1909–83) was a novelist and short-story writer. His most famous character is Arturo Bandini, an Italian-American writer at the centre of the so-called Bandini Quartet. Fante was a significant influence on Charles Bukowski, another chronicler of American low life.

E. M. FORSTER (1879–1970) explored class differences in his two best-known novels, *Howard's End* and *A Passage to India*. *A Room with a View* is probably the most accessible of his books. *Maurice*, which Forster wrote in 1913–14, and which explored homosexual love, was published for the first time only after Forster's death.

The work of DION FORTUNE (born Violet Mary Firth; 1890–1946) is almost entirely forgotten in the mainstream, though she still has a small circle of devotees. She was a prominent English mystic, with a very peculiar view of Christianity.

The bestselling writer TANA FRENCH (b. 1973) has published six psychological crime novels, the most recent of which is *The Trespasser* (2016).

NEIL GAIMAN (b. 1960) has written novels, graphic novels, comic books and film scripts, winning a wide range of prizes. He is considered one of the most important living writers of the fantastic.

ELIZABETH GASKELL (1810–65) was a Victorian novelist and short-story writer. *Cranford*, an episodic book about life in a small town (based on Knutsford, in Cheshire, where Mrs Gaskell spent much of her life), is probably her best-known work.

The Edinburgh-born KENNETH GRAHAME (1859–1932) worked for many years at the Bank of England, and was the author of the much-loved children's classic *The Wind in the Willows* (1908), part of which would later be adapted for the stage by A. A. Milne as *Toad of Toad Hall* (1929).

JOANNE HARRIS (b. 1964) is a bestselling, prize-winning author of novels that combine social commentary, magic realism and sheer originality.

JOE HILL (b. 1972) is the pen name of Joseph Hillstrom King. His novels, short stories and comic books have been widely acclaimed by fantasy readers.

ALICE HOFFMAN (b. 1952) is the author of twenty-six novels. *Time Magazine* wrote of her that she 'tells truths powerful enough to break a reader's heart'.

ZORA NEALE HURSTON (1891–1960) was an African-American writer who brought to her novels a deep feeling for characterisation and an anthropological understanding of human beings. *Dust Tracks on a Road*, her autobiography, was published in 1942.

GRAHAM JOYCE (1954–2014) was a writer of the fantastic and a World Fantasy Award winner. His books have an enduring appeal among genre and non-genre readers alike.

ROSALIND KERVEN (b. 1954) is an author and folklorist. She has published more than sixty books, and her work has been translated into twenty-two languages.

JOE R. LANSDALE (b. 1951) is an American writer. He is the author of the Hap and Leonard series of novels and novellas about two amateur investigators, which was adapted for television in 2016.

D. H. LAWRENCE (1885–1930) published his novel *Lady Chatterley's Lover* privately in Italy in 1928. When the unexpurgated novel, containing frequent uses of the word 'fuck', was published in Britain by Penguin Books in 1960, it became the subject of a famous trial – *R v. Penguin Books Ltd* – under the Obscene Publications Act 1959. The jury found for the defendant.

AMY LEACH is an American nature writer who plays bluegrass and piano in her spare time.

VERNON LEE (1856–1935) was the pseudonym of Violet Paget. Chiefly renowned for her supernatural stories, she was also an expert on aesthetics and a feminist. Her account of the Pontifical Mass appeared in *The Spirit of Rome*, published in 1906.

GIACOMO LEOPARDI (1798–1837) was one of the most prolific and influential Italian poets, and a philosopher, philologist and essayist.

KELLY LINK (b. 1969) is a cult author among readers of magic realism.

ROBERT MACFARLANE (b. 1976) is the author of a trilogy of award-winning books about landscape and the imagination: *Mountains of the Mind*, *The Wild Places* and *The Old Ways: A Journey on Foot*. He is a Fellow of Emmanuel College, Cambridge.

KATHERINE MANSFIELD (1888–1923) was the pseudonym of the New Zealand-born Kathleen Mansfield Murry. A writer of short stories, she later lived in Britain and continental Europe, and died early from tuberculosis.

DAPHNE DU MAURIER'S (1907–89) enduringly popular novels – including *Rebecca*, *My Cousin Rachel* and *Jamaica Inn* – remain stubbornly resistant to classification. Born in London, du Maurier spent much of her life in Cornwall, a place she loved deeply.

CATHERINE MILLET (b. 1948) is a French writer, art critic and magazine editor. *The Times Literary Supplement* said of her sexually explicit memoir *The Sexual Life of Catherine M.*: 'Millet writes extremely well... it is neither pornography nor her coy younger sister, erotica, but a work of libertine philosophy.'

DAVID MITCHELL (b. 1969) is an English novelist. His most famous work, *Cloud Atlas* (2004), was made into a film in 2012. He is widely appreciated for his capacity to merge realistic and fantastic themes.

JOHN MUIR (1838–1914) was a Scottish-born American naturalist and environmentalist who devoted a large part of his life to the preservation of America's western wilderness. In 1892, he co-founded the Sierra Club, which remains an important US conservation organisation.

EDITH NESBIT (1858–1924) was an author of books for children under the name E. Nesbit. A socialist and founder-member of the Fabian Society, her numerous works include the children's classics *The Railway Children* and *The Story of the Treasure Seekers*, and novels and short stories for adults.

ANAÏS NIN (1903–77) was an essayist and memoirist, born to Cuban parents in France. 'Manuel', the story included in our 'Pleasure' chapter, is one of fifteen erotic short stories that make up *Delta of Venus*, which Nin wrote on commission for a private collector in the 1940s.

GEORGE ORWELL (1903–1950), born Eric Blair, was the author of the novella *Animal Farm* and the dystopian novel *Nineteen Eighty-Four*. In the late 1920s and early 1930s he set out to explore low life in London. *Down and Out in Paris and London* is a memoir on the theme of poverty, chronicling his experiences of near-destitution in the French capital, and describing the lives of tramps in and around London.

OLIVE SCHREINER (1855–1920) was an early feminist in South Africa. She published her first novel, *The Story of an African Farm*, under a male pseudonym, but revealed her true identity when the second edition came out.

REBECCA SOLNIT (b. 1961) is an American writer, historian and activist, and the author of important books on environmental and feminist themes.

OLAF STAPLEDON (1866–1950) was a science fiction writer. His stories are imbued with philosophical ideas and notions of wonder and conflicting instincts.

H. D. THOREAU (1817–62) was a transcendentalist and immensely influential essayist. His *Walden: or, Life in the Woods*, chronicling the time he spent in a hut in woodland owned by his friend Ralph Waldo Emerson, near Concord, Massachusetts, is a classic of natural living and self-reliance.

J. R. R. TOLKIEN (1892–1973) was an academic philologist and author of the epic fantasy works *The Hobbit* and *The Lord of The Rings*. Their success was a major contributing factor in the growth of fantasy literature in the second half of the twentieth century.

ANTHONY TROLLOPE (1815–82) was a prolific Victorian novelist, and the author of *The Chronicles of Barsetshire*. He was successful in life, and is still widely read and appreciated.

MARK TWAIN (1835–1910), born Samuel Langhorne Clemens, was an energetic American writer, humorist and entrepreneur, and the author of the celebrated novels *The Adventures of Tom Sawyer* and *The Adventures of Huckleberry Finn*. He was particularly keen on public talks and lectures.

JO WALTON (b. 1964) is an award-winning fantasy writer. She has published thirteen novels, three poetry collections and an essay collection.

H. G. WELLS (1866–1946) was an early exponent of science fiction, but he wrote widely beyond the genre. *Kipps* was his own favourite among his many books.

The Irish dramatist, poet and aesthete OSCAR WILDE (1854–1900), author of such imperishable plays as *Lady Windermere's Fan*, *The Importance of Being Earnest* and *An Ideal Husband*, was perhaps the most quotable of all writers. He wrote *De Profundis*, a letter of lacerating self-criticism and admonishment to his friend and lover Lord Alfred Douglas, while imprisoned in Reading Gaol for homosexual acts in the 1890s.

The English humorist P. G. WODEHOUSE (1881–1975) created the memorable characters of the 'idle rich' Bertie Wooster and his sharply intelligent valet Jeeves, amongst many others. His numerous novels and short stories have never gone out of print.

The feminist VIRGINIA WOOLF (1882–1941) was part of the Bloomsbury group of writers, artists and intellectuals. She is famous for her use of the 'stream of consciousness' narrative technique in such novels as *Mrs Dalloway* and *To the Lighthouse*. 'Professions for Women' is an abbreviated version of a speech she gave to the National Society for Women's Service, on 21 January 1931.

DOROTHY WORDSWORTH (1771–1855) was a diarist and author and the sister of the Romantic poet William Wordsworth.

WILLIAM BUTLER YEATS (1865–1939) was an Irish poet and playwright with wide interests – folklore and magic among them – and a founder of the Abbey Theatre in Dublin. One of the major figures of twentieth-century literature, he was awarded the Nobel Prize for Literature in 1923.

CHRIS YATES (b. 1959) is an angler, photographer, tea connoisseur, broadcaster and writer. His book *How to Fish* is a classic in its field.

5. How to organise a 'Read Aloud party' in your home

If, like me, you dread bland dinner parties where absolutely nothing happens (no warm conversation, no hint of passion) and the evening drags, you might want to organise a *Read Aloud Party*.

All you need is:

- A number of chairs equal to the number of participants.
- A number of copies of the book equal to half the number of participants.
- Optionally, a number of blindfolds (scarves and scraps of fabric will do) equal to half the number of participants.

It is quite simple, and it works like this.

1. The Book. Ask your friends to bring over their own copy of *To Read Aloud*. You only need half of them to have one. If they don't, either buy them one, or pillage the local libraries, or find friends with better taste.

2. The Chairs. Take out as many chairs as there are guests, and put the chairs in groups of two, side by side, with their backs facing each other. If you have an

odd number of guests, simply put a third chair in one of the groups, in the same way.

3. The Beginning. Ask your friends to sit in the chairs, and introduce them to the party. Explain that you are going to have three rounds of Reading Aloud, and that everybody will change partner at the end of each round.

4. The *Reader* and The *Readee*. In each group one person will read, and one person will be read to. The person who is being read to – the readee – will select a chapter; then the reader will select a piece from that chapter. The reader will not reveal to the readee the name of the author of the piece until after she has read it.

5. Round One: *Warming Up*. A Read Aloud Party is structured in three rounds, starting with the Warming Up. In this first round you can only select writings up to 6 minutes long: this helps the party-goers to get into the mood, and to reassure those who might be sceptical about a new experience. When the reading is done, each couple can briefly discuss the piece, or meditate on it in a shared silence, as they see fit.

6. *The Swap.* Everybody stands up and changes partner. This is a fundamental rule of a Read Aloud Party, because it allows people to mingle and chat. It is not necessary for readers and readees to switch roles: some people love to read, others love to be read to, and others like to switch roles.

7. Round Two: *the Core*. When everybody is sitting with a new partner, the Core round begins. It works exactly like Round One, but this time there is no limitation as to the length of the pieces selected.

8. Once more, *The Swap*. Everybody changes partner again.

9. Round Three: *the Mystery*. In the last and final round, the person who is being read to has the option of wearing a blindfold. It is only an option: some might feel ill-at-ease. But my suggestion is to dare and accept the blindfold. Without the weight of sight, it is easier to get gently lost in the words read to us, and the experience of being a readee becomes even more intense.

10. *The Conversation*. The three rounds, with the introduction and a short break, take less than a hour in total. After the third round people will feel comfortable and relaxed: they will want to stand up, share some drinks and chat. I have seen the most amazing connections created after only three rounds of Reading Aloud. But of course, if you and your friends feel so inclined, nothing is stopping you from indulging in more.

11. *Strangers*. A Read Aloud party is a fantastic way of bringing strangers together. You might want to organise one in your local library or in a café, to meet new people: or you might invite friends you had always wanted to introduce to each other, without ever having found quite the right occasion to do so.

Text acknowledgements

JORGE AMADO: *Gabriela, Clove and Cinnamon* (originally published as *Gabriela, Cravo e Canela*, by Livraria Martins Editora, São Paulo, 1958), translated by James L. Taylor and William L. Grossman. Reprinted by permission of Penguin Books USA and Souvenir Press.

JANE AUSTEN: *Pride and Prejudice*, 1813.

MAURICE BARING: 'Half a Minute's Silence', from *Half a Minute's Silence and Other Stories*, 1925.

GREGORY BATESON: 'Why Do Things Get in a Muddle?' from *Steps to an Ecology of Mind*, 1972. New edition published by University of Chicago Press, 2000.

LILLIAN BECKWITH: *The Hills is Lonely,* Hutchinson, 1959. Reprinted by permission of Curtis Brown.

ISABELLA BIRD: *The Hawaiian Archipelago*, 1875.

ALAIN DE BOTTON: 'What Nice Men Never Tell Nice Women'. Reprinted by permission of Alain de Botton.

ALGERNON BLACKWOOD: 'The Messenger', from *Pan's Garden*, 1912. Reprinted by permission of United Agents.

RAY BRADBURY: *Dandelion Wine*, Doubleday, 1957. Reprinted by permission of Abner Stein.

LEWIS CARROLL: Letter to Isabel Standen, from Stuart Dodgson Collingwood, *The Life and Letters of Lewis Carroll*, 1898.

KATE CHOPIN: 'A Respectable Woman', from *A Night in Acadie and Other Stories*, 1897.

CICERO: *De Amicitia* , 44 BC. Translation by W. A. Falconer for the Loeb Classical Library, 1923, adapted by Francesco Dimitri.

JOHN CLELAND: *Fanny Hill or, Memoirs of a Woman of Pleasure*, 1748.

ROB COWEN: *Common Ground*, 2015. Reprinted by permission of The Random House Group Ltd © Rob Cowen 2015.

ALEISTER CROWLEY: *The Confessions of Aleister Crowley: An Autohagiography*, edited by John Symonds and Kenneth Grant, Jonathan Cape, 1969.

SIMONE DE BEAUVOIR: *A Very Easy Death*, translated by Patrick O'Brien, translation copyright © 1965 André Deutsch Ltd, Weidenfeld & Nicolson and G. P. Putnam's Sons. Used by permission of Pantheon Books, an imprint of Knopf Doubleday Publishing Group, a division of Penguin Random House LLC. All rights reserved.

CHARLES DICKENS: *Great Expectations,* 1861.

FRANCESCO DIMITRI: *The Oak in my Garden* © Francesco Dimitri 2017.

JIM DODGE: *Stone Junction*, Canongate, 2004. Reprinted by permission of Canongate Books and Grove/Atlantic Inc.

DAPHNE DU MAURIER: *Rebecca*, Victor Gollancz, 1938. Reprinted by permission of Curtis Brown.

ARTHUR CONAN DOYLE: *The Coming of the Fairies*, 1922.

RALPH WALDO EMERSON: 'Nature', 1836.

EPICURUS: *Letter to Menoeceus*, translated by Robert Drew Hicks.

JOHN FANTE: *The Brotherhood of the Grape*. Copyright © John Fante 1977. Copyright © John Fante 1988. Reprinted by permission of HarperCollins Publishers.

TANA FRENCH: *The Secret Place*, Hodder & Stoughton 2014. Reprinted by permission from Penguin Random House.

E. M. FORSTER: *A Room with a View*, 1908. Reprinted by permission of The Provost and Scholars of King's College, Cambridge and the Society of Authors as the E. M. Forster Estate, and Penguin Random House.

DION FORTUNE: *Glastonbury: Avalon of The Heart*, 1934. Copyright © 1995, 2000 Society of Inner Light, London. Reprinted by permission of Red Wheel Weiser.

NEIL GAIMAN: 'The Sweeper of Dreams', from *Smoke and Mirrors*, Avon Books, 1998. Reprinted by permission of Writers House.

ELIZABETH GASKELL: *Cranford*, 1893.

KENNETH GRAHAME: 'The Piper at the Gates of Dawn', from *The Wind in the Willows*, Methuen, 1908.

JOANNE HARRIS: *Chocolat* © Joanne Harris 1999. Reprinted by permission of The Random House Group Ltd and Viking Books, an imprint of Penguin Publishing Group, a division of Penguin Random House LLC. All rights reserved.

JOE HILL: 'Sheherazade's Typewriter', from *20th Century Ghosts*, Gollancz, 2007. Reprinted by permission of The Choate Agency.

ALICE HOFFMAN: *Practical Magic*, G. P. Putnam's Sons, 1995. Reprinted by permission of ICM Partners.

ZORA NEALE HURSTON: *Dust Tracks on the Road*, copyright © 1942 by Zora Neale Hurston; renewed © 1970 by John C. Hurston. Reprinted by permission of HarperCollins US and Little, Brown.

GRAHAM JOYCE: *The Limits of Enchantment*, Gollancz, 2005. Reprinted by permission of the Orion Publishing Group and Sue Joyce.

ROSALIND KERVEN: *The Dead Moon*, National Trust Books/Anova Books, 2008. Reprinted by permission of Pavilion Books.

JOE LANSDALE: *Captains Outrageous*, Weidenfeld & Nicolson, 2002. Reprinted by permission of the Orion Publishing Group.

D. H. LAWRENCE: *Lady Chatterley's Lover*: published privately, 1928; first unexpurgated edition published by Penguin Books, 1960.

AMY LEACH: 'Radical Bears in the Forest Delicious', from *Things That Are*, 2012, Milkweed Editions. Reprinted by permission of Milkweed Editions.

VERNON LEE: 'A Pontifical Mass at the Sixtine Chapel', from *The Spirit of Rome*, 1906.

GIACOMO LEOPARDI: *Dialogue of Torquato Tasso and his Familiar Genius*, from *Operette morali*, 1827. Translated by Francesco Dimitri.

JULIE DE L'ESPINASSE: 'Letter to Hippolyte de Guibert', 1770s; in Antonia Fraser, *Love Letters: An Anthology*, Weidenfeld & Nicolson, 1976. Reprinted by permission of the Orion Publishing Group.

CATHERINE MILLET: *The Sexual Life of Catherine M*, copyright © 2001 Editions du Seuil; translation copyright © 2002 Adriana Hunter. Used by permission of Grove/Atlantic Inc. and Profile.

KELLY LINK: 'Going to Hell. Instructions and Advice', from 'Flying Lessons' copyright © 1995 by Kelly Link. Originally published in *Asimov's* and reprinted in Kelly Link's *Stranger Things Happen* (Small Beer Press). Excerpt used by permission of the Author.

ROBERT MACFARLANE: *The Old Ways*, Hamish Hamilton, 2012. Reprinted by permission of Penguin Books Ltd and Penguin Random House.

KATHERINE MANSFIELD: 'Bank Holiday', from *The Garden Party and Other Stories*, 1922.

DAVID MITCHELL: *Black Swan Green*, Sceptre, 2006. Reprinted by permission of Hodder & Stoughton.

JOHN MUIR: *My First Summer in the Sierra*, Houghton Mifflin Company, 1917.

EDITH NESBIT: 'Uncle Abraham's Romance', from *Grim Tales*, 1893.

ANAIS NIN: 'Manuel', from *Delta of Venus*, published posthumously, 1977. Reprinted by permission of the Anais Nin Trust and Houghton Mifflin Harcourt.

JOYCE CAROL OATES: 'The Scarf', from *Faithless: Tales of Transgression*, 2001. Copyright © 2001 by the Ontario Review, Inc. Reprinted by permission of HarperCollins Publishers.

GEORGE ORWELL: *Down and Out in Paris and London*, Victor Gollancz, 1933. Copyright © George Orwell 1933 and renewed 1961 by Sonia Pitt-Rivers. Copyright © The Estate of the late Sonia Brownell Orwell, 1986. Reprinted by permission of the Orwell Estate and Houghton Mifflin Harcourt Publishing Company. All rights reserved.

OLIVE SCHREINER: 'The Woman's Rose', from *Dream Life and Real Life*, 1893.

REBECCA SOLNIT: *A Field Guide To Getting Lost*, Canongate, 2006. Reprinted by permission from Canongate and Bonnie Nadell.

OLAF STAPLEDON: *Star Maker*, 1937. Reprinted by permission of The Orion Publishing Group.

J. R. R. TOLKIEN: : Excerpt from *The Lord of the Rings* by J. R. R. Tolkien, edited by Christopher Tolkien. Copyright © 1954, 1955, 1965, 1966 by J. R. R. Tolkien, Michael H. R. Tolkien and Priscilla M. A. R. Tolkien. Copyright © Renewed 1993, 1994 by Christopher R. Tolkien and Priscilla M. A. R. Tolkien. Reprinted by permission of Harper Collins and Houghton Mifflin Harcourt Publishing Company. All Rights Reserved.

H. D. THOREAU: *Civil Disobedience*, first published in 1849 as *Resistance to Civil Government* in *Aesthetic Papers*; and with the present title in a posthumous anthology of Thoreau's works: *A Yankee in Canada, with Anti-Slavery and Reform Papers*, 1866.

ANTHONY TROLLOPE: *An Autobiography*, 1883.

MARK TWAIN: Seventieth Birthday speech, Delmonico's restaurant, New York, 5 December 1905; published in a supplement to *Harper's Weekly*, 23 December 1905.

JO WALTON: *Among Others*. Reprinted by permission of Little, Brown Book Group and Macmillan.

H. G. WELLS: *Kipps*, Macmillan, 1905.

OSCAR WILDE: *De Profundis*, first published 1905.

P. G. WODEHOUSE: 'The Secret Pleasures of Reginald'. Published by *Vanity Fair*, 1915. Copyright © P. G. Wodehouse. Reproduced by permission of the author's estate c/o Rogers, Coleridge & White Ltd.

VIRGINIA WOOLF: 'Professions for Women', paper read to the Women's Service League, 1942; published in *The Death of the Moth and Other Essays* (1942).

DOROTHY WORDSWORTH: *Recollections of a Tour Made in Scotland, A.D. 1803*. G. P. Putnam's Sons, 1874.

CHRIS YATES: *Nightwalk: A Journey to the Heart of Nature*, 2013. Reprinted by permission of Harper Collins.

William Butler Yeats: 'Enchanted Woods' from *The Celtic Twilight*, 1893.

Every effort has been made to contact copyright holders for permission to reproduce material in this book. In the case of any inadvertent oversight, the publishers will include an appropriate acknowledgement in future editions.

Toasts

It takes a village to raise a child, and it takes at least a small crew to make a book. The one that made *To Read Aloud* was not only effective, but also a great fun to work with. Let me raise a glass to all of them in turn.

The first toast goes to Piers Blofeld, my agent, who was there since day one, when I sent him an odd email with an odd idea. He helped me to refine it and make it sensible, going through a number of drafts and emails that would have put off a lesser man. Piers is a creative powerhouse, and he is stubborn enough to crack diamonds with a head-butt: you would say he is too good to be true, but he is true indeed, in all senses. To Piers!

My next toast is to Richard Milbank, my editor. We went through countless conversations about what to include and what not, and we had most of them face to face, over lunch, in a perfect *To Read Aloud* spirit. Richard is not only an exceedingly erudite and pleasant conversationalist, he can also spot a good restaurant, and has the guts to take an Italian to Italian places in London. He showed me the best ones, and I am every bit as grateful for that as I am for the hard work he put into this book. To Richard!

Allow me now to raise a glass to my wife, Paola Filotico.

With her training as a psychotherapist she made me focus some of the ideas in *To Read Aloud*. With her care she helped me see through the darkest moments (there are always dark moments when you work on a book). And with her general awesomeness she inspired me at every twist and turn. To Paola!

These are the three main players in the crew. There are many others, but if I had to raise a glass to all of them, one by one, the hangover tomorrow would fill us all with profound regret. So, here is a collective toast to the London Library staff, that gave me shelter and books and made the research for *To Read Aloud* such a pleasant endeavour. And here is one to the Head of Zeus staff: Ellen Parnavelas with her painstaking chasing of rights holders, the communication trimurti of Blake Brooks, Kaz Harrison, and Jennifer Edgecombe, with their capacity to come up with ideas and make them happen, Amanda Ridout with her true grit.

To close the circle, my last toast goes to Kat, James, and Bella Priddis: they came visiting on a winter weekend, bringing with them a book on a witch. It all started there. Without them, *To Read Aloud* wouldn't exist. You know what I mean.

If you don't like *To Read Aloud*, take it up with them!